Practical Marketing Research

PRACTICAL MARKETING RESEARCH

New, Updated Edition

Jeffrey L. Pope

amacom
American Management Association

New York • Atlanta • Boston • Chicago • Kansas City • San Francisco • Washington, D.C.
Brussels • Toronto • Mexico City

Library of Congress Cataloging-in-Publication Data

Pope, Jeffrey L.
    Practical marketing research / Jeffrey L. Pope. — New, updated
ed.
        p.   cm.
    Includes index.
    ISBN 0-8144-5086-5
    1. Marketing research.   I. Title.
HF5415.2.P63   1993
658.8'3 — dc20   92-30310
                                                  CIP

Printing number

10   9   8   7   6   5   4   3

To my partner, **Judy Corson,** with whom I've shared
many of the best times of my career in research.

And to all the people at CRI who contributed their ideas
and efforts to this book.

Contents

Introduction

If your job involves marketing research, then you've probably already figured out one thing: Most marketing research books don't help you much to do your job. Most of the ones around are *textbooks*, and they talk mostly about *why* research works or should work. But you already know that research works. That's why you're in this business, right?

What you really want to know is *how to do* research. You know research could help make a packaging decision, but you need to know how to conduct a packaging test. You know research could help you screen new product concepts, but you need ideas about how to do new product screening. How do you research a new product name?

This book didn't start out as a book; it began as a notebook for staff members of our company, Custom Research Inc., a marketing research firm that works every day for a large number of clients on a wide range of research problems. We needed a notebook that described what we'd learned from experience about the best way to approach different kinds of studies. As the notebook was being written, we found clients asking for copies of chapters. That told us there was interest in a practical, real-world-oriented research guide, so the notebook was revised to become a full-size book.

The goal of this book is simple: *to serve as a reference source for many of the things you need to know either to be a competent professional marketing researcher yourself, or to be successful at marketing when you rely on marketing research done by others.* To accomplish this goal, the book is designed to focus on:

- *Applications.* What's really happening in the research world? This book deals with research on actual marketing problems.
- *Real-world issues.* To be usable, the principles laid down must deal with how to get things done in the real world. This book is based on experience with thousands of actual research projects involving hundreds of different companies.
- *Practitioners.* This book is designed for readers with responsibility for the research function within a company, either as part of their

job or as their primary responsibility. This is not a student text-book.

- *Specific problems.* The contents of the book are organized around the kinds of marketing problems the techniques are designed to solve: new product concepts, packaging, advertising, sales testing, and so on.

The principles in this book apply, with only minor variations, to most types of businesses. In all markets, the research principles are largely the same. The approaches are similar; only the details differ. So the book focuses on these common principles, then includes individual chapters (on business-to-business and service markets, for example) that illustrate how the same approaches can be applied to those types of markets.

If you're new to marketing research, this book will help orient you to the field. If you already have some experience, it will broaden your base of knowledge. And if you're a senior researcher, it will give you information on facets of the business you've probably never encountered.

Finally, this book is designed as a handbook. Each chapter stands by itself. It's meant to be used as a reference source for dealing with specific problems.

Most marketing researchers are puzzle solvers—people who like to analyze problems and figure things out. The puzzle presented by every study is unique in some way. This book gives you the tools to tackle the research puzzles you encounter every day in the real world.

Part I
The Role of
Research in Business

1

The History and Role of Marketing Research

"History is more or less bunk," declared Henry Ford. But it can also be very interesting if the history happens to involve *you*.

Little children ask, "Where did I come from, Mommy?" If you're involved with marketing research, you probably have a similar curiosity about how the field developed.

Many other business disciplines, such as sales, production, and finance, have existed in some form for thousands of years. But the history of marketing research is much shorter, because all the real growth in the field has come in this century—most of it within the past fifty years.

Early Beginnings

The following names and figures are the result of one of the earliest known examples of research, a "straw poll" taken by the *Harrisburg Pennsylvanian* during the 1824 presidential campaign.

Andrew Jackson	335
John Quincy Adams	169
Henry Clay	19
William H. Crawford	9

Do you know how the election turned out? If you look it up, you'll find this poll was wrong. None of the three top candidates received a majority of electoral votes, so the election went to the House of Representatives. There Clay threw his support to Adams, who was elected.

(Jackson came back and won in 1828, so perhaps this first poll was more predictive than anyone realized at the time.)

The accuracy of polling and other research has increased considerably since the 1800s. Political polling is now very sophisticated and quite accurate in forecasting election results. This early example shows that surveys have long seemed a logical way to predict things, whether the matter at hand was an election or the introduction of a new product.

Marketing Applications

Research, however, wasn't used as a business tool until many years later.

In the first quarter of this century, formal research departments started to appear around the country. The first groups were found in four types of organizations:

1. *Manufacturers.* DuPont, General Electric, and Kellogg were among the first to begin doing research.
2. *Publishers.* The *Chicago Tribune* and Curtis Publishing were early pioneers.
3. *Advertising agencies.* Lord & Thomas Advertising and N. W. Ayer Advertising are generally credited with having the first agency research functions.
4. *Universities.* Harvard and Northwestern each established a Bureau of Business Research before 1920.

Then during the 1920s and 1930s, research departments became more common in businesses of all types.

Growth Factors

Why is research in such widespread use today? Why do most companies of any size have a marketing research function of some type? Growth can be linked to four factors:

1. *Company size.* Businesspeople used to conduct their own first-hand research, although few would have called it that. The shoemaker in colonial America had no need for research. He knew the wants and

needs of his customers by dealing directly with them every day. The local druggist and grocer in 1900 had the same firsthand contact with their "markets."

But things have changed today. Companies are bigger—much bigger—and the managements of most multimillion-dollar businesses have little or no direct contact with the end users of their products or services. Marketing research has replaced firsthand experience as the link between businesspeople and their customers. It has become the management tool for staying in touch with the wants and needs of the market. So growth in the size of businesses has created the need for marketing research.

2. *Computers.* While business size created the need for research, computers created the capability for doing it efficiently. Most of the marketing research done today would be impossible without the computer. Even a simple study involving ten or fifteen questions and 300 respondents would be extremely tedious to tabulate accurately by hand. And large-scale studies of several thousand respondents would be virtually impossible to handle even in total—forget about the cross-tabs or any multivariate analysis. People who were in the business thirty or forty years ago tell about rooms full of people working to tally survey results. A task that is now done in minutes or seconds by a computer routinely took hundreds of labor hours.

Computers have been widely available to business only since the mid-1950s and early 1960s, and that's when marketing research began to blossom.

3. *Scanners.* Product code scanners have revolutionized retail auditing in recent years. Scanners provide a way of measuring almost perfectly the product sales in supermarkets and drug stores. And the use of scanners is rapidly expanding into other types of research situations.

4. *Communication and transportation technology.* Imagine trying to conduct a typical research study today without telephones, cars, fax machines, or airplanes. Planning the study would be hard enough; conducting it would be almost impossible. If you really want to shudder, think about producing questionnaires, instructions, and reports in the years "B.X."—before Xerox!

In short, the need for research by large companies that use more sophisticated management techniques has coincided with the technological developments that have made large-scale research feasible. That's what has made marketing research the large and growing industry it is today.

The Four Ps

Just as education has its three Rs, marketing has its four Ps (Figure 1-1). Marketing comprises *all* the business functions involved in getting goods and services from the producer to the user. In other words, marketing is getting the right *product* to the right *place* at the right *price*—and letting people know about it through *promotion*.

These same factors apply to every type of product and service, not just to advertised consumer products. For example, *Time* magazine, in a cover story on the Boeing Company, quoted an executive of Germany's Lufthansa Airlines as saying, "There is no secret at all about Boeing's success. The company just keeps coming up with the right plane, at the right price, at the right time."

The goal of the marketer is to put all these components together in a way that will maximize profits. This is no simple task, since each of the components has several subparts that all need to work together. The total of these parts for a product or service is called its marketing mix (Figure 1-2).

Figure 1-1. The four Ps of marketing.

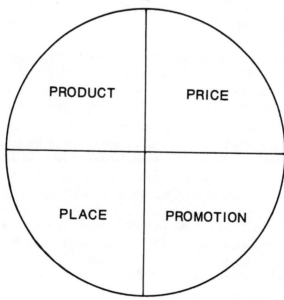

Figure 1-2. Details of the marketing mix.

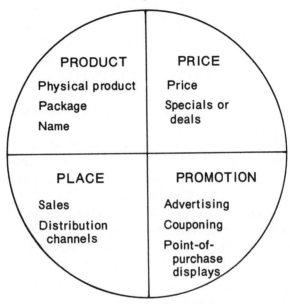

Production or Marketing?

There are two alternative philosophies that can be used to select the components of the marketing mix: the production concept and the marketing concept.

A company that follows the *production concept* says essentially, "We sell what we can make." In the early days of the industrial revolution, this was the prevalent philosophy of business, and it worked just fine.

Goods were in short supply, and people were anxious to buy almost anything. Henry Ford used to say that people could have any color of car they wanted as long as it was black. And in the early 1900s that view was adequate to build one of the world's largest companies. There was little need then for research in companies operating under the production concept.

But as manufacturing techniques improved, producers developed the capacity to supply more of most products than consumers could buy. Today, goods are no longer in short supply; there's an excess of supply over demand. Since the end of World War II, the focus in most companies has shifted from production to marketing.

The *marketing concept* says that a company's total effort—product, place, price, and promotion—should be adapted to the needs and wants of customers rather than based on what the manufacturer can most easily produce.

Trial and Error or Research?

There are two basic ways to discern the market's wants and needs: (1) trial and error and (2) research.

Trial and error involves simply putting a product or service on the market and seeing if it sells. On a small scale for small companies, this may be cheaper and easier than research. The simplest way for the local corner restaurant to see if a new item will sell is to add it to the menu and watch what happens. But for a large chain like Burger King, the "try it and see if it sells" approach is much too costly and risky.

Today, marketing research provides a tool for most large marketers

Figure 1-3. The marketing process.

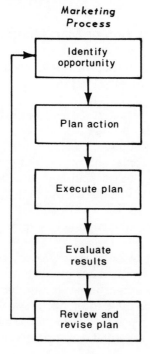

of goods and services to reduce their risk by anticipating the wants and needs of their markets.

The Marketing Planning Process

Every marketing decision involves some variation of the process depicted in Figure 1-3. A good practical definition of marketing research would be that it's a tool to help make better decisions at each step in the marketing process. There are a lot of fancy, technical definitions of marketing research, but they all come down to one thing: *helping to make better marketing decisions.*

For example, a typical new product introduction would involve the steps shown in Figure 1-4. At each step in the process, research can help

Figure 1-4. Marketing process for a new product.

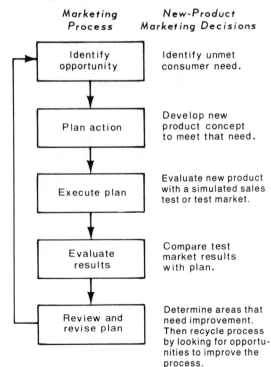

Figure 1-5. Contributions of marketing research to the marketing process.

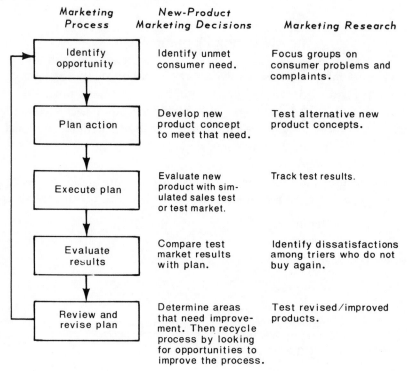

Marketing Process	New-Product Marketing Decisions	Marketing Research
Identify opportunity	Identify unmet consumer need.	Focus groups on consumer problems and complaints.
Plan action	Develop new product concept to meet that need.	Test alternative new product concepts.
Execute plan	Evaluate new product with simulated sales test or test market.	Track test results.
Evaluate results	Compare test market results with plan.	Identify dissatisfactions among triers who do not buy again.
Review and revise plan	Determine areas that need improvement. Then recycle process by looking for opportunities to improve the process.	Test revised/improved products.

give direction to the marketing decisions that have to be made. Figure 1-5 illustrates this for a new product introduction. Comparable steps would be taken for advertising, packaging, or pricing decisions, or for any other component of the total marketing mix. And research can be done to help reduce the risk at each step in the process.

2

Research Strategy and Planning

People have different needs as they move through the stages of life—childhood, adolescence, adulthood, and old age. So do products. And that's where the concept of a research strategy comes in. It means tailoring the research to the needs of a product at each point in its life cycle.

The concept of product life cycle is well accepted. It usually breaks down a product's development into four stages, as shown in Figure 2-1. While the concept of *product* life cycle is well accepted, the idea of *research* life cycle isn't as obvious. Nevertheless, it's important to develop a research strategy that is adapted to the unique needs of the product at each stage.

Introduction Stage

This is the "childhood" of a product. The product is just getting started. Things are developing fast. It's a crucial period: Like a child's, a product's future is strongly influenced by what happens here.

The research strategy should focus on developing and building issues. At this stage, research studies most commonly concentrate on the following areas:

- *Concept testing.* Does the concept have sufficiently broad appeal to be successful? To what market segments does it appeal most? What are the benefits that are most attractive to potential buyers?

- *Product testing.* Is the physical product as good as it can be? How does it compare with the competition?

Figure 2-1. The four states of a product's life cycle.

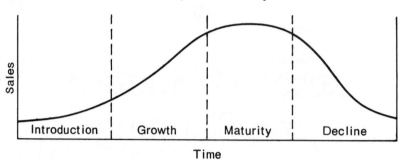

• *Concept fulfillment.* Does the physical product meet expectations created by the concept? (Good products and good concepts don't necessarily go together. It's always a good idea to check.)

• *Name testing.* This should be done early, since the name actually becomes part of the "concept" once the product hits the market.

• *Package testing.* This is the stage at which the majority of packaging decisions are made and most package testing is done. Once a product is on the market, it's unusual to make a package change. It's better to do the research up front and get it right the first time.

• *Advertising research.* An advertising strategy (as well as actual ads) that executes the concept and is consistent with the name and package must be developed.

• *Simulated sales testing and test marketing.* These are typically the last two steps before a product goes on the market. They're the last checkpoints on the final, complete bundle of product, ad, name, and package.

• *Tracking.* From the beginning, it's important to set up a system for tracking the key sales components of customer awareness and trial and repeat purchases. This is often done through periodic waves of telephone interviewing. (Purchase panel data, which monitor consumers' purchases of product categories and brands, can also be used, although they don't give a measure of customer awareness.) Tracking these components gives a basis for deciding whether sales are building as expected or whether changes need to be made. (For example, if customer awareness is lower than expected and trial purchases are low as a result, the advertising may need to be reevaluated. If repeat purchases are low, product quality may be a problem.)

Growth Stage

This is the "adolescence" of a product. Sales are beginning to take off. And as with a teenager, growth for a product can come too fast and may be painful. The research strategy at this stage should deal with tracking issues. The components of the marketing mix are usually well set by this point. A tracking program (monitoring customer awareness and trial and repeat purchases as components of volume) should be maintained. The objective of this tracking is to look for either of two kinds of accidents:

1. *Unexpected successes.* Things are sometimes—not often, but sometimes—more successful than expected. What is planned as a modest new product may turn out to be a runaway success. The tracking research should be designed to spot this quickly, determine why it happened (that's critical), and look for ways to expand, multiply, or accelerate the unexpected success. Believe it or not, many extremely successful products started as ideas that simply found unexpected success when they hit the market.

2. *Repairable failures.* In the early stages of a product's growth cycle, most of the volume comes from first-time trial purchases. Later, an increasing share comes from repeat purchases. If this *isn't* happening, something is wrong. A supply of first-time buyers can't be maintained forever. So if the sales components of awareness and trial and repeat purchases aren't developing as planned, action needs to be taken to fix the element that's a problem.

It's common for sales to take a slight temporary dip during the growth stage as trial purchases trail off but before repeat purchases pick up the slack. At this point, management's conviction and commitment often get tested, unless the dip has been forecast. If it hasn't been predicted, there's a risk that a good product and a sound marketing plan will be abandoned just before a new sales spurt develops. That's another reason why good planning and good tracking must go together.

Tracking competitive products is the other function of a tracking system during the growth phase. The period before its success and market position are established is when a product, even a good one, is most vulnerable to competition. The same measures (customer awareness and trial and repeat-purchase levels) should be collected on competitive products to see how much of a threat they pose. In addition, samples of competitive products should be purchased and tested to see how they compare with your own product. Your objective should be to know as much about the strengths and weaknesses of competitive products as you know about your own.

Maturity Stage

This is "adulthood" for a product. As with a person, there's a risk that things will get stale and go flat. The objective is to manage the "mid-life crisis" of the product and find new ways to build interest, excitement, and sales—without abandoning the elements that made the product successful in the first place. Accordingly, the research strategy should focus on *finding opportunities.* Research can help identify ways to bring new interest to a product. Here are some of the ways this can be done:

• *Product line extensions.* New products in a line (new flavors, colors, and sizes) are usually introduced during the maturity stage. They should be tested before introduction to make sure they're up to the quality standards of the existing line. And estimates should be developed to make sure the sales generated by the new items represent some add-on volume and aren't totally the result of "cannibalizing" existing products.

• *New positioning.* Sometimes new volume can be built by changing a product's position and appealing to a broader market or a different set of needs.

• *New advertising.* When a product's sales begin to plateau, companies typically look for new advertising to generate renewed interest. So advertising research is often done, beginning with qualitative research and moving through quantitative copy testing.

• *Package testing.* A new or redesigned package that gives a product a new look is another way to try to increase sales. Package testing should be done to make sure the new package is really better (in impact, visibility, and connotations) and not just different.

• *New uses.* Category studies may uncover additional uses for a product that can be promoted to stimulate new sales. (The promotion of baking soda as a refrigerator deodorizer some years ago is a classic example of this approach.) This is usually a long shot, and real successes are rare, but they can happen.

Decline Stage

This is the "old age" of a product, when sales begin to drop off. By this point, improved products or technologies have come along, or the public has simply grown tired of the product and moved on to others. Research strategy should focus on *salvaging* the product—or attempting to salvage it. Realistically, this is not a stage at which much research usually gets done. When sales start to drop off, the first reaction is usually to cut expenses—research expenses included. It's rare for a company to undertake a large, expensive research study on the slim chance that a "secret" will be uncovered that can turn the product around. When a product starts to decline, management usually tries to slow the drop-off but rarely expects to stop or actually reverse it.

What are the areas in which research could help? Go down this list and evaluate whether changes in any of the following areas are likely to have a significant impact on product sales:

- Physical product
- Positioning
- Market segments
- Advertising
- Name
- Package
- Pricing
- Distribution

If these are candidates for significant changes, evaluate whether the impact of the change has a good chance of paying back the cost of the research and more. If it does, propose it. If it doesn't (which is more likely), accept that fact and don't propose that more research costs be added to the overhead burden the product already has to support.

In summary, people have different needs and interests at different points in their lives. Similarly, products have changing research support needs as they grow, mature, and decline. One research program can't fit all the needs. Different research strategies must be developed for products to fit them at each stage in their product life cycles.

The Planning Process

The marketing plan is the document that guides all the marketing activities for a company or a product. It sets out objectives, defines how success is to be measured, and describes the strategies and tactics that will be used. Although products and markets vary substantially from one industry to the next, the type of information in a marketing plan is very similar across different businesses.

The fundamental purpose of planning is to give the total marketing program a focus that is well thought out. This keeps the pieces of the program from becoming fragmented or from conflicting with one another. For example, the product, the packaging, and the advertising must all contribute to the accomplishment of a single goal, such as positioning the item as a convenient, old-fashioned product or as a "new improved" product. That goal and the reasoning behind it are contained in the marketing plan.

The planning process usually involves four steps: opportunity identification, planning, execution, and evaluation. This process represents a *cycle* that's repeated over and over, usually on a yearly basis. A marketing opportunity is identified, and a plan is developed to take advantage of it. That plan is executed, and the results are evaluated. Often that evaluation identifies a new opportunity, and the process starts over again. At each step along the way in this process, research plays a crucial role.

Opportunity Identification

This first step in the planning process is key, since it determines the direction for everything that follows. It usually requires some creativity or insight to identify an opportunity that may not be obvious. The types of opportunities that could form the basis for a marketing program include:

- Introducing a new product or service
- Developing an improved product or service
- Adding "flanker products" (additional flavors, colors, sizes, and so on) to a product line
- Repositioning a product or service
- Targeting a product at different or additional market segments
- Changing packaging
- Using couponing or sampling
- Revising advertising in a significant way

How are these kinds of opportunities identified? Creative insight can come from almost any source, even ones seemingly unrelated to the product or the market. But opportunity identification most often occurs through three types of research studies:

- *Group interviews.* But be careful with these because it's easy to turn the comments of one vocal person into a consumer "mandate" for a new product, new package, or revised ad campaign.
- *Market segmentation studies.* This type of study can help identify homogeneous segments of the market that look like promising targets.

- *Product positioning research.* These studies describe consumers' perceptions of a product category and the relative positions of brands in it. Such research is a useful method for identifying "holes"—needs unfilled by other brands—that could represent opportunities for effective advertising or new products.

Planning

At this point, the marketing action needs to be selected and a plan developed for its execution. Whatever the action, it's usually researched first to increase the plan's odds of success. So the research that's done is typically a test of the effectiveness and impact of the marketing variable on which the plan will focus. Here are some examples of such research:

- *Product testing.* Is the new or improved product really better than the current product or competitive product?
- *Package testing.* Does the new package have more shelf impact than the current package or competitive packages?
- *Advertising testing.* Which new ad claim seems most important to consumers? What is the persuasion power of the new ads? Are they memorable?

Execution

At this step of the planning cycle, research moves into a monitoring and measuring role. The execution step is where line marketing people become busiest as they translate the plan into action. Research's role here is to begin collecting the information that will make evaluation of the plan's results—and improvement of the plan if necessary—easier.

The most common survey research tool here is some type of AAU (awareness, attitude, and usage) study. This usually takes the form of a series of periodic waves of telephone research to measure:

- Customer awareness
- Trial purchases
- Intent to make a trial purchase
- Repeat purchases
- Intent to make a repeat purchase
- Attitudes of buyers toward the product and their reactions to using it
- Advertising recall

In addition, some type of syndicated market data (IRI or Nielsen for consumer packaged goods) is often purchased to supplement company sales information. These sources provide data on total category sales and market share that aren't available from a company's own sales data.

Evaluation

This is an analytical step and usually doesn't require collecting additional survey data. It involves comparing actual results with the results projected by the plan to see if the effort succeeded or failed.

But this shouldn't be just a matter of ruling "thumbs up" or "thumbs down." It's important for the researcher to stay in the role of player and not become just a scorekeeper. The researcher should ask: If the plan didn't succeed this time, how can it be made better next time? In this way, the evaluation step feeds right back into the opportunity identification step of the next planning cycle. From every evaluation should come the seeds of identifying the next opportunity.

How can the plan be improved and modified to be made more effective? If all the research can be focused on this question, then research will play a valuable role in the marketing planning process. Otherwise it risks providing nice-to-know but essentially useless information.

Part II
Choosing the Interviewing Method

3

Using Personal Interviews

Before discussing the subject of personal interviews, I must point out one thing: There's no one interviewing method that's always better. That's why selecting the type of interview to use is often the most important decision you make in designing a survey research project.

You have three basic choices: in-person, telephone, or mail interviewing. Once you make that decision, many aspects of the interview are fixed. And a wrong decision risks wasting money and time or, worst of all, producing misleading results. So it's important to choose the right method.

If one method were always more accurate than the others, the decision would of course be easy. But studies have shown that well-conducted studies of each type *can* produce similarly accurate results. No one type is always better. Instead, the choice among interviewing methods for each project depends on which offers the best combination of two factors: suitability for the study's objectives, and feasibility (cost, timing, execution). Consequently, the decision requires a good understanding of the advantages and disadvantages of each type of interview.

This and the next two chapters provide a summary of the strengths and weaknesses of each method of interviewing: personal interviews, telephone interviews, and mail questionnaires.

When to Use Personal Interviews

When you form a mental picture of an interview, what do you see? If you're like most people, you've been conditioned by years of newspaper and magazine cartoons to think of someone, clipboard in hand, asking questions on a doorstep.

And that used to be the way most research was done. In the 1930s and 1940s, if you wanted to conduct an interview, you rang the doorbell and asked your questions.

While the classic door-to-door interview isn't extinct, today it's clearly an endangered species, for several reasons:

- With a majority of women employed outside the home, it's diffi-cult for interviewers to find respondents at home during the day-time.
- This means that most door-to-door interviewing has to be done at night or on weekends. It's often difficult to find interviewers who are willing to walk door to door at night through unfamiliar neigh-borhoods.
- Increasing crime rates, especially in large cities, have made many people reluctant to let strangers into their homes, even if those strangers are survey interviewers.

Nevertheless, personal interviews have some important advantages that keep the method alive for certain kinds of research. And personal inter-views are still quite common in many other countries around the world.

Advantages of Personal Interviewing

Personal interviewing comes closest to being the universal research ap-proach. It is usually used when you have to show or give the respondent something. The most common examples of this kind of study are prod-uct tests, advertising tests, and package tests.

Other common types of personal interviewing studies are complex attitude and opinion studies in which the length of the interview or the types of questions asked make mail or telephone questionnaires imprac-tical. Theoretically, personal interviewing could be used on almost every study, if cost considerations didn't make that impractical. Here are the major advantages of this approach:

- *Flexibility and versatility.* The key advantage of personal interview-ing is that with this format you can do almost anything. You have the greatest freedom in questionnaire length and format. A personal inter-view is often most effective for getting detailed attitude and opinion in-formation. And interviewers can sometimes do a better job of probing and clarifying open-ended questions in a face-to-face interview. In short, virtually any type of question can be asked in a personal interview.

• *Exhibits.* Another key benefit of personal interviewing is that you can show or give things to respondents. This means that you can expose them to advertisements and ask their opinions about them. You can hand respondents test packages to open. Or you can give them samples of test products to use at home. So if it's necessary to show some type of exhibit during the interview, a personal contact is usually required.

• *Observation.* An interviewer has the option of observing things the respondents do in addition to asking them questions. For example, you might observe whether the respondent opens a test package correctly or whether the test product spills when the respondent tries to pour it. Another time you may want to measure how much time women spend in a supermarket examining bacon packages before making a final selection. These kinds of observation measures are possible only in a personal interview.

• *Sampling.* In theory, at least, it's possible to draw a very representative sample of the total population using households (or "dwelling units," as they're called in sampling terminology) as a basis for the sample. In practice, of course, actually executing a door-to-door sample and interviewing everyone in it presents problems that often make it unfeasible or not worth the very high cost involved.

• *Speed.* By dividing the total sample among several markets and conducting the interviews in each city simultaneously, it's possible to complete large studies very quickly. Personal interviewing conducted this way is usually faster than doing a study by mail, although it is usually not quicker than doing it by telephone.

Disadvantages of Personal Interviewing

Offsetting these important advantages are two major drawbacks that limit the applicability of personal interviewing. The first is cost. Personal interviewing, especially door-to-door interviewing, typically costs several times as much per interview as mail or telephone research. So, except where a personal contact is absolutely necessary, budget considerations argue against door-to-door personal interviewing.

The second problem—execution—is more serious. While door-to-door sampling may often be desirable, consider this:

- Any large, representative national sample will invariably include many sampling points in the inner cities of major metropolitan areas, such as New York, Atlanta, Chicago, Dallas, and Los Angeles.
- With a majority of all adult women employed outside the home, most contacts on any project will have to be made on weekends or at night.
- Obtaining a truly representative sample of these households will require that several callback attempts be made on respondents who are not at home or who are unavailable to be interviewed. This can mean repeated visits to distant neighborhoods in a city to try to complete a single interview.

Would *you* want to be the interviewer on a study like this? Probably not. And if you'd consider taking the job, how much would you charge? Probably a lot. That's why door-to-door studies are so expensive—and it's virtually impossible to hire interviewers to go into certain neighborhoods of some cities at any price. High cost, along with risks to interviewers' safety, are the reasons that large, nationally representative door-to-door studies have almost disappeared.

Trends in Personal Interviewing

Still, for some kinds of research (those involving ads or packages, for example), it's necessary to talk personally with respondents. This has generated a new kind of personal contact: intercept interviews. These involve contacting or "intercepting" respondents in high-traffic locations, such as shopping malls or stores. This is one of the fastest-growing—and, today, one of the most common—kinds of research.

Intercept Interviews

The concept behind this interviewing method is simple: It's more efficient to let respondents come to the interviewer, in a shopping mall or store, than it is to send the interviewer out to the respondents' homes.

Of course, the drawback to intercept interviewing is that it can't, theoretically, produce a sample that's as representative of the population as the best door-to-door study is. Intercept studies also must usually be limited to thirty-minute interviews.

On the other hand, given the problems of actually executing door-to-door studies, those samples aren't usually perfectly representative to begin with. And samples of respondents in intercept studies are often more representative than you might expect.

Many large, regional shopping centers (which typically contain several major department stores) attract a large cross section of shoppers to sample from. Similarly, it's possible to find respondents from a wide range of socioeconomic groups by conducting interviews in several supermarkets in different types of neighborhoods.

All in all, the samples developed from intercept studies often reflect the total population closely enough for purposes of marketing decision making. And the cost per interview of intercept studies is usually only a fraction of what it is for going door to door. Adequate sample control and dramatically lower costs are why intercept studies have largely replaced door-to-door samples for personal interviews.

Prerecruited Central-Location Studies

For some types of projects it may be most efficient to screen respondents ahead of time by telephone, for example, then invite those who qualify to come to a test location at a specific time to be interviewed. This method is often best when two things are present:

1. *The incidence (the proportion of qualified respondents) is low.* If only 5 percent or 10 percent of all people contacted will qualify to be interviewed, it's usually best to do this screening in advance, then conduct the full-scale interviews all at once.
2. *The interview is long.* Many people find it inconvenient to spend forty-five minutes or an hour on the spur of the moment to be interviewed. Prerecruiting allows them to make an appointment to be interviewed at a convenient time.

Mail/Telephone Combinations

On projects for which it's still necessary to make some contact in person, it's often possible to reduce costs by using the telephone or mail on portions of the study.

Product tests are an example. A personal interview (intercept or door to door) is usually needed at the beginning of an in-home use test to qualify respondents for the study and give them samples of the test product. But instead of conducting the callback interview in person to get an after-use evaluation of the product, you may find it more efficient to obtain reactions by telephone, through the mail, or by a combination of telephone and mail.

4

Doing Research by Telephone

AT&T used to claim, "Long distance is the next best thing to being there." Not true. In some kinds of marketing research studies, the telephone is actually *better* than being there. In other studies, of course, it may be far less than "next best"; it may be totally unacceptable. But as the use of door-to-door interviewing has declined, telephone research has replaced it for most large, national studies.

Advantages of Telephone Interviewing

Telephone research has several important advantages that account for its widespread popularity today as a method of interviewing:

• *Ease of sampling.* A key advantage of telephone interviewing is that it makes it relatively easy to draw a large, geographically dispersed sample. And the use of random digit dialing makes it possible to reach even newly moved households and homes with unlisted numbers. (See the section in this chapter on "Trends in Telephone Interviewing" for a description of random digit dialing.)

• *Callback ability.* A drawback of door-to-door interviewing is the need for an interviewer to travel across town to make a second attempt to reach a respondent—perhaps only to find that he or she isn't available. With telephone interviewing, callbacks can be made much more easily, which makes it relatively simple to follow good callback sampling procedures.

• *Ease of supervision.* When interviewing is done from a central telephone facility, it's possible for a supervisor to monitor a portion of each interviewer's work to make certain the questionnaire is being administered properly. This close supervision is impractical for most personal interviews.

• *Questionnaire flexibility.* Compared with mail questionnaires, telephone research can use more complex questionnaires (skip patterns, probes, refer-backs, and terminations), because an interviewer is at hand to control the questioning.

• *Ready access to hard-to-reach people.* In any study using personal interviewing, it is difficult to reach consumers in small towns or rural areas. There are few professional interviewing services available in such places. With telephone interviewing, however, these consumers are just as easy to reach as respondents in large cities.

• *Speed.* When a central interviewing facility is used, it's possible to assign enough interviewers to a study to complete hundreds of interviews each day. This makes it possible to complete even large, national studies in a short time.

• *Pretesting ability.* You can pretest a telephone questionnaire in the morning and begin full-scale interviewing on a nationwide basis that afternoon. Obviously that isn't practical with personal interviewing or mail studies.

• *Lower cost.* Telephone research usually costs only a fraction of the cost of studies involving personal interviews, especially door-to-door contacts. It's usually more expensive than mail research, however.

Disadvantages of Telephone Interviewing

At the same time, telephone research has some characteristics that limit the kinds of studies for which it can be used. These include:

• *Limited length of interview.* The ideal length for a telephone interview is between ten and fifteen minutes, with thirty minutes being about the maximum that's feasible. If it isn't possible to obtain the information required in this length of time, then telephone research isn't a good alternative.

• *Lack of exhibits.* It's impossible, of course, to show a respondent anything during a telephone interview. This can be a major limitation on certain studies. It makes it totally impractical to conduct certain types of research (advertising-copy testing and package testing, for example) by telephone. Sometimes this obstacle can be overcome by mailing the respondent an exhibit, then calling to conduct the interview. Even if you're creative, however, this remains an inherent problem with telephone research.

• *Limitations on types of questions.* It's difficult to administer lengthy scales by telephone, which in many cases limits your ability to measure the issue at hand with any degree of sensitivity. Also, the repeated use of similar scales in a questionnaire becomes tiresome to the respondent more quickly on the telephone than it does in person.

Trends in Telephone Interviewing

As telephone interviewing grows, it continues to develop and make more use of technology.

Centralized Interviewing Centers

Years ago, when telephone interviewing was starting, interviewers usually conducted the work out of their homes. Today, however, most telephone interviewing is done from large, central telephone interviewing centers, where dozens of interviewers work at the same time calling people all over the United States. These central facilities offer much better supervision and sampling control than the old-fashioned "kitchen" approach did. Moreover, the economies of scale made possible by centralized telephone service usually make this type of interviewing surprisingly competitive in cost with less well supervised approaches.

Random Digit Dialing

Although sampling from telephone books is adequate for many telephone studies, there are always a number of households (probably at least 20 percent) not listed in even the most current telephone directory. Some families have moved into the area since the directory was compiled, while others have chosen to have unlisted numbers. Random digit dialing is a technique that can be used, if the study objectives require it, to reach some households that aren't in the directory.

Random digit dialing is based on this concept: Every possible telephone number in America can be sampled by randomly generating ten-digit numbers (a three-digit area code plus a seven-digit telephone number). In reality, of course, many of these randomly generated numbers do not have telephones assigned to them. But companies that sell samples of randomly generated numbers try to concentrate those numbers in banks of numbers that are known to be assigned and in use.

Another variation of this is known as "plus one" sampling, where one is added to the last digit of a number in the directory. (For example, 934-3456 becomes 934-3457 with this method.) This is a way to add some "randomness" to the sample and reach some households not in the directory without going to completely random digit dialing.

Random digit dialing is more costly than sampling from telephone books, but it offers a way to reach consumers who might not be included in a sample drawn only from telephone books. Are the people who aren't listed likely to differ significantly from those in the directory in their attitudes toward or usage of the product being studied? That's the question you have to ask yourself to determine whether random digit dialing makes sense for a study. Because of the improved sample coverage it can provide, random digit dialing is gaining acceptance for use on studies where the best possible sample is desirable—and worth the higher cost.

Computer-Assisted Telephone Interviewing

In most modern telephone interviewing centers, paper questionnaires are being replaced by computer-assisted telephone interviewing (CATI) systems. These look like personal computers and are often wired directly to a large computer. The screen displays questions for the interviewer to read over the telephone to the respondent. The interviewer then types the respondent's answer directly into the computer on the keyboard. The elimination of paper questionnaires—which also cuts out editing, keypunching, and data cleaning—and direct interaction between the interviewer and the computer result in faster turnaround, greater accuracy, closer control, and often lower cost. As a result, CATI is fast becoming the major approach to telephone interviewing.

Projects That Typically Use Telephone Interviewing

Telephone research is an efficient way to collect facts and opinions from a broad national sample of people. For this reason, it has become the preferred technique for many attitude and usage studies, particularly tracking studies, which are repeated periodically to monitor customer awareness, attitudes, and usage in a product category.

In addition, telephone research may be an efficient way to conduct callback interviews with people who have previously been contacted in person—participants in product tests, for example. Telephone interviews can be used after a test period to obtain respondents' opinions of the product they have been testing.

Finally, telephone research is often used to contact respondents drawn from a specific list (coupon redeemers, for example). When there are a limited number of potential respondents and they are geographically dispersed, telephone interviewing is the only practical way to reach them. For this reason, the use of telephone research is growing in business-to-business and medical studies.

5

Pros and Cons of Mail Questionnaires

When government makes a mistake, it is a
big one, like the post office or Vietnam.

—Ben Heineman, president of Northwest Industries

Sending out a questionnaire in the mail often seems like an attractive alternative. It's relatively easy to do and usually quite inexpensive compared with telephone interviewing.

Advantages of Mail Research

While mail research has some major limitations that make it unreliable for many types of studies, its benefits can be significant.

- *Low cost.* Using address labels and a cover letter addressed "Dear Respondent" is an inexpensive way to distribute a large number of questionnaires. This is the main appeal of mail research.
- *Efficiency of large samples.* Not only is mail research inexpensive to begin with, but it gets relatively more efficient as the sample size grows. For example, the cost difference between mailing out 2,000 and 1,000 questionnaires may be only the costs of the postage and of a little printing.
- *Ready access to hard-to-reach respondents.* You can reach geographically dispersed respondents or hard-to-reach people (farmers, for example) at the same cost as that of reaching geographically concentrated, easy-to-reach people. In this respect, mail research is similar to telephone research.

- *No interviewer bias.* Because there is no interviewer present, there can be no interviewer bias. Unfortunately this can also be a problem, because there's no interviewer to probe or clarify incomplete answers.
- *Potential for exhibits.* Although it's impossible to include large exhibits in a mailing, it's quite feasible to incorporate drawings or photos into a mail questionnaire. It's also possible to include such things as fabric swatches in a mailing. This can be an important advantage in certain types of studies over telephone interviewing.

Disadvantages of Mail Research

For most projects, the limitations of mail research far outnumber the advantages, which accounts for mail studies being rarer than either personal or telephone research. For most types of studies, the following limitations make using a mail questionnaire inappropriate:

- *Low rate of return.* On a typical mail study sent to a cold list of randomly selected respondents, no more than 5 percent or 10 percent of the questionnaires will be returned. This can sometimes be increased—occasionally increased dramatically—but it's always a potential problem with mail studies.
- *Nonreturner bias.* This is a major weakness of mail questionnaires: Not only is the percentage of respondents small, but the respondents who do return complete questionnaires are often not typical of the total sample.

For example, on a mail survey about a new product, consumers who return questionnaires are likely to be those who either like the product intensely or have a complaint about it they want to voice. It's common for older, retired people to have a higher return rate than younger, busier consumers; yet it's often the younger consumers you are most interested in studying.

In short, the typically low rate of return, along with serious questions about the representativeness of the respondents who do reply, make mail questionnaires unreliable for many purposes.*

- *Poor control.* You can't control who fills out the questionnaire—or

---

*A bit of research trivia: In 1896, Professor Harlow Gale, of the University of Minnesota, sent a mail questionnaire to 200 Twin Cities advertisers to survey their opinions of what made advertising successful. Unfortunately, his efforts were hampered when he achieved only a 10 percent return rate—a problem that still plagues mail studies.

even who gets it. Many mailing lists of names aren't up-to-date, which means that someone other than the person to whom you've sent the questionnaire may complete and return it.

• *Limitations on questions.* Because there is no interviewer present to administer a mail questionnaire, each question must be carefully structured; there's no way to clarify a question the respondent doesn't understand. Perhaps more important, there's no opportunity for probing or following up on incomplete or unclear answers.

• *Oversimplification of format.* Because a mail questionnaire is always self-administered, it must be very simple and straightforward. If there are too many complex questions or difficult skips, many potential respondents will simply get frustrated and throw the questionnaire away. Newspapers are said to assume only a sixth-grade education among readers, which is probably a good guideline for mail questionnaires too.

• *Slowness.* With mail surveys, it usually takes several weeks for returns to come in, and even longer when follow-up mailings are made.

• *Lack of pretesting.* Because it takes just as long to pretest a mail questionnaire as to conduct the full-scale project, a pilot study often isn't feasible.

• *Difficulty of obtaining names.* For consumer studies, it's best to have a specific name to address the questionnaire to. And having an individual's name is even more important on industrial, executive, or medical studies. Addressing a questionnaire to "Engineer" at a large company or "Floor Nurse" at a hospital isn't adequate. Unfortunately, a list of such names, especially on industrial or medical studies, may be nearly impossible to obtain.

Trends in Mail Questionnaires

Mail questionnaires are suitable only for certain kinds of tests, with medical and industrial markets being among the most frequent users.

Because low response rate is a primary weakness of mail questionnaires (along with the nonreturner bias resulting from low response), many of the efforts to improve mail questionnaires center on increasing return rates. Doing that makes mail research a more acceptable alternative for some kinds of studies.

The first step in any mail study is to make sure that the "package" you send to the people on your list is designed to encourage response. To that end:

1. Make the package look attractive.
   - Use first-class postage.
   - Mail an incentive, such as a dollar bill, with the questionnaire to show how important you consider each individual's response.
   - Personalize your cover letter by addressing it to the respondent by name.
   - Make the entire package look professional. Don't skimp on paper or printing quality. Avoid the look of a bulk mailing.
2. Make the questionnaire look easy to answer and return.
   - Enclose a postage-paid return envelope.
   - Keep the questionnaire from looking cluttered.
   - Try to keep length to under four pages.
   - Consider putting the questionnaire on both sides of a folded 17" × 11" page, which tends to look less intimidating than a four-page, single-sided questionnaire.
3. Make sure you use a mail questionnaire only on a study where the limitations of mail don't make it inappropriate.

Consider doing something unusual, creative, or dramatic to increase the return rate on your mail questionnaire. If it's important to reach a small number of specific respondents, as is typically the case in industrial or medical studies, this creativity is often particularly useful as a tactic.

For example, one company used a combination of mail and telephone techniques on a study among upper-management executives. A small lockbox containing survey materials was sent to each respondent. A letter was attached, informing the person that he or she would be called in a few days, given the combination for the lockbox, and interviewed on the basis of the contents of the box. The lockbox, of course, was a strong attention-getting device. Who could throw it away unopened? The box added enough interest to the questionnaire to induce a large proportion of the respondents to agree to take part in the study when they were contacted by telephone.

With all the junk mail most people receive each day, it takes something special to make a mail questionnaire stand out and motivate the respondent to return it.

Projects That Typically Use Mail Questionnaires

Mail questionnaires are most often used on business-to-business or medical studies, where respondents share a relatively high interest in the products being studied. In these studies, there is often only a small, geographically dispersed sample to draw from, so the extra effort and expense of special incentives or unusual approaches (such as the lockbox) can be justified.

It is rare, however, for a mail survey to be used on general studies of consumer products and services. The response rate on these projects is usually too low to produce reliable results.

Mail Panels and Purchase Panels

Because of the cost appeal of mail research, two approaches have been developed to retain the economies of mail studies yet overcome the low-response problem. Both use respondents who have previously agreed to take part in mail studies, usually in return for a token gift as an incentive.

Mail panels periodically send custom-designed questionnaires to their panel members, while consumers who are on *purchase panels* agree to keep diaries of all their purchases in several product categories each month.

The question most frequently asked about these two methods is whether diary panel members are representative of the population. ("Who would agree to keep track of everything they buy at the grocery store?") Nevertheless, the record shows that these panels generally provide a good way of developing straightforward information on large samples of consumers at relatively low cost.

The major mail panel companies are Home Testing Institute (HTI), National Family Opinion (NFO), and Market Facts.

Part III

Step by Step Through a Research Project

6

The Steps in a Survey Research Study

How do you get from the beginning to the end of a project without forgetting any important steps along the way?

Well, it helps to have an overview of the process, which can then serve as a checklist to make sure everything gets done—or at least, omitted on purpose and for good reason.

A project's flow could be viewed a number of different ways. The basic steps needed to complete a typical project are shown in Figure 6-1. While there are many other steps and activities along the way, these fifteen steps are the major ones. Some things can be done simultaneously (such as scheduling interviews and writing the questionnaire), while others have to happen in sequence (writing the questionnaire and writing the instructions, for example).

In addition to these steps, test materials (ads, product samples, packages, and so on) must be ordered and ready on time.

Project Management

Each project should have one person (usually with a title such as "project director") responsible for coordinating and managing the study from beginning to end. This person must be:

- Organized
- Detail-oriented
- Able to handle a lot of things at one time
- Able to keep things moving and get things done
- Deadline-conscious

Figure 6-1. Fifteen steps in a research project.

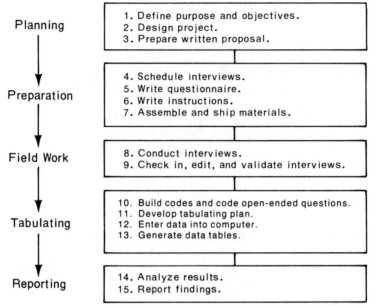

Planning	1. Define purpose and objectives. 2. Design project. 3. Prepare written proposal.
Preparation	4. Schedule interviews. 5. Write questionnaire. 6. Write instructions. 7. Assemble and ship materials.
Field Work	8. Conduct interviews. 9. Check in, edit, and validate interviews.
Tabulating	10. Build codes and code open-ended questions. 11. Develop tabulating plan. 12. Enter data into computer. 13. Generate data tables.
Reporting	14. Analyze results. 15. Report findings.

If you're running a project yourself, make sure someone's designated to act in this role. If you're working with an outside research supplier, be sure to meet, then stay in touch with, the project director. The project director is like the quarterback of the team and will play a key role in getting the project done properly and on time.

The Steps

Many companies have flowcharts or checklists of the detailed steps in a research project to serve as reminders of the tasks to be done and to keep the study on track. Many of these steps are the subjects of whole chapters in this book. However, here's a capsule description of each phase:

1. *Define the project's purpose and objectives.* "If you don't know where you're going, any road will get you there." Everything that follows in the project (and since this is the first step, that's *everything*) will go more smoothly if you take time at the very start to clearly determine why the

project is being undertaken, what the study should be designed to measure, and what decision will be taken on the basis of it.

2. *Design the project.* You then need to develop a plan for a study that will meet that purpose and those objectives. This is the place to put in "head time" on a project to make sure that the design really fits the problem and isn't just the closest thing you can think of quickly.

3. *Prepare a written proposal.* Are you sure that *everyone* in the project understands what's to be done? Movie mogul Samuel Goldwyn said, "Verbal contracts aren't worth the paper they're written on." Verbal descriptions of research designs can have comparable value. They're just too easy for people to misinterpret. The written proposal pins things down and provides the means of ensuring that everyone agrees and understands.

4. *Schedule interviews.* Do this as far ahead of time as possible, since it becomes a deadline around which most of the other steps must be planned.

5. *Compose the questionnaire.* You now have the difficult task of translating your objectives into specific, clear, unambiguous questions. (That's why there are two chapters on this subject.)

6. *Write instructions.* Don't forget to give the interviewers and supervisors detailed instructions on how to conduct the study in exactly the way you want it done. Don't assume anything.

7. *Assemble and ship materials.* If possible, avoid leaving this until five o'clock on the afternoon before the morning that interviewing is set to begin 2,000 miles away. Be skeptical of the miracles promised in ads by freight companies and the U.S. Postal Service.

8. *Conduct interviews.* This is what the whole study is set up to accomplish. It seems so simple, but there are seven steps before it and an equal number to follow.

9. *Check in, edit, and validate interviews.* These three little steps can spare you a lot of problems later.

> *Check in:* Simply count the number of completed interviews received.
>
> *Edit:* Check within the questionnaires for internal consistency. For example, people who never heard of a brand shouldn't have been asked when they last bought it. But on a big study you can almost bet that the questionnaires will show that this has happened a few times.

Validate: Spot-check to make sure that the people whose names are on the questionnaires were actually interviewed and were asked the questions properly.

10. *Build codes and code open-ended questions.* Answers to all the "why?" questions, as well as to any other questions calling for discussion-type answers, must be translated into numerical responses that the computer can tabulate. This can be tricky (which is why there's a chapter on coding too).

11. *Develop a tabulating plan.* Now's the time to think about how you want the computer to deliver the results. What format do you want? What subgroups of people do you want to look at in detail? Develop the tabulating plan by going back to the purpose and objectives of the study and then looking for ways to lay out the results to meet those objectives.

12. *Enter the data into the computer.* This puts the information gleaned from the questionnaires where you can use it and work with it.

13. *Generate data tables.* Here you get the results of the study back from the computer in the form specified by your tabulation plan.

14. *Analyze results.* Now you spend "head time" trying to translate all the numbers into answers to the key questions posed by the study.

15. *Report findings.* Finally, the payoff! Now you bring the results of the project to bear on the problems that started it all. This is the part that's really fun. It's what research is really all about—but (unfortunately) it constitutes only a small part of the total process.

Background, Purpose, and Objectives

Understanding the *background,* the *purpose,* and the *objectives* of a study is critical. The initial design of the project is determined by this information, and the report of the results is usually organized around answering the questions posed under these headings.

The three topics are related, but they differ in important ways. Each can be most easily defined by a question:

Background: How has this problem come to exist?
Purpose: What decision will be made on the basis of the research?
Objectives: What information must the research provide to help make that decision?

An example can help clarify the distinction between a study's purpose and its objective. The *purpose* of a product test could be to help decide which of two new products, A or B, should be introduced. The *objective* of the same study might be to determine which product, A or B, is preferred by consumers—but that preference alone might not determine which product is introduced. Differences in cost or profitability, production capacity, requirements for new equipment, and many other factors could also play an important role in the decision.

So while it is important to keep the decision to be made (the purpose) in mind, it's also important to clearly define the specific information that is expected from the study (the objectives).

If you're dealing with research problems within a company for which you've worked for a while, much of the background of a problem will be understood. You don't need to review it for every project.

But if you're working in a new company, on an unfamiliar product, or with a new outside research supplier, you should go over the background issues in detail. And the purpose and objectives checklists bear review on every study.

Here are the basic questions you should ask regarding background, purpose, and objectives:

Project Background Checklist

1. Briefly, what is the company's history? What is the company's personality—go-go, conservative, or what?
2. What are its major product lines? What is the relative importance of each product line?
3. What is the product's sales history? Is it growing, stable, or declining?
4. What are the competitive products? What is the market share of each? What new products have entered the market?
5. In one sentence: What is the problem? Then expand on that one sentence by asking who? what? when? where? why? how?
6. Is this a big problem or a little problem?
7. What previous research has been done on this subject? What did it show?

Project Purpose Checklist

1. What decision will be made or what action will be taken as a result of the research?

2. What are the implications of this action? Is it a big deal or a little deal?
3. What are the alternatives available?
4. What are the risks in the decision or action?
5. What are the potential payoffs of the decision?
6. When will the decision be made? Are there externally enforced deadlines on the decision?

Project Objectives Checklist

1. What *specific* information should the project provide?
2. If more than one type of information is to be developed from the study, which type is most important? What are the priorities for the information?
3. What results are expected? Is there agreement among those involved with the project? If not, why not?
4. Have criteria been established for evaluating the results? If so, what are they? If not, why not?

Discussing these questions should provide enough understanding to permit you to begin designing the study.

7

How to Estimate
Research Costs

Never ask of money spent
Where the spender thinks it went.
Nobody was ever meant
To remember or invent
What he did with every cent.

— Robert Frost, "The Hardship of Accounting"

Wouldn't it be nice if cost were no object and we could do all the research we pleased without being asked to account for where the money went? Well, welcome back to reality. Cost is always an object in research; it sometimes seems like *the* object.

Although it's true that good design and careful execution shouldn't be sacrificed to cost considerations, realistic budget constraints cannot be ignored. They're a basic fact of research life.

Here is a step-by-step description of how research costs are estimated by research companies and a list of the factors that most directly influence costs. (The next chapter describes specific ways to *cut* costs.)

Principles of Cost Estimating

Most research companies estimate costs for projects using some variation of this basic formula:

$$\text{Total costs} = \frac{\text{labor hours required}}{\text{to conduct study}} \times \frac{\text{dollar billing}}{\text{rate per hour}} + \text{expenses}$$

It's really that simple. Even though the specific methods used by different research companies can become very complex, the principles involved are quite simple. Let's look at all the pieces of a cost estimate and at how they are assembled to develop a final budget figure.

Labor

A large part of the cost of any survey research project is labor—the charges for the time people spend conducting the study. On most projects there are two kinds of labor involved:

1. *Interviewing and data entry.* These are directly related to the size and complexity of the study—the number of people interviewed, the number of questions to be coded and keypunched, and so on.
2. *Administration and project management.* These include the time required to design, direct, and supervise the study.

Interviewing. The key factor in determining the cost of the interviewing is time. How many interviewing hours will it take to conduct the interviews, or how many interviews can an interviewer complete in one hour's time? So many factors affect this completion rate that it would be impossible to list them all, but these are the major ones:

- *Qualifications and incidence.* How many people does the interviewer have to screen before a qualified respondent can be found?
- *Length of questionnaire.* How long does it take to administer the questionnaire to a qualified respondent?
- *Type of interviewing method.* What type of interviewing is to be used—telephone, door to door, intercept, or central location?

Other factors, such as time of day of the interviews, quotas of hard-to-reach people, and the need for specially trained interviewers, can also affect the cost of the interviewing.

The actual interviewing done by research companies is either conducted at a central telephone facility or, if it involves personal interviews, these are conducted in several cities and then subcontracted to independent interviewing services in each city. Each location has supervisors and other office staff who are responsible for training and supervising the interviewers. So in addition to the cost of interviewing hours, there are also costs for supervision of the project. These supervision costs are charged directly on an hourly basis or by adding a percentage to the cost of interviewing. In addition, automobile mileage, location rental, respondent fees, and charges for equipment may be part of the total interviewing costs.

Data entry. If the interviews are collected on paper questionnaires rather than CRTs, the information on the questionnaires must be entered into a computer for data processing. If there are unstructured answers from open-ended questions, these answers have to be coded into an answer structure. All closed-ended or structured answers can be entered directly into the computer by keypunch or from a keyboard or CRT terminal.

Some of the major factors affecting the cost of coding and data entry are:

- Number of questionnaires to be tabulated
- Number of answered questions on each questionnaire
- Number of open-ended and closed-ended questions on each questionnaire
- Complexity of questionnaire format

Administration and project management. The final (and in most cases smallest) part of the total labor cost is the time spent in setting up the project, typing and assembling the questionnaires, and supervising tabulation of the results.

Even though most of this time is spent by the higher professional levels within the company, the total number of hours is small in comparison to the time spent on interviewing and data entry.

Some of the factors influencing project and data processing management are:

- Amount of time spent on the design of the project and questionnaire.
- Size and complexity of the project. The test design and number of interviewing locations are examples of things that affect the time needed to coordinate a project.
- Changes in design, or implementation problems.
- Amount and complexity of data processing required.
- Complexity of analysis and report.

Once the total number of hours and each type of labor are determined, the hourly rate charged for each type of job is multiplied by the number of hours to calculate the total cost of labor.

Expenses

The other part of the project cost is expenses. Most projects, regardless of type, have the following expenses:

- Printing
- Long-distance telephone tolls
- Postage and shipping
- Computer time
- Travel expenses

Other expenses, which vary by type of project, are:

- Location rental
- Equipment rental
- Incentives for respondents
- Product costs
- Product storage and delivery costs
- Field supplies

The labor costs and expenses are usually computed and recorded on a cost estimating form or put into a computer program.

Contingency Allowance

Because it is difficult to estimate costs precisely, most research companies include a contingency of plus or minus (±)10 percent. This means: "If the project is conducted the way we've assumed, we believe the actual costs will be within 10 percent of what we've estimated." If costs are more than 10 percent higher, the research company makes less profit. If costs are less than 90 percent of the estimate, it makes a higher profit.

This ± 10 percent contingency range is meant to cover normal estimating uncertainty with the original specifications. It is *not* intended to provide for changes in the specifications. If the specs are changed, the base estimate should change too.

Evaluating Cost Estimates

It's not unusual for clients to get competitive bids from different suppliers. That's the American way. But clients should keep several things in mind when comparing the cost estimates of different research companies:

1. *The total estimates are the only things that can be compared directly.* Some companies use hourly billing rates that incorporate profit; others add a profit margin to the total. Looking at the pieces will make comparison confusing. The bottom line is the key to comparing estimates.

2. *Large differences in competitive cost estimates may reflect different assumptions by the suppliers.* If you get four bids on the same project, chances are that the difference between the high and the low bidder will be no more than 10 or 15 percent. If one is too high or low, check to make sure that the research company is basing its estimate on the same assumptions and specifications as the rest.

3. *Lowball bids can be risky.* As in all businesses, research companies sometimes submit lowballs to get business, keep business, or bolster sagging volume. As a client, go into this type of situation with your eyes open and protect yourself if you take a lowball bid. The risk of the lowball bid is that the supplier may try to cut corners, so be especially careful that quality control procedures are followed on these types of projects.

4. *The research company and the client are partners regarding costs.* It's fair to say that most research companies don't plan to get rich on a single project, and most clients recognize that their suppliers have to make a reasonable profit to stay in business. The best arrangement between client and supplier is based on trust and recognition of the shared goal of producing professional, action-oriented research.

8

Ten Ways to Cut
Research Costs

Most companies' marketing research budgets are being squeezed by managements that suspect there's some fat in there that could come out. They're generally right. The budgets for most research projects could be cut and still enable the project teams to accomplish their objectives.

Costs for many types of research have at least doubled over the past ten years. That wasn't a big problem when times were good and budgets were fat, but the current economic situation seems to have sharpened marketing directors' memories. They suddenly recall that today's $20,000 project cost $10,000 when they were assistant product managers.

For a variety of reasons, we can never get back to yesterday's cost level, but clients usually can do better at cutting costs than they're doing. In that our company makes a living selling research, I feel a little like the chicken telling the fox where the holes are in the barnyard fence. But openness about costs has always been part of our philosophy. If a client asked me, "How can I cut my research costs?" here's what I'd tell him:

1. *Change the cities where you do research.* Too often the cities for a sample are selected by naming the first three or four that come to mind. The most predictable candidates using this method are New York, Chicago, Los Angeles, and Atlanta. Unfortunately, all cities are not created equal in research costs. On a recent study, we found that the costs per interview in New York were more than twice those in Pittsburgh and

Adapted with permission from *Marketing News*, June 6, 1975. Published by the American Marketing Association.

Denver, among others. These differences exist for a number of reasons, some more understandable than others. But regardless of their legitimacy, the differences are real.

Sometimes you're locked into the cities where you have to work (when you're researching products in test market, for example). But if you've got flexibility in the selection of markets, don't necessarily use the first ones that you think of.

2. *Do more multiproduct studies.* For some clients this is about as simple as suggesting that all the countries in the Middle East get together on a peace agreement. As a supplier, I'm scared by the thought of trying to coordinate this type of project; but if a company can put one of these projects together internally (on products within a division, for example), there's a lot of money to be saved.

3. *Eliminate open-ended questions.* It may not be possible to cut out all open-ended questions, but it's almost always practical to eliminate some of them from a study. An open-ended question costs three to five times more to ask, code, and tabulate than a structured question. Some clients continue to ask the same "why do you like it?" questions on the same products project after project, long after they've learned all that consumers have to say on the subject.

Related money wasters are such redundant open-ended questions as "What would you like to see changed about it?" and "Why haven't you bought it?" A good rule is: If you can use a single set of codes for more than one question—as you almost invariably can for the two questions just mentioned—then you've really got just one question, not two. Useless open-ended questions are one of the biggest sources of wasted money in marketing research.

4. *Cut questionnaires to the bare essentials.* A lot of research dollars are spent on fishing expeditions in the hope that consumers will say something profound that no one has even suspected before. These long-shot questions are almost always suggested at research planning meetings by the phrase, "As long as we're there, let's ask them . . ." Just about every study has at least a few of these that could be cut with no appreciable effect on the results. The instinct to include these questions is the same one that built Las Vegas and made state lotteries lucrative. And the odds of being successful are about the same too.

5. *Be careful about sample sizes.* This is a tough area to evaluate because there's no such thing as the "right" sample size. It's largely a matter of judgment. But sampling statistics being what they are, doubling the sample size (and the interviewing costs) doesn't come close to cutting your confidence intervals in half. Are great big sample sizes

worth it? Often not. The point is to avoid oversampling "just to be safe." It costs money, and it's usually not all that safe, anyway. Instead, consider an alternative.

6. *Do sequential research.* By this I mean you should consider doing a small-scale study first to see if it produces any surprises. Go ahead with a full-blown study only if it does.

For example, if you're doing a periodic product test to check quality against the competition and all tests in the past have shown you're about equal, start with a modest-size project to see if anything has changed. Chances are good that nothing has, and you can save yourself the cost of a big test. A lot of money is wasted on big studies verifying with great statistical certainty what companies already suspect or know for sure.

7. *Process only the information you really need.* There's something in most researchers that tells them information isn't available unless it's on paper somewhere. So they tabulate everything they can think of from a study just to have it on file. As a result, they end up with stacks of expensive computer printouts that they can't find time to read through, let alone understand.

We need to realize that most research data are retained for a long time. Our company, for example, saves data tapes for at least seven years—longer if the client requests it. Long after the study is completed, you can go back and tabulate any piece of information you need.

The most efficient approach to tabulating a study is to determine what information you must have to understand the subject, then tabulate only that. Leave the rest on the tape, and go back to it only if you find you need it. This takes some hard thinking, which is why it rarely gets done. Unfortunately, computers have made us all a little sloppy about this kind of planning because they spit out tabulations so easily. But they don't do it free!

8. *Ask: "Is this technique really necessary?"* Tough times are good times to take a hard look at the need to experiment with expensive quantitative techniques of analysis. Is this really the time to try out a factor analysis, cluster analysis, or multidimensional scaling just to see what it might show? If you've got good reason to believe it will help you, go ahead. These techniques can save money in the long run. But is this the time to play hunches? Maybe not.

9. *Leave your suppliers alone.* Obviously, a certain amount of coordination and planning is necessary on any research project. But at some point, demanding too much coordination (even if you think of it as "client service") turns into hand-holding; and somewhere, somehow, you're going to have to pay for that. The best approach is to find a sup-

plier you can trust, give clear instructions about what you want done, then leave that supplier alone to do the work. Since you're paying a research company primarily to do research, you'll save by keeping meetings, reviews, and revisions to a minimum.

10. *Challenge your research suppliers to save you money.* By this I *don't* mean that you should hassle your suppliers about costs. It's funny how some clients are raising prices to their customers and asking us not just to hold, but actually to lower, our prices to them. What I do mean is, stop, after outlining a project to suppliers, and ask them, "Now what could be done to cut the cost of this project?" I think you'll be surprised at the good ideas they have.

These aren't perfect solutions. You always have to give up something to save money. But in most cases, what you're saving is much more than what you're losing. Unfortunately, few research users are close enough to the day-to-day mechanics of the business to know the kinds of savings that are possible. But the times may be right to start digging in and finding the soft spots.

9

How to Develop a Questionnaire

Vigorous writing is concise. A sentence should contain no unnecessary words, a paragraph no unnecessary sentences, for the same reason that a drawing should have no unnecessary lines and a machine no unnecessary parts.

—William Strunk, Jr., *The Elements of Style*

Does the exact wording of a question really matter that much? Yes, it matters a great deal, probably more than you imagine. Studies have shown that exactly how a question is worded and asked can even determine the results of opinion polls. For example, in the late 1970s, the *New York Times*–CBS News Poll asked this question: "Do you think there should be an amendment to the Constitution prohibiting abortions, or shouldn't there be such an amendment?" The responses were:

Favor amendment	29%
Uncertain	9
Oppose amendment	62

Later in the survey, the same people were asked a slightly reworded question, which produced a very different result: "Do you believe there should be an amendment to the Constitution protecting the life of the unborn child, or shouldn't there be such an amendment?"

Favor amendment	50%
Uncertain	11
Oppose amendment	39

The two wordings produced opposite indications of the direction of public opinion. So using the right question and the proper wording clearly does make a difference—often a crucial difference.

A questionnaire must do two basic things: (1) translate the objectives of the research project into specific questions the respondents can answer and (2) motivate the respondents to cooperate and give their information correctly so that it reflects their attitudes accurately. All the rules, guidelines, and tips about writing questionnaires are nothing more than ways to accomplish those two purposes.

Steps in Writing a Questionnaire

Each researcher develops his or her own approach to writing a questionnaire. Whatever the technique, however, it usually includes the following six steps:

1. Consult your statement of the study objectives and develop from it a list of information to be obtained. This can take the form of specific questions, phrases, or key words (such as "likes" or "dislikes" of product). This list will form the basis for developing your questions. This step is critical. Don't bypass it. A questionnaire cannot be written until you understand precisely what information you need to get.

2. Consider the method of data collection—mail, telephone, or personal interviews. This obviously affects the ways in which questions are asked, their order, and how the questionnaire should be formatted.

3. Draft the questionnaire.

4. Get someone else—preferably someone who is not directly involved in the study—to read through your questionnaire draft and critique it.

5. Pretest the questionnaire.

6. Make the necessary revisions and proceed with the study.

A useful learning device is to debrief the interviewers at the conclusion of the study. While it's too late to do anything about this study, interviewers' comments on what worked and what didn't work well during the study can be helpful in improving your next project.

Checkpoints

Once the questionnaire is drafted and you read it over, there are some points to double-check:

☐ *Does the questionnaire answer your objective for the study?*

☐ *Are all the questions necessary?* Extra questions add to expense and increase the demands made on the respondent.

☐ *Will respondents be able to answer the questions?* This means, are they likely to have the information you are asking for? Can they remember it? Questions that ask respondents to mention things they can't remember accurately usually lead to bad information, because respondents will try to furnish the information even if they have to guess.

☐ *Will the respondent be willing to answer the questions?* Sensitive, private issues can be a problem in this respect, although people are often more willing to discuss such issues than you would expect. Questions that are too much work or require the respondent to expend extra effort in collecting the information needed for an answer can bring the interview to an abrupt halt.

☐ *Does it flow?* Does it sound more like a natural conversation than just a series of unrelated questions? Is it internally consistent and logical? In other words, does it make sense?

☐ *Is it reasonable in length?* The only way to really test this is to read it through *aloud* and have someone answer it. Just reading it over to yourself is not a good indicator of length.

☐ *Can an interviewer or a respondent fill it out?* Can someone who knows less about the study than you do complete the questionnaire? A pretest can help determine this, but often you can avoid problems simply by being honest with yourself about this.

☐ *Is the sequence of questions right?* Be sure you have arranged questions so that the answer to one will not influence the response to another.

☐ *Have you included transitions and introductions?* If the questionnaire is going to seem conversational, you need to build bridges between questions and sections in the questionnaire.

Sections of a Questionnaire

There are three basic sections to most questionnaires.

1. *Qualifying questions.* These are the questions that must be asked in order to determine if you are talking with the proper type of person for this study. Examples would be:

"What brands of soft drinks have you purchased within the past week?"

"Do you own a dog?"

"Do you, or does any member of your immediate family, work for a food product manufacturer, marketing research company, or advertising agency? [This is called a security screen.]"

The answers to these questions determine whether the respondent is qualified for participation in the study. The questions immediately following the qualifying questions are critical. These questions must:

- Capture attention and create an interest in what you are researching. You need to get the respondent involved right away.
- Build rapport between the interviewer and the respondent. The more comfortable they feel with each other, the smoother the interview will go and the more complete the information will likely be.
- Make it seem easy for the respondent to answer the question. This is usually done by including some general, simple, nonthreatening questions early in the interview to help the respondent to warm up and feel it is easy to answer the questions.

2. *Basic questions about the category being studied.* This category includes all the questions, both open-ended and closed-ended, that constitute the body of the questionnaire. This is usually the largest section.

3. *Classification or demographic questions.* These include information about the respondent's age, sex, and income, as well as his or her name, address, and telephone number. Classification questions tend to be the least interesting to the respondent and are likely to be the most sensitive, so they are usually placed last.

Guidelines on Questionnaire Writing

As mentioned before, questionnaire writing is an individual thing, and each person does it a little differently. But here are some tips on putting together questionnaires. They are so basic that they apply to almost anyone in virtually any study.

1. *Because one question may influence another, always proceed from the general to the specific.* Consequently, open-ended questions are put at the beginning of the questionnaire. It is best to ask a "likes" and a "dislikes"

question before you bias or educate the respondent with a list of twenty product attributes. Always remember that every question can influence every other question that follows.

2. *Arrange questions in a logical order.* The flow should be similar to the way the respondent would think about a subject. Make sure there are proper transitions and introductions. For example, if you are going from a general category such as cake mixes to questions concerning the brand last used by the purchaser, you might say: "I'd like you to think about the cake mix you used last time you baked a cake. You mentioned you used Betty Crocker cake mix. In the next few questions, I'd like you to think only about the Betty Crocker mix you used last time."

3. *Be sure the respondent won't have to work hard to get the information you're asking for.* If an executive has to dig for sales volume information on a line of individual products, you are unlikely to get an accurate answer. If respondents are asked how many times they've ever waxed their car or made popcorn, they will probably guess at the answer.

We frequently make assumptions that our respondents know—or care—as much as we do about the subject we're researching. Many of the products we research are low-involvement products for the people who buy them. That is, people usually are not involved with cereal, floor wax, or pizza. So make sure you are not asking consumers to tell you more than they can about the category.

4. *Determine if you need several questions instead of one.* Some questions ask for more than one decision by a respondent, making interpretation difficult. If one question can be broken down into several more specific questions, that's usually the best way to do it.

5. *Be careful that respondents don't neglect to state their most important reasons simply because they feel they are so obvious.* This is particularly important with questions about price. If you ask, "Why do you buy Private Label dog food instead of Alpo?" many respondents may neglect to explain that they do so because it's cheaper. That seems so obvious to them that they assume you are looking for other reasons.

6. *Respect the respondent's privacy.* We believe we have a right to ask people questions, but they also have the right to refuse to answer them. Researchers have no inherent "right" to make people talk to them, so don't coerce or pressure people who don't want to take part in a study, whatever their reasons are.

7. *Decide how to handle sensitive issues.* For example, there may be questions that respondents are reluctant to answer. First, recognize that people often provide more information than you might expect if the in-

terview tone is straightforward and businesslike. Tampons and other feminine sanitary products, for example, are routinely researched and tested. So sensitivity is not always present where you think it might be. But let's assume you are studying subjects you think people might be reluctant to discuss openly. Here are some ways to minimize the problem:

- Ask the question within a group of less difficult questions. Then, if the interview is going along smoothly, respondents may be more willing to give an answer.
- Use a general introduction indicating that the behavior asked about is not unusual, that many people have the problem or use the product.
- Depersonalize the question or make it objective. Use phrases like "other people" or "some people" to make the responses easier.
- Use exhibit cards with letters or numbers that correspond to the answers. Because the respondent has only to mention the code letter or number, this helps maintain a certain sense of privacy.

8. *After you've finished writing the questionnaire, read it out loud.* That way, you can be sure you've included all the instructions for the interviewers. This will help you uncover any cumbersome or unclear wording. Let others read the questionnaire too. They can bring a fresh perspective to it and spot things you can't. Finally, be personally involved with pretests and monitoring whenever possible. You're sure to learn something.

Pretesting: Researching the Research

After the questionnaire has been drafted, and reviewed by someone other than the person who devised it, it is always a good idea to pretest it.

A pretest is a small sample of interviews (usually ten to twenty) conducted as a final check before you go ahead with a large-scale study. It's a way to double-check on possible problems and make corrections before you proceed with a study.

What Is Being Tested?

A pretest is used primarily to evaluate the questionnaire and determine the following:

- Does the questionnaire flow naturally and conversationally?
- Are the questions clear and easy to understand?
- Can the questionnaire format be followed by the interviewers?
- Do respondents seem to understand what they're being asked? Can they answer the questions easily?

But in addition to testing the questionnaire, a pretest can also be used to:

- *Test the study methodology.* If many exhibits are being used, for example, a pretest may help determine the best procedure for handling them smoothly.
- *Check on the sampling procedure.* Can interviewers follow the sampling instructions? Is the procedure efficient? Does it have holes in it that become apparent in the field?
- *Establish a completion ratio or interview length.* This can help verify the costs and timing before the full-scale study is begun. Since this is a key factor in estimating costs, a pretest can be especially useful for this purpose.
- *Measure an expected return rate for a mail study.* Then you can decide if your planned sample size is too big, too small, or about right.

Ways of Pretesting

The most straightforward way to pretest, of course, is simply to conduct a few interviews and evaluate them. This is a standard pretest, and it's often done. But sometimes another approach works better. Here are two of these approaches:

1. *Using the first day's work as a pretest.* This is commonly done in telephone studies. Plan to interview for a day, then pause a day to evaluate and make any changes needed before going ahead with the rest of the study. Centralized telephone studies permit this kind of flexibility. And assuming everything works well on the first day, the results can be counted toward the final quota and used in the total sample for the study. This approach allows you to get a running start on the project.

2. *Using one city as a pretest.* If a study involves a large, elaborate setup of displays, it may not be practical to arrange all this for only ten or twenty interviews. A compromise that still retains some of the value of a pretest is to conduct the interviews in one city first (assuming it's a multicity study), then evaluate that before going ahead with the inter-

viewing in other cities. This gives you a chance to check on how things are working while there's still time to make changes before the bulk of the interviewing is done. This is not as good as a standard, separate pretest, but often it's the only alternative that's feasible.

Rules of Thumb

As the researcher in charge, follow these guidelines for conducting a good pretest:

• *Interview people as similar as possible to the actual respondents to be included in the study.* Contacting experts or special authorities in the field doesn't tell you how the questionnaire will work with more typical respondents.

• *Use typical interviewers to conduct the pretest.* Don't use only your best, most experienced interviewers for a pretest, or your results will not indicate how the larger-scale study is likely to go.

• *Actively involve yourself in the pretest.* This may involve monitoring some pretest interviews or debriefing the interviewers after the pretest and getting their reactions to the questionnaire. Because interviewers are an excellent source of feedback on how well a questionnaire is working, don't miss a chance to get their reactions. The more involved the researcher is in the pretest, the more useful it is likely to be.

Validation: Was the Research Done Right?

After the interviewing is completed comes an important quality control step: validation. Validation is the final step to ensure that the interview was done well and the questionnaire was administered correctly. Validation is most often used for personal interviews conducted away from the research company facilities. In central telephone facilities, monitoring of the interviewing as it proceeds is typically used in place of validation.

Validation involves recontacting a portion of the respondents and conducting a brief follow-up interview to confirm that the original interview was, in fact, conducted and that it was handled properly. Usually 10 percent of each interviewer's completed questionnaires are validated.

This step is designed both to ensure the quality of the data and to evaluate the performance of the interviewers. The validation of each study should answer two basic questions:

1. Was the interview actually conducted?
2. Did the interviewer follow the correct procedures?

It is usually difficult to re-ask specific questions from the study. The time that has elapsed since the study was conducted may change some answers, and people's responses to attitude questions can vary from day to day. For these reasons, validation usually covers general areas, such as:

- *Method of contact*—to be sure a personal interview wasn't actually handled on the telephone, for example.
- *Questions asked*—to verify that no important questions, such as qualifying or demographic questions, were skipped.
- *Exhibits/products shown*—to make sure people saw any concept boards or products they were supposed to see.
- *Respondent's familiarity with interviewer*—to determine that the interviewer did not contact friends or acquaintances. A basic rule for interviewers on every study is never to interview anyone they know. It destroys objectivity.
- *General reactions to the interview*—to check on the general quality of the contact.

Sample Validation Questions

The validation form for a study should be based on the objectives of the study. It should check on the most critical questions and qualifications—things that would seriously damage the results if not handled properly.

Ideally, a validation form should include both direct and follow-up questions. The follow-up questions are designed to help clarify a respondent's answer when it does not agree with the expected or "correct" answer.

Here are some typical validation questions and the follow-up questions that might be used:

- *"Could you please describe the study and how you were interviewed?"* This is usually the first question asked during a validation interview. It should yield information about how, when, and where the interview was conducted.

If there were any irregularities in procedures, they are often uncovered here. The respondent may say, "This nice lady telephoned me and asked if I'd like to try some free samples of a new product." If the test was supposed to be a personally administered concept and product test, this shows there is obviously a problem. But the respondent may not give all the information you need, so some follow-up questions must be included:

"Where did the interview take place?"
For a concept test: "Do you remember seeing any descriptions of products or advertisements for products?"
For a product test: "How did you obtain the product? Did you both prepare and taste the product?"

• *"Did you know the interviewer?"* Interviewers are instructed not to interview their neighbors, their relatives, or people they have interviewed in the last six months. If the respondent answers yes to this question, the validator should follow up to clarify with a question such as:

"Have you been interviewed by the interviewer before?"
"How many times have you been interviewed by the interviewer?"
"How long ago were you interviewed by the interviewer?"

Answers to these follow-up questions can be misleading unless you remember that if there was a placement questionnaire and later a callback questionnaire, it is possible that the respondent will say that he or she has been interviewed by the same interviewer before. There are other types of tests where situations similar to this one can arise. Warn the validators of these possible situations.

• *"Did you see any cards from which you selected answers?"* If exhibit cards were used in the study, it is important that the respondent actually saw the cards and selected answers from them and was not merely read the questions by the interviewer. It takes more time for the interviewer to shuffle these cards, but more consistent replies are gathered when each respondent selects an answer from a prepared list of choices.

• *"Were you asked to give your total family income?"* This is an important validation question to ask because sometimes interviewers shy away from asking demographic questions. It also fits nicely into the validation after a question asking respondents if they saw cards from which they selected answers, because income categories are usually listed on cards.

In addition, income is usually one of the last questions asked on the questionnaire, and it is good to take a sample of questions from different parts of the questionnaire to make sure that the interviewer went through the entire questionnaire with the respondent.

• *"Do you have any suggestions that might be helpful in designing a simi-lar study in the future?"* It's important for respondents to feel that their opinions regarding the interview count. This question serves the pur-pose of letting them know this. If the respondent was irritated by some part of the test, it is important that you know about it, and this is one way to find that out. This is usually the last question asked in the vali-dation.

Qualifying questions are also validated. On most studies it is critical that only certain types of people be included in the sample. Qualifica-tions could include age ranges in which the respondent must fall and frequency of use of product types. In some cases, it's important to make sure that only homemakers or grocery shoppers were interviewed. Ask the respondent if he or she remembers the interviewer asking this ques-tion, or ask the respondent, "Is this the answer you gave the inter-viewer?"

What If Validation Uncovers Problems?

After the validation is completed, a validation report should be filled out to summarize the quality of work done by the interviewing service or research company.

If the validation indicates that the interviewing was not conducted properly, the interviewing service or research company should be noti-fied immediately and asked to explain the problem.

Often, apparent problems in validation turn out to be nothing more than communication problems between the validator and the respon-dent. These can be clarified once the validator understands exactly what was done in the field.

However, if any interviewer's work is called into question, the nor-mal procedure is to validate additional questionnaires, up to 100 percent of that interviewer's questionnaires. In most cases, to be safe, if there is a question about any of an interviewer's work, all of that interviewer's questionnaires will be excluded from the study.

Cheating or improperly done work is very rare in research, much rarer than people outside the business would expect. Systematic valida-tion is one procedure that helps prevent these problems from occurring. If interviewers know that their work will be validated, most will follow interviewing procedures carefully and conscientiously.

10

How to Pick the Right Kind of Question

Remember the parlor game (also a radio and TV show) called Twenty Questions? In this game, one team picked the name of a person, place, or thing, and another team had to guess the first team's choice by asking only questions that could be answered yes or no. More often than not, the guessing team won—sometimes in fewer than twenty questions.

In some ways, an interview is like a game of Twenty Questions. As the researcher, you're trying to learn something from the respondent through a series of questions. And just as in the parlor game, the exact wording and sequence of the questions can be crucial to your success.

That's really what questionnaire writing is all about: putting the right questions together in the right order. Of course, you're not limited to twenty questions or to yes/no answers. But if it's possible to guess almost anything with only twenty simple questions, it seems likely that many marketing research questionnaires are longer and more complicated that they need to be. Or perhaps we're trying to find out too many things at once.

Questions are the tools of the survey researcher. And like other craftspeople, researchers ought to use their tools for the job they were designed to do. The tip-off to a questionnaire written by an inexperienced person is usually that the questions don't quite fit. They aren't precisely the right questions for obtaining the information that's being sought. That's where a knowledge of all the types of questions available comes in handy. The more choices you have, the better your chances of selecting the best question.

Types of Questions

There are really only two types of questions: open-ended and closed-ended. You can let the respondent answer in his or her own words (open-ended), or you can have the respondent select an answer from your words (closed-ended).

It's a little more complicated than that, of course, because there are many variations on these two basic types. This chapter describes the kinds of questions most often used in survey research studies for business. If these questions were arranged into natural groupings, the categories would look like this:

I. Open-ended questions—allow respondents to answer entirely in their own words
   A. Basic questions
   B. Follow-up questions
      1. Probing
      2. Clarifying
II. Closed-ended questions—offer preset alternative answers
   A. Multiple-response questions
      1. Dichotomous
      2. Multiple response
   B. Scales—reflect both direction and magnitude
      1. Unipolar
      2. Bipolar
      3. Hedonic
      4. Buying intent
      5. Agree/disagree
   C. Ordering questions—attempt to force respondents to pick one response over another
      1. Preference
      2. Ranking
   D. Miscellaneous
      1. Semantic differential
      2. Constant sum

The following pages provide an overview of these types of questions.

Open-Ended Questions

Examples:
- "What did you like most about the product?"
- "Why do you say that?"

Uses:

- Collects information with a minimum of direction to the respondent.
- Useful where the range of possible responses is very broad and can't be elicited by a closed-ended question.
- Captures the respondent's own words.

Things to Remember:

- Expensive to ask, code, tabulate, and analyze, so should be used sparingly, only where it serves a specific purpose.
- Be sure the questions include written instructions to the interviewer to "probe" and "clarify" the responses.
- Interviewers must record responses absolutely verbatim.
- Results depend heavily on the quality of interviewing and coding.

Probing Questions—ask for additional answers or ideas

Examples:

- "What else?"
- "What other things?"
- "What else did you like about the product?"

Uses:

- A standard technique for getting a full, complete response to an open-ended question.
- Should be used routinely by interviewers as a follow-up to open-ended questions until the respondent has nothing more to add.

Things to Remember:

- Must be completely nonleading.
- Never ask about subjects not already volunteered by the respondent. For example, don't probe with "What did you think about the texture?" if the respondent has not mentioned texture.

Clarifying Questions—ask for more information about answers that respondents have already given

Examples:

- "In what way was it too oily?"

- "What exactly do you mean when you say the bottle was difficult to handle?"
- "Can you explain what you mean by that?"

Uses:

- A standard technique for getting a clearer explanation of a response to an open-ended question.
- Should be used routinely by interviewers as a follow-up to any vague or general term used by the respondent.

Things to Remember:

- Must be completely nonleading.
- *Never* suggest a response or direction to the respondent when clarifying:
    Correct: "What didn't you like about the color?"
    Incorrect: "Was the color too dark?"
- Interviewers often aren't sure what words need to be clarified. It's helpful to provide a list, as part of the instructions for any open-ended questions, of key words to be clarified.

Dichotomous Closed-Ended Questions—elicit opposite, mutually exclusive answers

Examples:

- "Do you do most of the grocery shopping in your household?"
    Yes   ☐
    No   ☐
- "Have you ever eaten Cheerios brand cereal?"
    Yes   ☐
    No   ☐

Uses:

- One of the most basic types of questions.
- Many types of information split naturally into two categories.
- Easy to ask, answer, and tabulate.

Things to Remember:

- Be sure the question *really* has only two answers. Often "don't know" and/or "both" are also legitimate responses.
- If there are more than two possible responses, consider including

them in the question if that will make it easier for the respondent to answer. At the least, list the other answers on the questionnaire for the interviewer to use in recording, and include a "do not read" instruction next to those responses.

Multiple-Response Closed-Ended Questions—offer the respondent an opportunity to give more than one answer

Examples:

- "Which of the following brands of cake mix have you purchased within the past twelve months?"
  Betty Crocker ☐
  Duncan Hines ☐
  Pillsbury ☐
- "Was the product better than you expected, not as good as you expected, or about the same as you expected?"
  Better than expected ☐
  Not as good as expected ☐
  About the same as expected ☐

Uses:

- Should generally be used instead of an open-ended question wherever all the responses can be determined beforehand.
- Easier and less expensive than open-ended questions to ask and to tabulate.
- Ensures that all respondents will answer on the same dimension because it is more directed than open-ended questions.

Things to Remember:

- Be sure it really is a closed-ended question. You must be able to anticipate and list all possible responses.
- *Never* prelist categories of answers to an open-ended question and ask interviewers to code responses into the correct categories. Interviewers are trained to record verbatim answers, not to code.
- Can be followed by an open-ended question (such as "why") to obtain more detailed information.

Unipolar Scales—range essentially from good to bad

Examples:

- "Which statement best describes the *color* of the french fry? Was the *color* of the french fry . . ."

Excellent   ☐
Very good   ☐
Good   ☐
Fair   ☐
Poor   ☐
Very poor   ☐
Extremely poor   ☐

- "How interesting did you find this advertisement? Was it . . ."
  Extremely interesting   ☐
  Very interesting   ☐
  Quite interesting   ☐
  Somewhat interesting   ☐
  Slightly interesting   ☐
  Not at all interesting ☐

Uses:

- Best for measuring product attributes where there is no opposite end point that's equally desirable or undesirable. Where there are equal end points, use a bipolar scale.
- All well-constructed scales share the quality of being adaptable to statistical tables. Numerical values can be assigned to each point and statistical routines run (means, standard deviations, analysis of variance, and so on). This is not possible with nonscale data such as open-ended questions.

Things to Remember:

- Try to include another product as a benchmark or reference point for interpreting results.
- Can be more difficult to interpret than a bipolar scale. In the example given, is "quite interesting" good or bad? It's difficult to tell without using another product for comparison.

Bipolar Scales—have extremes at each end, and the "best" response is in the middle

Examples:

- "Which of the following statements best describes the *color* of the bacon? Was the *color* of the bacon . . ."
  Much too dark   ☐
  Somewhat too dark   ☐

　　　　Just about right　　　☐
　　　　Somewhat too light　☐
　　　　Much too light　　　☐
- "Which of the following statements best describes the *spice level* of the salami? Was the *spice level* of the salami . . ."
　　　　Much too spicy　　　　☐
　　　　Somewhat too spicy　☐
　　　　Slightly too spicy　　☐
　　　　Just about right　　　☐
　　　　Slightly too bland　　☐
　　　　Somewhat too bland　☐
　　　　Much too bland　　　☐

Uses:

- Usually the best way to evaluate attributes in product tests because it gives some general direction for improvement.
- Easy and efficient to ask, answer, and tabulate.

Things to Remember:

- A benchmark competitive product is often needed for comparison with test products.
- Usually better for comparing alternative products than for providing absolute measures.

Hedonic Scales—measure how well something is liked

Example:

- "Considering everything about this product, which statement best describes how you like or dislike this product *overall?*"
　　　　Like it extremely　　　　　☐
　　　　Like it strongly　　　　　☐
　　　　Like it very well　　　　　☐
　　　　Like it fairly well　　　　☐
　　　　Like it moderately　　　　☐
　　　　Like it mildly　　　　　　☐
　　　　Neither like nor dislike it　☐
　　　　Dislike it moderately　　　☐
　　　　Dislike it intensely　　　　☐

Uses:

- Good way to measure overall "liking" for a product, especially its physical attributes.
- Six positive points usually provide sensitivity to differences, even among similar products.

Things to Remember:

- Does not necessarily reflect buying intent. For example, a premium product may have a high hedonic score but, because of its price, generate lower buying intent.
- On a food product, hedonic and overall-taste scales usually mirror each other.

Buying-Intent Scales—reflect a likelihood of purchase

Example:

- "Which of these statements best describes how interested you would be in buying this product?"

    Definitely would buy it   ☐
    Probably would buy it   ☐
    Might or might not buy it   ☐
    Probably would not buy it   ☐
    Definitely would not buy it   ☐

Use:

- Because sales are usually the end measure of a product's success, this type of question comes closest to evaluating sales potential in a survey setting.

Things to Remember:

- Respondents need to be given enough information (e.g., price, color, or size) about a product to form an intelligent opinion about buying.
- These scales do not perfectly reflect sales. Responses must be discounted somewhat; not all respondents who say "definitely buy" will actually buy.
- When talking with someone who is *not* the actual purchaser (e.g., a child about a product Mom or Dad would buy, or a nurse about a product the purchasing department would buy), you need to

rephrase the question to ask: "How likely would you be to recommend (or ask for) this product?"

Agree/Disagree Scales

Example:

- "For each statement, please indicate whether you . . ."

Agree strongly	☐
Agree somewhat	☐
Agree slightly	☐
Neither agree nor disagree	☐
Disagree slightly	☐
Disagree somewhat	☐
Disagree strongly	☐

Use:

- Getting the degree of agreement or disagreement with a series of statements is a common way to measure attitudes.

Things to Remember:

- Interpretation can be difficult. For example, disagreement with a negative statement doesn't necessarily mean agreement with the opposite positive statement.
- Listed responses may not accurately reflect respondents' feelings.
- Statement wording is very critical.

Preference Questions

Examples:

- "Overall, which of the two products that you used do you prefer, product 72 or product 74? Or do you like them both equally?"
- "Which flavor do you prefer, mint or regular? Or do you like them both equally?"
- "Which of these colors do you like best for a paper towel in your kitchen?"

Uses:

- A logical way to collect information in most product tests.
- Tends to direct respondent toward choosing one as better regard-

less of the magnitude of difference. Small, but perceptible, product differences can result in lopsided preferences.

Things to Remember:

- It's usually best to offer a "no preference" choice because there's nearly always a group that can't differentiate or doesn't care.
- Preference data can be very volatile, since small perceived differences can result in large swings in preference.
- If there are more than two items to choose among, ranking questions may provide more useful information than preference questions.

Ranking Questions

Example:

- "Please rank these characteristics from most important to least important to you, with 1 being the most important and 7 being the least important."

Uses:

- An easy way to collect information on any group of items (e.g., brands or characteristics).
- Relatively simple to ask and tabulate.

Things to Remember:

- Ranking questions do not reflect intervals between the items ranked. (First may be far superior to second; second and third may be nearly equal to one another.)
- Assumes respondent is aware and knowledgeable enough to rank all the items.
- Can become tedious for the respondent, especially if done repeatedly and/or on a large number of items.
- To prevent misunderstanding, tell respondents whether 1 represents their first choice or their last.

Semantic-Differential Questions

Example:

- "Please place an X in the box that best represents your opinion of the First National Bank:"

| Friendly | | | | | | | | Unfriendly |
| Old-Fashioned | | | | | | | | Modern |

Use:

- Used mostly for collecting attitude information, especially "image profiles" of products, brands, or companies.

Things to Remember:

- Questions contain few verbal clues: Points between ends are not labeled or numbered. This is theoretically desirable, but it can be confusing to some respondents if not clearly explained.
- Some scales have no clearly "preferred" end point, so analysis can be difficult. In the example given, which is better for a bank, being "old-fashioned" or being "modern"?
- Precise wording of end points is critical. They should be opposites.

Constant-Sum Questions

Example:

- "Please divide these eleven chips among the six brands of cake mix according to your preference for the brands."

Uses:

- Provides a quantified measure of preference among several brands.
- A useful way to quantify attitude shift on a before/after basis, such as in advertising testing.

Things to Remember:

- It can be difficult to clearly describe the task to respondents.
- Be careful to specify whether you want respondents to allocate on the basis of preference, expected next X purchases, or some other basis.
- Tabulation and analysis can be complex.

Tips on Questionnaire Writing

Chapter 9 gave you some general guidelines for preparing questionnaires. Here are five technical tips:

1. *Avoid harsh, extreme end points on scales.* Most people are reluctant to select harshly worded scale points, especially end points. This means that the number of points on your scale is effectively reduced.

2. *Use exhibit cards, especially on closed-ended questions with more than four or five alternatives.* Listing the answers so that the respondent can look at them makes the interview more comfortable and improves the accuracy of the information obtained.

3. *Rotate the order in which multiple responses are read to respondents if there's no logical order.* In a long list of items—brands, for example—there tends to be a bias toward the first and last items. So rotate the point at which the interviewer starts reading the list to eliminate such a bias.

4. *Be aware of question order.* Each question influences all the ones that follow. For example, you should generally ask about:

- Appearance before taste. It's difficult to evaluate the appearance after you've already eaten all the test product!
- Overall evaluations before specific attributes.
- Buying intent before specific attributes.
- Open-ended "like" and "dislike" questions before scale questions or questions about product attributes.

5. *Keep self-administered questionnaires absolutely as simple as possible.* Try to avoid complicated question patterns, especially questions to be skipped. It's also wise to assume that respondents will read through the whole questionnaire before completing any of it. This makes unaided awareness questions, followed by an aided brand list, virtually impossible to ask on a self-administered questionnaire. In some cases, it may be possible to control jumping ahead by separating the questions into two completely different questionnaires.

Questionnaire Format Tips

The wording of questions in a questionnaire is the most important concern, but it's also important to lay out the questions in such a way that the interviewer can easily understand and handle them. Here are some tips on questionnaire format:

1. *Include all parts of a question on one page whenever possible.*
2. *Don't split an answer list, with part on one page and part on another.*

The same applies to open-ended questions. Don't put the question on one page and the space for the answer on the next.

3. *Type all interviewer instructions on the questionnaire in capital letters.* Anything *not* in capital letters should be read to the respondent. Always put "Read list" or "Do *not* read list" by every closed-ended question.

4. *If a "skip" instruction involves skipping to a different page, have the questionnaire laid out so that the interviewer begins at the top of the new page.* A skip occurs when a respondent's answer to one question means the interviewer should skip some of the following questions because they won't apply. If it's a skip that will be used a lot, it helps to print the key page on paper of a different color. That way your instruction can say: "Skip to Q. 10 *on blue page.*"

5. *Put a box around answers that will be referred to later in the questionnaire.* For example, if you have a question that will be answered only by people who got a free sample, set up the sample question like this:

3. "Did you receive a free sample of Gobbledygook in the mail?"

Yes   [1]
No   2

Then later on, when your instructions say, "Refer to Q. 3. If respondent answered yes, continue. If not, skip to Q. 19," the interviewer can quickly see where he or she is supposed to look.

6. *Use double-spacing or at least a space and a half when setting up questionnaires.* By squeezing questions together you increase the chance of confusing the interviewer, and that creates errors.

7. *Keep the materials an interviewer has to handle in a personal interview to a minimum.* For instance, use exhibit cards only when needed. You usually don't need an exhibit card for short scales with only four or five choices. The interviewer can easily read the choices to the respondent. Exceptions to this are the buying-intent scale (it's usually a critical part of the study, and you want *no* chance of misunderstanding) and income questions.

8. *Always have a space on the front of the questionnaire for the interviewer's name, the date of the interview, and the city and state in which the interview took place.* If you're interviewing at more than one location in a city, identify which location the questionnaire came from.

9. *Have a study title and date on each questionnaire.* Make the title as specific as possible to avoid confusion with similar projects. Also include

the type of study: telephone, mall intercept, door to door, and so on. Here's an example:

PERSONAL PRODUCTS
TELEPHONE TRACKING STUDY
APRIL 1992

10. *Be sure the project number appears on every separate document connected with the study (questionnaires, contact sheets, instructions, and so forth).* This provides a clear reference point if materials get separated.

11. *Use different-colored questionnaires to identify different parts of a study.* This will make the instructions easy to follow, as in this example:

A. "If respondent has used Hi-C drink, go to *pink* questionnaire."
B. "If respondent has heard of, but *not* used, Hi-C, go to *yellow* questionnaire."
C. "If respondent has not heard of Hi-C, go to *white* demographic section."

11

Guidelines for Interviewing

Being an interviewer is, and always has been, a demanding job. But if you think people are difficult to interview today, consider this: During the 1920 Soviet census—taken only three years after the 1917 revolution—dozens of enumerators were beaten up, and thirty-three were murdered. That's hostility!

Fortunately, things are a little more friendly these days, but interviewing still demands skill. As in many fields, experience is the best way to develop interviewing skills. Nevertheless, there are some guidelines for interviewing that will help make you a better interviewer faster.

General Attitude

Rapport is an important part of the interviewing relationship. To help establish rapport, an interviewer should be:

• *Friendly.* Be friendly and assertive enough to talk to people and get them to talk to you, but not so pushy that you frighten people. Don't become so chatty that the interview gets too lengthy or wanders off the subject. Try to be the kind of person respondents feel they can trust.

• *Patient and flexible.* Because you're interviewing respondents in their homes or places of business, you'll have to adjust yourself to the environment. You must wait patiently if the respondent has other interruptions, such as caring for a crying child, answering the telephone, or whatever. Don't become angry or offended and ruin any good relationship you might have established.

• *Unbiased.* Always remember that a respondent's answers will be influenced by his or her perceptions of you. Respondents should feel relaxed, not that they must answer to please you. Sighing, changing your tone of voice, or looking bored or impatient can bias a respondent's answer.

Sometimes a new interviewer, eager to encourage and win over a respondent, will make affirmative exclamations: "You're so right," "I certainly agree with you," and so on. Although the intention is to show interest, more often it results in biasing the respondent. If you concur with one attitude, the respondent may later be reluctant to express another. Remember that you are there to acquire information, not to color it.

Asking Questions

Read all questions verbatim, clearly, and slowly so that the respondent is able to understand every word. Questions are carefully thought out, and a particular wording is chosen for good reason, so read questions as written. This also ensures that each respondent is asked exactly the same questions.

If a respondent does not understand a question, *never* interpret it unless specifically instructed to do so. Reread the question, but don't try to explain it. If the respondent is still unable to answer, make a note of the circumstances in the margin and go on to the next question.

When doing in-person interviews, don't let respondents read the questionnaire over your shoulder. There may be parts of the questionnaire that they should not see, because premature knowledge of those parts could bias their responses.

Be sure to follow all procedures and instructions. Much thought goes into the procedure for conducting an interview, and it is very important that each interview be conducted in the same way by all interviewers.

At the end of an interview, before you hang up on or leave the respondent, quickly look over the questionnaire to be sure that all questions are answered and that the answers are clear, meaningful, and legibly recorded. Be sure to thank the respondent for his or her cooperation at the end of the interview.

Open-Ended Questions

Open-ended subjective questions such as "Why do you think so?" or "Why do you say that?" give respondents a chance to express themselves freely. Often answers given in a respondent's own words are not clear at first. For example, a respondent may say that the "appearance was nice," but this really doesn't tell you *what* is liked about the appearance. In these circumstances, you should record the initial answer in the exact words, including any slang expressions used by the respondent. Never summarize or paraphrase what is said.

To get at the full meaning of these sometimes mysterious responses, the interviewer must rely on techniques designed to pierce the fog.

The techniques of probing and clarifying are the two basic techniques used to ensure that a respondent's answers become clear and meaningful. *Probing* is the procedure used to get further information and obtain a complete response. It involves asking respondents for information in addition to what they have already given. *Clarifying,* as the name suggests, is a procedure used to get a clearer or more specific meaning from a respondent's answer than has been given. Respondents often speak in ambiguous terms. It is your responsibility as interviewer to clarify the ambiguous statement and find out more precisely what the respondent means. For example, if the respondent says, "It smells nice," you must find out what about the smell is nice.

Interviewers must not ask leading questions when clarifying and probing. The important thing is to clarify and probe without putting words in the respondent's mouth or inserting your own ideas. Probing and clarifying questions must never suggest answers to the respondent. You are to ask only nonleading questions. Here are some examples of nonleading probing questions:

"What else?"
"Is there anything else?"
"What else [*repeat appropriate phrase from question*]?"

You must *never* lead respondents by asking about subjects that they have not voluntarily mentioned. For example, do not ask, "What did you think about the color?" if the respondent has not brought up color. Some examples of nonleading clarifying questions are:

"Can you explain what you mean by that?"
"Why do you say that?"
"What are your reasons for saying that?"
"In what way was it [*repeat respondent's exact words*]?"

Finally, never suggest how the respondent may feel. For example, if the respondent says the product has a poor appearance, do not say, "Was the color too bright?" Instead, find out what the respondent means by "poor."

12

Coding: The First Step in Analysis

GIGO—"garbage in, garbage out"—is an axiom of the computer field. It means that the results that come out of the computer won't be any better than the information that goes in.

In research, what goes into "the system" is the individual answers of all the respondents in a study. What comes out is a set of nicely categorized and organized tables, ready to be analyzed and to be used to develop conclusions and recommendations.

The process of translating the actual individual responses into categories is called coding. Coding determines whether the results are useful information—or simply garbage.

What Is Coding?

Open-ended questions are discussion-type questions that elicit such a wide range of responses that the possible answers are too varied and numerous to be prelisted on the questionnaire. An example of an open-ended question is: "Why do you like pizzeria pizza better than frozen pizza?"

For these questions, a space is left on the questionnaire for the interviewer to record the answer *verbatim;* later the responses are categorized or coded. Never attempt to have interviewers do on-the-spot coding of answers to open-ended questions. Interviewers are not trained for this task and shouldn't try to make snap judgments about categorizing responses. And unless the answers are recorded verbatim, the respondents' actual answers are lost forever, and it's impossible to check the quality and accuracy of the coding.

The purpose of coding is to reduce all the varied responses to a question to a few types of answers that can be tabulated and then analyzed. On the sample question ("Why do you like pizzeria pizza better than frozen pizza?"), it would be important to know how many people mention crust, compared with the number who mention cheese. And, for those who mention crust, what's the importance of crust thickness compared with crust texture? And, of those who mention crust thickness, do more prefer thin crust or thick?

From this it should be obvious that coding open-ended questions to provide different levels of detail—crust versus cheese, thickness versus texture, thick versus thin—is very demanding. Reducing all the responses to a few important categories without losing the "feel" of the results in meaningless generalities is tricky business. Coding and code development are very demanding steps in the flow of a survey research project.

Developing Codes

The first step in coding is to determine the kinds of responses that have been given to a question. This is normally done by taking a sample from the completed questionnaires—25 percent is typical—and listing the answers and their frequency.

Next, the comments listed are organized into logical groupings. These groupings are determined by the frequency of the responses as well as by the objectives of the test. For example, in a product test of two products with different spice levels, detailed codes would typically be developed to pick up spiciness comments.

Finally, these categories, or codes, are assigned numbers corresponding to computer column numbers so that the questionnaires can be tabulated after they're coded.

For example, in a product test on furniture polish, one of the variables tested might be gloss. All the comments relating to shine would be put into one grouping with a code for each detail mentioned about the shine.

The code might look like this:

Shine—Column 68

Furniture shined as soon as product applied	1
Shine lasted a long time	2

Shine was like glass/mirror	3
Shine was easy to get	4
Shine looked real	5
Shine wasn't greasy	6
Other miscellaneous shine comments	7

Tips on Coding

Here are a few practical tips for doing better coding.

1. *Code ideas, not words.* This is critical. Coding is not simply coding the words people say but rather understanding the *meaning* of what is said.

2. *Check prior studies for codes already developed.* Don't reinvent the wheel. Most companies ask similar questions about their products or services from study to study. Using the same codes not only is easier but also makes the different projects easier to compare.

3. *Be sure to cover critical issues—even if no one mentions them.* If a product test involved a change in the sweetness level of two cereals, for example, you'd want to be sure to include a sweetness code—maybe even several more detailed codes within a sweetness category—regardless of whether the prelisting of responses from the sample of questionnaires showed any mention of sweetness. Sometimes it's important to know for sure that not one person in a study gave a certain response. You can do this only if you include a code based on the study's objectives. Then you can say with certainty that no one mentioned it, because there was a code set up to catch any such responses if they occurred.

4. *Review the objectives of the study with those doing the coding before they start to work on a project.* They should thoroughly understand what the study is about and what they should look for.

5. *Read each respondent's answer completely before coding anything.* That's the only way to understand all ideas correctly and in the right context.

An Example

How the coding process works, as well as how demanding it can be, are best illustrated by a brief example taken from an actual test of a shampoo product (see Figure 12-1).

(*Text continues on p. 87*)

Figure 12-1(a). Sample codes for coding "likes" questions.

TEST NO. _____ Shampoo _____

QUESTION: Likes

COL. 10 Gentleness	COL. 11 Results on hair
11 Gentle/mild/not harsh	21 Good for hair/helps hair
12 Wouldn't strip hair of natural oils	22 Leaves hair manageable/no tangles/ no need for cream rinse
13 Wouldn't dry out hair	23 Gives hair body
14 Wouldn't make skin/scalp break out	24 Mends split ends
15	25 Leaves hair not flyaway
16	26 Leaves hair silky/smooth
17	27 Leaves hair soft
18	28 Leaves hair shiny
19	29
20	30
1 –	2 –
1 + Other gentleness	2 + Other results on hair

Question:

COL. 12 Cleaning	COL. 13 Miscellaneous
31 Leaves no oil/keeps hair dry	41 Cheaper/economical/good price
32 It cleans well/hair looks/feels clean	42 Smells good/nice/clean
33 Lifts out oil/dirt/artificial conditioners	43. Hairdresser recommended
34 Don't have to scrub as much	44 Comes in different formulas
35 No need to wash as often/ keeps hair cleaner longer	45 Concentrated/use only a small amount
36 Doesn't leave a residue on scalp	46 Good for whole family (unspecific)
37 Good lather	47
38 Good for oily hair	48
39	49
30	40
3 –	4 – Other miscellaneous
3 + Other cleaning	4 + Don't know/nothing

Figure 12-1(b). Sample codes for coding "dislikes" questions.

TEST NO. _____ Shampoo _____

QUESTION: Dislikes

COL. 14 *Harshness*	COL. 15 *Cleaning*
51 Too strong	61 Doesn't clean well
52 Strips hair/takes too much oil out	62 Leaves a residue on scalp
53 Dries hair out	63 Poor lather
54 Skin reacts badly to it	64 Not good for oily hair
55	65
56	66
57	67
58	68
59	69
50	60
5 –	6 –
5 + Other harshness	6 + Other cleaning

Question:

COL. 16 *Comparison to others*	COL. 17 *Miscellaneous*
71 Prefer herbal/organic shampoo	81 Don't like the name
72 Prefer medicated/dandruff shampoo	82 Too expensive
73 Same as other shampoos — doesn't work any differently	83 Not economical for long hair
74 Prefer one with a cream rinse	84 Use what hairdresser recommends
75 Prefer another brand (unspecified)	85
76	86
77	87
78	88
79	89
70	80
7 –	8 – Other miscellaneous
7 + Other comparison to others	8 + Don't know what/disliked/nothing

On this study there are two separate codes: Columns 10–13 are for coding the "likes" and columns 14–17 are for coding the "dislikes." The column headings relate to the different attributes of a shampoo. If you were coding, you'd first look for the correct category heading, then look for the correct comment under that column and code that number in that column. There can be more than one number in a column, and not all columns will always have numbers in them.

For example, if, in the "likes" questions, a respondent said, "The shampoo was gentle and mild," you would look at column 10, since this is the "gentleness" column, and find the comment "gentle/mild/not harsh." You would then write an 11 next to the comment. If someone said, "I would rather have a shampoo with a cream rinse," you would look in column 16 for comparison to other shampoos and write in a 74 ("prefer one with a cream rinse") beside that response.

The three sample questionnaires from this study (shown in Figure 12-2) illustrate how different responses to the "likes" and "dislikes" questions would be coded.

Figure 12-2(a). Sample questionnaire 1.

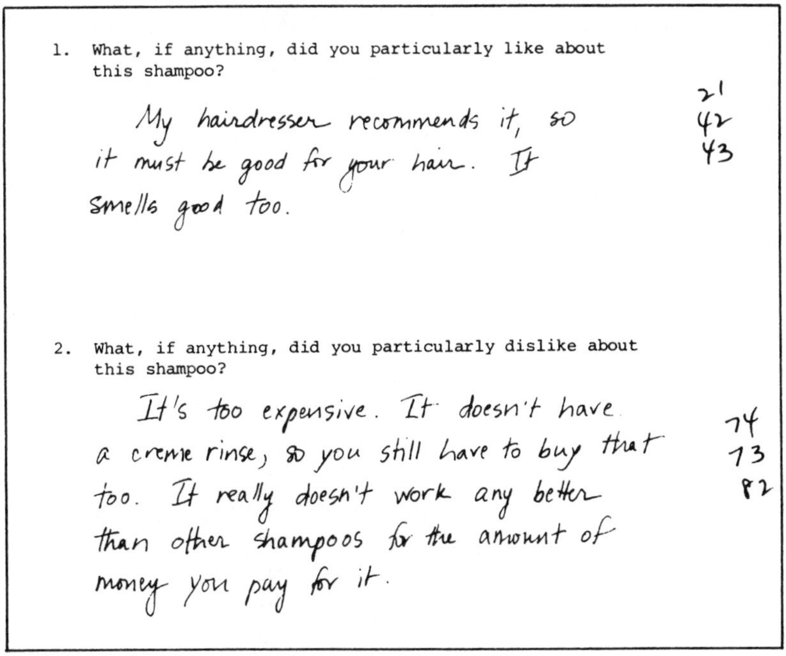

1. What, if anything, did you particularly like about this shampoo?

   My hairdresser recommends it, so it must be good for your hair. It smells good too.

   21
   42
   43

2. What, if anything, did you particularly dislike about this shampoo?

   It's too expensive. It doesn't have a creme rinse, so you still have to buy that too. It really doesn't work any better than other shampoos for the amount of money you pay for it.

   74
   73
   82

Figure 12-2(b). Sample questionnaire 2.

1. What, if anything, did you particularly like about
   this shampoo?

   there are different kinds for different   13
   types of hair. I use the one for dry   27, 28
   hair. It doesn't dry out my hair.   44, 45
   It leaves it soft and shiny.
   It works so well & only have to   (else)
   use a little bit for each shampoo.

2. What, if anything, did you particularly dislike about
   this shampoo?

   Nothing. I liked it.   8+

Figure 12-2(c). Sample questionnaire 3.

1. What, if anything, did you particularly like about
   this shampoo?

   I have limp, oily hair and have to
   wash it real often. With this shampoo   23
   I found it stayed cleaner longer, so   35
   I don't have to shampoo as often
   and my hair has more body.

2. What, if anything, did you particularly dislike about
   this shampoo?

   I like the shampoo but I don't
   think the name is very appealing.   81

Checking the Coding

As the coding is being done, each coder's work should be checked periodically. When the coding is completed, the study is ready to be "check coded." Essentially, check coding is done by actually *recoding* 10 percent of each coder's work. The check coder's coding is then compared with the coder's coding to make sure that the same judgments were made.

After the check coding is completed, the information on the questionnaires is ready to be entered into the computer for editing and tabulating.

13

How to Develop a
Data Processing Plan

Computers are fast, reliable, stupid, and rigid.

—Richard J. Harris, *A Primer of Multivariate Statistics*

Everyone would agree that the development of computers has helped create the marketing research field as we know it today. It's difficult to imagine processing most of the studies done today, even simple ones, by hand.

At the same time, computers have the potential drawback that they can be *too* efficient. The author of the quotation at the top of this page continues: "An aspect of computers' 'behavior' which deserves more emphasis than is popularly accorded is their high reliability, that is, their ability to (indeed, their inability not to) perform any set of instructions programmed into the computer hundreds of thousands of times without once departing from those specifications in the slightest detail."*

In other words, if you're not careful, the computer can easily bury you in paper. That's the purpose of a data processing plan: to help you get all the paper (tables) you need, but nothing more.

Purpose of a Data Processing Plan

A data processing plan should be designed to accomplish three goals:

1. Provide data for the total sample.
2. Determine, through cross-tabulation, what differences exist among demographic or attitudinal subgroups within the sample.

*Richard J. Harris, *A Primer of Multivariate Statistics*, 2nd ed. (San Diego, Calif.: Harcourt Brace Jovanovich, 1985).

3. Select any other complex types of analysis (statistical tests or multivariate techniques) that are needed to help interpret the results.

The specifications for tabulating the data from the study to accomplish these goals are contained in the data processing plan.

The data processing plan for each study should focus on getting an answer to the question that is the key overall issue for that study. For example, different projects might attempt to answer any of these major questions:

Are any of the proposed new products better than the current product?

What are the levels of customer awareness and trial and repeat purchases in the test market?

Which of the new product concepts have the broadest appeal?

Which package is most visible on the shelf?

Begin with this primary question, taken from the project proposal, and design the data processing plan to answer it. All the tables run for the project should contribute to clarifying that key issue.

Editing and Error Reports

The first step after coding the questionnaires is to do editing and error reporting. This is a quality control step to make sure that no questionnaire has information missing. *Editing* means checking the questionnaires for completeness and accuracy. It can be done manually, by looking through every questionnaire, or it can be done by computer. It is generally more accurate and efficient to have the computer do this checking.

Edits are simply checks of logic conditions, usually described as "if," "and," "or," and "not" conditions. For example, suppose question 6 on a questionnaire were the following:

6. "Have you purchased a new car within the past six months?"
   Yes ☐ continue
   No ☐ skip to Q. 8

An edit would be done of question 7 to determine that all the people who said yes to question 6, but only those who said yes, answered question 7. If any who said no to question 6 mistakenly answered question 7 (instead of skipping to question 8), their answers to question 7 would be deleted as part of the editing process.

Most comprehensive computer tabulating programs can do this checking. Obviously, most questionnaires require so many edits that it would be very tedious to do them by hand. Instead, a set of editing instructions is fed into the computer with the questionnaire data. The computer checks every question on every questionnaire against the logic conditions and prints an *error report* of the questionnaires with errors. The error report is used to correct errors according to a set of guidelines set up for each question.

A final check should be run after all the corrections have been made to make sure that the data are "clean" (free of logic errors). If they are, you're now ready to tabulate the results.

Cross-Tabulating Results

Figure 13-1 is an example of what a typical computer-generated table looks like. The banner is the series of column headings that run horizontally across the top of the table. In this case, the banner shows age, income, presence of children, and employment. The terms *banner, break,* and *cross-tab* are used interchangeably.

The stubs are the responses to the question being tabulated and usually run vertically down the left side of the table. In this example, the stubs show the rating-scale points of "definitely would buy," "probably would buy," and so on.

The primary purpose of cross-tabulations is to provide information on whether there are differences in responses among subgroups within the sample. If there are, then additional tables can be run and a more detailed analysis made. Some of the most typical breaks for cross-tab purposes are:

1. *Demographics*—by age, sex, income, education, household size, presence of children in the household, and employment of the female outside the home
2. *Geography*—by city or region
3. *Usage*—by awareness or usage of a brand or product category

These standard breaks are common to all types of studies. On product or concept tests, it's often helpful to run two additional types of breaks:

Figure 13-1. Computer-generated table showing buyer intent.

	TOTAL	AGE			INCOME			CHILDREN UNDER 13 IN HOUSEOLD		EMPLOYMENT	
		UNDER 35	35–44	45–54	UNDER $45K	$45K–$59K	$60K PLUS	YES	NO	EMPLY	NOT EMPLY
TOTAL	150	33	49	68	55	50	45	44	106	115	35
NO ANSWER	1	–	–	1	–	1	–	–	1	–	1
BASE	149	33	49	67	55	49	45	44	105	115	34
	100.0	100.0	100.0	100.0	100.0	100.0	100.0	100.0	100.0	100.0	100.0
DEFINITELY/PROBABLY WOULD BUY (NET)	54	11	18	25	27	14	13	17	37	42	12
	36.2	33.3	36.7	37.3	49.1	28.6	28.9	38.6	35.2	36.5	35.3
(5) DEFINITELY WOULD BUY	17	5	2	10	9	4	4	5	12	14	3
	11.4	15.2	4.1	14.9	16.4	8.2	8.9	11.4	11.4	12.2	8.8
(4) PROBABLY WOULD BUY	37	6	16	15	18	10	9	12	25	28	9
	24.8	18.2	32.7	22.4	32.7	20.4	20.0	27.3	23.8	24.3	26.5
(3) MIGHT OR MIGHT NOT BUY	45	15	13	17	13	20	12	17	28	38	7
	30.2	45.5	26.5	25.4	23.6	40.8	26.7	38.6	26.7	33.0	20.6
(2) PROBABLY WOULD NOT BUY	35	5	10	20	8	12	15	6	29	24	11
	23.5	15.2	20.4	29.9	14.5	24.5	33.3	13.6	27.6	20.9	32.4
(1) DEFINITELY WOULD NOT BUY	15	2	8	5	7	3	5	4	11	11	4
	10.1	6.1	16.3	7.5	12.7	6.1	11.1	9.1	10.5	9.6	11.8
PROBABLY/DEFINITELY WOULD NOT BUY (NET)	50	7	18	25	15	15	20	10	40	35	15
	33.6	21.2	36.7	37.3	27.3	30.6	44.4	22.7	38.1	30.4	44.1
MEAN	3.04	3.21	2.88	3.07	3.25	3.00	2.82	3.18	2.98	3.09	2.88
STANDARD DEVIATION	1.16	1.08	1.17	1.20	1.27	1.02	1.15	1.11	1.18	1.15	1.20
STANDARD ERROR	.10	.19	.17	.15	.17	.15	.17	.17	.12	.11.	.21

1. *Purchase intent*—to determine how and why those who express interest are different.
2. *Order of product use*—to check whether the order of use affected product evaluations. When everything is rotated properly, this bias should be eliminated or, at the least, it should affect all products equally. But it's always a good idea to check.

Percentaging and Bases

The data processing plan must specify how the data are to be percentaged. The plan's specifications should be consistent with the way the project will be analyzed. The alternative is for the person preparing the report to spend many tedious hours repercentaging with a hand calculator.

Percentaging can be done vertically, horizontally, or in both ways. Vertical percentaging is the most common way and normally the most helpful to the analysis. It quickly shows whether there are different responses to each question among the cross-tab groups.

Bases also need to be specified for each question. Most questions are based (percentaged) on only the number of respondents who were asked the question. That usually makes the most sense for the analysis.

Should "don't know" responses and "no answers" (respondents who erroneously fail to answer a question) be included in the bases for percentaging? "Don't knows" should usually be included, in that "don't know" represents as legitimate a response to most questions as "yes" or "no." Knowing what proportion of people "don't know" will usually add to your understanding of the results. That's not true of "no answers." These most often represent interviewing errors—a question was accidentally skipped. The number of these people is shown on the table, but it adds nothing to the analysis of the study results to include them in the base. So "no answers" should usually be excluded from the base used for percentaging.

Some questions need special bases. For example, evaluation of a "why?" question following a preference question should be based only on the number of respondents preferring each product. And evaluation of a "how often" question following a product purchase question should be based only on the number of people buying each product.

Net counts can add considerably to the analysis of open-ended questions. A "net" is simply the number of people making one or more comments in a broad response category. For example, a respondent might say he or she thought a product was "easy to hold and easy to use."

That person would be counted for both of those detailed comments in the following example but would be included only once in the net count of "convenience" comments:

Convenience (net)	31%
Easy to hold	25
Easy to use	17
More convenient size	14
Other convenience comments	5

In other words, "nets" count people rather than the total number of comments. In this example, 31 percent of the respondents made some reference to convenience, although it's clear from the numbers that many made more than one comment about convenience.

The final check on the data processing plan is to examine the sample size in each of the proposed banner points or breaks. If only a handful of respondents turn out to fall into one of the categories included in the banner, the break will be useless for analysis. This is checked through a report called an "80-column dump" or "marginals." This is simply a listing of the distribution of answers to every question on the questionnaire.

Finally, before the tables are run, all simple statistical functions to be run on some or all of the tables should be specified. These include:

- Mean
- Median
- Standard deviation
- Standard error
- Analysis of variance (ANOVA)
- Student's t-test
- Chi-square test

Planning these ahead of time will avoid the necessity of going back and running extra tables later. It's less costly if they're run at the same time as the rest of the data.

A bit of philosophy and a word of warning: There is nearly always a temptation in working up a data processing plan to want to run "everything by everything," to cross-tab every question by the responses to nearly every other question. The computer makes this feasible, and it often seems like a good precaution "just in case." This is nearly always the wrong approach. It wastes money, of course; but more important, it buries you under piles of tables that become an obstacle to thorough analysis. It's usually impossible to get an overview and understanding of the results when you're slogging through hundreds of computer tables.

As an alternative, try this approach:

1. Run the questionnaire with one banner first to get the total and a few basic cross-tab breaks. Even better yet, do your first analysis from the totals shown on the marginals. Chances are that you can get most of what you need from that, even before you run the first table.

2. If you think other breaks might be useful, select one or two questions for which you expect the breaks to make the greatest difference, and run them first as a sort of pretest. If you see no differences on those questions, you can probably save yourself the trouble and expense of running and analyzing the whole study by those breaks. On the other hand, if you do see differences on those questions, go ahead and run more tables, because you now know that the extra tables are likely to be useful to your analysis.

14

Writing Research Reports That Get Read

The results of marketing research are often intangible. A decision (maybe a very important one) usually gets made, but afterward there's often little physical evidence of all the time, money, and effort that went into the project. That's why reports are so important: They're often the only documentation of a study. So it's important that they be done well.

Of course, every company and each person go about it a little differently. There's no one right style for a report. But you need *some* style, some viewpoint to give your writing consistency. This chapter discusses some ideas that will help you to write better research reports.

What a Report Should Be

In the research business, the written report of the findings of a project is extremely important. It has immediate use in making decisions, and it also serves as a historical record. Before launching into it, you should think about the purpose of the report and your role in writing it. Here are some guidelines.

• *Interpret and explain the study's results rather than just summarizing them.* Too many reports just translate into words what is clear from looking at the data. "Overall, 73 percent of the homemakers in the test prefer product A." That doesn't help much in understanding the results. You should go a step further and draw a conclusion about what the results mean: "Most consumers prefer product A." You conducted some research among a sample of people. They prefer product A, so you assume that most others in the population do too.

• *Don't be afraid to draw conclusions.* Researchers are often overly timid about reaching conclusions. It's true we shouldn't jump to conclusions on subjects we know little about, but if you're writing the report, you probably know more about the project than anyone else. That puts you in the best position to know what the results mean. Furthermore, the user of the research is expecting you to use your judgment, not just to restate the facts. Your judgment is probably better than you think, and you're being paid for your interpretation. So don't be too modest about your ability to give an analysis of what the results mean.

• *Let the report be complete enough to stand by itself.* It shouldn't require the tabulations or the proposal to clarify what you did or what you learned. For many of the people who read the report, it will be their only exposure to the project—or they will have forgotten whatever they heard before. So it should be a complete story all by itself.

• *Think of your readers as product managers, not as fellow researchers.* In planning studies, you deal most often with other marketing researchers, but projects are ultimately conducted for managers, who use the results to make decisions. Direct the tone and content of your report to them. If you write to other researchers, your report will be overly technical and use too much research jargon.

• *Go back to the proposal to help you organize your thinking about the report.* By the time you get to the end of a project, you may be too immersed in the details of the fieldwork or tabulating to remember precisely why the project was undertaken in the first place. Read over the proposal to get the project back in perspective.

• *Focus the report on the basic purpose of the project.* All your findings and interpretations should be organized in relation to that purpose. If the purpose, as stated in the proposal, was to determine whether the revised version would replace the current product, all the findings should focus on that issue. Other results should be put either in a separate section of the report or in the appendix. The purpose of the study—*not* the order of the questionnaire—should determine the organization and focus of the report.

• *Make sure you understand the results before you write about them.* By the time you finish reviewing the data you should have a grasp of the findings. You should understand in an overall sense what the results mean and be able to describe them verbally to someone in a few simple sentences. If you don't understand the results, you'll wind up simply restating facts when you start to write instead of interpreting them.

• *Think of the report as having three sections: the report digest, the detailed findings, and the tabulations.* This mental outline will help you decide what to include in each section:

1. *Report digest.* This is something the president of the client company should be able to read in five minutes and understand why the project was undertaken, how it was conducted, and what was learned from the study. Your tendency will be to make this section too long. Concentrate on the basic findings.
2. *Detailed findings.* View this section as being written for the product manager or the person directly responsible for the product being studied. Include the things and the amount of detail a product manager would want and be able to understand. Remember, he or she has only a general knowledge of marketing research and even less of statistics.
3. *Tabulations.* The tabulations from the project, which are usually bound separately, are for the client's researcher. If a lot of detail is wanted, it can be found here. While the tabs aren't physically part of the report, viewing them as the part of the report intended for the researcher helps you to realize that every little bit of detail doesn't have to be in the written report.

The relationship of report sections to your target readers is summarized in Figure 14-1.

Report Mechanics

Here are some guidelines on how the report should look and how it should be organized:

- *Remember, the appearance of a report is very important.* If it looks interesting, people will want to read it. If it looks dull, they won't. If it looks well organized, they'll assume your thinking is organized. If it's disorganized and rambling, they'll assume it reflects sloppy thinking. Finally, a neat, attractive-looking report says that you are a professional. No one likes to deal with slobs.
- *Make sure that the title on the report is complete and descriptive.* Something like "Cheerios Research" isn't very good, because General Mills has a warehouse full of research that would come under that title. Generally, make the title a description of the subject investigated, such as "Cheerios Nutritional Advertising." Use simple terminology; avoid jar-

Figure 14-1. Relationships between report sections and intended readers.

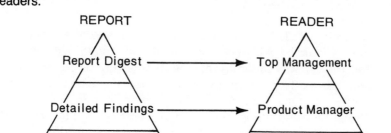

gon or technical words. Do not include the research technique (taste test or in-home test, for example) in the title unless it helps clarify a subject on which many types of research have been conducted.

• *Keep the report digest brief, restricting it to no more than two or three pages.* It's a digest, so it should be complete but not detailed. The absence of detail in the report digest is the key to making it readable. Consider printing the report digest on colored paper to help set it apart from the rest of the report.

The report digest usually contains three sections:

1. *Background and purpose.* This should be only a paragraph or two long, usually about half a page. It should contain brief statements on the external and internal conditions leading to the need for the project and on the project's purpose (i.e., the decisions to be made on the basis of the findings).
2. *Research procedure.* This section typically includes a description of the data collection methods (in very general terms) and a sentence referring the reader to the appendix or tabulations for details. This should usually be no longer than half a page. There is a tendency to make this section too long and to go into more detail than most readers will care about. If you have an elaborate sample and are obliged to discuss it, put it in the appendix and only mention in the digest where the details can be found.
3. *Major conclusions.* This section usually consists of a couple of pages (rarely more) that summarize the principal conclusions, interpret the results in terms of the study's purpose, and recommend or suggest action if that's appropriate.

• *Group related subjects in the report, regardless of where they appeared in the questionnaire.* Don't be tied to the questionnaire order in your report. That order was developed to make the questions easy for the interviewer to ask. The readers of your report usually won't be interested in your questionnaire sequence. They want to relate associated pieces of information in order to come to a conclusion about a subject on which they must make a decision. If possible, go back to the proposal for the project to get an outline of the major issues or subjects dealt with in the study.

• *Use "sentence conclusions" to summarize findings.* These should be interpretive conclusions about the information reported in the text and/or illustrated in the exhibits. Such a sentence may summarize findings from several exhibits. Underline or italicize these points to make them stand out.

• *Break up the report format with different kinds of exhibits.* A report full of nothing but numerical tables looks dull. Try to use bar charts, pie charts, graphs, and other types of exhibits to provide a change of pace from the tables and to enhance the physical attractiveness of your presentation. In thinking about your report's format, remember that there are three kinds of people who will be reading it:

1. *Number people*—who are best communicated with by numbers
2. *Word people*—who better understand ideas expressed in words than numbers
3. *Picture people*—who need pictures (charts or graphs) to help them understand the findings

A finding such as that in Figure 14-2 communicates with all three types of readers because it uses numbers, words, and pictures. Some readers grasp the pie chart, others like the numbers, and others best understand the sentence conclusion.

• *Try to simplify exhibits rather than pack in every fact you can think of.* In particular, avoid throwing in technical details about how the results were obtained. Usually they add nothing to the findings and may even confuse them. Your readers assume that you conducted the study in a proper and professional way, so you don't need to keep proving it. Figure 14-3, for example, contains all the information that an exhibit normally requires.

To improve the usefulness of your illustrations, here are four tips:

1. Use the word *exhibit* in preference to *table.* It's broader, and your exhibits shouldn't all be tables.

Figure 14-2. Report exhibit geared to number, word, and picture people.

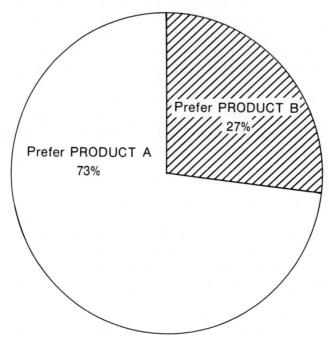

(No. of respondents: 302)

2. Give each exhibit a simple title that describes its content.
3. Show only percentages; don't also show the number of people giving each response. If readers really care, they can figure out the number giving a response from the base. If the base is very small, then show the number only, not the percentages. There is almost never a need to show both.
4. Indicate the base at the bottom of the exhibit, not the top. It's a minor point of reference, not a finding, so put it out of the way. "Number of respondents" is a little more descriptive than "base."

• *Put copy and the exhibits that illustrate it on the same page, if at all possible.* The reader usually has to see the exhibit to fully understand the copy. Use the facing page, if necessary, to get copy near an unusually large exhibit. As a last resort, go to the previous page. For an exhibit to

Figure 14-3. Typical report exhibit of test product preference.

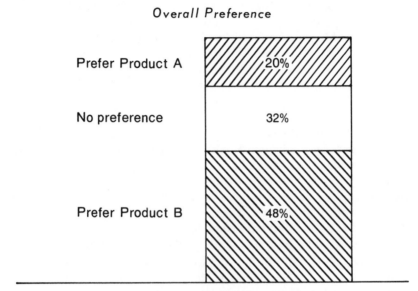

Overall Preference

Prefer Product A — 20%

No preference — 32%

Prefer Product B — 48%

(No. of respondents: 239)

be effective in illustrating a finding, the copy and the exhibit must be physically together.

Steps in Writing a Report

It's easier to describe a report format than to prescribe how to write what's to be put in that format. Nevertheless, there are a few points on how to go about organizing and writing a report that are worth considering.

Preparing a report involves three steps: understanding, organizing, and writing. Notice that the process *ends,* rather than begins, with the writing step. You first have to develop an understanding of the results. You need to have an overall grasp of the findings and what they mean.

One way to do this is to go through the data, pulling out the key findings and making up pencil tables of them. This accomplishes two things: (1) It serves as a device to help you understand what's in the tabulations, and (2) it gives you the tables as raw material for the report. Once you finish going through the tabulations in this way, you'll usually have a pretty good understanding of what's there.

Next, organize what you've got into a more logical sequence by grouping related subjects together and by putting the subjects in an order that naturally develops the most important conclusions.

At this point, you should have a good idea of what the report will say, even though you haven't written a word yet. Now start writing. Begin with the sentence conclusions, then add copy to explain or clarify the conclusions. Remember, these are conclusions, not just restatements of facts.

Write the report digest last. You can't write up the major conclusions until you know what the conclusions are. You'll find it easier to be concise in the digest if you've worked through all the details first. At that point, it's much easier to tell what's major and what's not.

Develop your own routine for writing reports. This is probably the most personal thing we do, and no two people do it just alike. Work on an approach to putting together reports that's comfortable for you, then stick with that routine. But have some kind of routine.

Use an appendix. The appendix is probably the greatest thing ever invented for report writing. It provides a place to put all those things that don't have a home anywhere else. As a rule of thumb, use the appendix for things that you want to save as part of the project's history but that have no direct impact on the findings. Here are some examples of materials that ordinarily belong in the appendix:

- Data used to make projections or estimates
- Lists of competitors and their products or prices
- Product descriptions and illustrations
- Packages or promotional materials
- Ad samples or storyboards
- Explanations of complex research procedures or techniques
- Tables on respondent characteristics (age, income, and so on)
- Project exhibits

These kinds of materials add value and credibility to the report, but they only obscure a straightforward statement of the findings. So put them in the appendix.

Part IV

Solving Specific Marketing Problems

15

Product Testing

Every good cook is an expert on product testing: tasting the soup, adding a little more salt, tasting again, and so on until it's just right. That process—test, revise, and test again—is the same one that multibillion-dollar corporations use to develop and improve their products.

Product testing is one of the most basic and most widely used types of marketing research. It deals with the very basic question, "How does this product compare with that one?" The best way to get an answer to that question is to let the customers who will actually purchase and use the product give their opinions. Furthermore, the application of product testing is clear, since the results usually lead directly to a management decision.

Testing is particularly important in the area of frequently purchased consumer products (food, health and beauty aids, household products, and so on), where an improvement in the physical product can quickly lead to changes in market share in a product category. But product testing is also used for industrial products, office supplies, and even medical products. In the hospital market, for example, it is important to know if your tape product is an improvement under actual use conditions before you try to market it.

The Role of Product Testing

Product testing is usually done to answer such questions as:

- Which product is better?
- How much better is it—just a little or a lot?
- Why is one product better than the other?

Testing is most often done in the early stages of a product's development, before either the introduction of a new product or the development of an improved product. Typically, several product tests are run during the period in which a product is being revised or redesigned; then the product is moved into a test market after product testing indicates that it has been optimized.

How is performance in a product test measured? Usually in one of three ways:

1. *Testing against a standard, either a current product or a competitive product.* This is the comparison most often made for an improved product or a product being developed for introduction into a market with a clear leader.

2. *Horse-racing alternatives.* When several alternatives are being developed by a company, it is common to test the alternatives against one another to see which has the greatest consumer acceptance.

3. *Testing versus a historical standard.* Occasionally testing is done against the performance, on a set of standard scales, of a product that has been successful on the market, but that may not be directly involved in the test. This is an unusual type of standard, however, because the costs required to interview the large samples needed for comparability, together with the execution problems of conducting exactly comparable tests over time, often make this testing impractical.

Types of Questions

Three types of questions, each of which has a specific role, are most often used in product testing:

1. *Closed-ended questions and scales.* These are the most common questions in product testing because they give the clearest direction for product revisions and are less dependent on the other products that happen to be included in the test. An example would be, "How do you feel about the seasoning level in this product? Would you say it is . . ."

Much too spicy	☐
Slightly too spicy	☐
Just about right	☐
Slightly too bland	☐
Much too bland	☐

This type of bipolar scale is especially helpful for giving direction to product development. It not only tells whether the seasoning is "right" or not but also indicates the direction that should be taken (more or less spice) to make it better.

2. *Preference questions.* These questions, which probe either overall preferences or preferences with respect to specific attributes, are used to obtain direct comparisons between products. While this is a simple, easy-to-understand method, its weakness is that it gives no indication of the magnitude of difference between two products. If A is preferred over B, for example, was A great and B awful, was A just the lesser of two evils, or were both good, with A being just relatively better? Preference measures depend heavily on the products being tested, so they are difficult to compare from one test to another.

3. *Open-ended questions.* Open-ended questions are useful for getting at the "why" behind closed-ended or preference questions. "Why do you say that?" can be a useful follow-up to a preference question. Because open-ended questions can be difficult to code and interpret precisely, however, their use in product testing is generally limited to providing the reasons behind the responses to scalar questions.

Methods of Testing

Companies sometimes use expert panels, most often personnel from R&D laboratories, to determine whether there is a perceived difference among products. Unless the experts can detect a significant difference between the test samples, the product should not be evaluated by consumers.

However, because their expertise makes them very unrepresentative of the population, experts should be used only to determine whether differences do in fact exist. They should *not* be used to evaluate which of two products is better or even whether either of the products is acceptable to consumers.

Taste Tests

All things being equal, taste tests are the most efficient kind of testing because respondents come to the interviewers instead of interviewers going to the respondents. Taste tests can be conducted either as a mall intercept or as a prerecruited central location. If the test is done as a mall intercept, respondents are intercepted in the mall and qualified. Qualified respondents are then taken to a room to participate in the taste test. If it is done as a prerecruited central location, consumers are recruited by telephone and invited to the research location where they take part in the research. Generally, a mall intercept methodology is significantly less expensive than a prerecruited central-location methodology. However, a prerecruited central location may be necessary if: (1) difficult or lengthy product preparation is required; (2) the project timing is tight; or (3) the incidence of qualification is very low.

The efficiency of this type of test, by comparison with an in-home product test, makes it faster and cheaper to conduct. The drawback to this approach is that the products are prepared not by the consumers themselves but by home economists or trained kitchen personnel. In addition, this testing usually provides evaluations by homemakers only and does not include the opinions of other family members. For these reasons, it is appropriate primarily as an early-screening device, when several alternatives that present similar preparation problems are being considered. For products that involve any preparation or in-home use problems—cake mixes and furniture polish are examples—some type of in-home test should be conducted before a final decision is made.

In-Home Tests

With this method, consumers are given one or more products for actual use in their homes. This testing is most often used when the product must be either handled or actually used by the consumer or when the reactions of all family members to the product are important. Products are usually placed "blind," that is, in blank packages showing only the *type* of product contained. The packages are marked with a letter or number so that they can be identified by the interviewer and so that the respondent can use them in the right order if more than one product is being tested. But manufacturer and brand name are not shown on the package.

In-home testing has the advantage of being the most realistic type of testing inasmuch as consumers use the products in nearly the same way they would have if they had purchased the products themselves. Because of the complexity of making the placements and doing callback interviews in-home, however, it is also the most expensive form of product testing. To help control the cost of in-home tests where this method is the only one practical, consider these alternatives:

• *Use intercept interviews, instead of door-to-door contacts, for screening consumers and placing the product.* Interviewing consumers in shopping malls, for example, then giving them the product to take home and use, accomplishes the placement for an in-home test without the inefficient, high-cost step of sending interviewers door to door.

• *Use the telephone for making callbacks instead of conducting in-home interviews.* Test participants can be given a questionnaire or "diary" on which to record their reactions to the product as they use it. Then interviewers can telephone after the usage period to obtain the information from the questionnaire and ask any additional questions. Because personal callbacks can be difficult to arrange and usually involve considerable travel time by interviewers, this step often saves substantial time and money.

Methods of Evaluating

Within the taste test or in-home testing format, there are several ways products can be evaluated, ranging from monadic testing to multiple-product test designs.

Monadic Testing

This type of testing involves giving consumers one product only to use and evaluate. No other product is used for comparison, though respondents may remember similar products they have used. More than one product can be evaluated in a monadic test, of course, by having different samples of respondents test different products simultaneously. Comparative results can also be obtained by having consumers compare the test product with their usual brand, as best they remember it.

The real world is monadic, so this is the most realistic kind of test. In real life, consumers usually try a new product, evaluate it against their recollection of the product they currently use, then decide whether they will buy the new product a second time.

But since different groups of consumers test each product, possible differences in respondents must be minimized through large sample sizes. As a result, monadic testing is very costly. Because so large a share of the total interviewing cost on any product test goes into recruiting respondents, it is inefficient to use individual respondents to test only one product.

Overall, monadic testing is the safest way to test, but it is too costly to be used regularly by most companies.

Paired Comparisons

Paired-comparison tests are common because most often a new product is being evaluated against either the maker's current product or a competitor's product.

Paired comparisons can be conducted either side by side, where consumers are given more than one product to use at the same time, or sequentially, where consumers are given first one product, then another.

Direct, side-by-side comparisons are not widely used, since they may highlight differences that wouldn't be noticed in the marketplace. In reality, of course, consumers almost never use products side by side.

The *sequential* product test blends many of the advantages of the paired-comparison test and the monadic test. Respondents are usually given one product, as in a monadic test, then interviewed about their reactions to it. They are next given another product and interviewed about their reactions to it. Finally, test participants usually are asked about their comparative reactions to the two products—which they liked best and why. Sequential product testing is economical, since it yields both single-product and paired-comparison information from the same group of respondents. This method also minimizes sample differences, because all respondents use both products, and there is no problem of matching two parallel testing groups.

At the same time, even sequential monadic testing has some drawbacks. Products may be used in more rapid succession than they would be normally, which may bring out differences that wouldn't be important in the marketplace.

If several products are involved, the paired-comparison procedure gets unwieldy if all the products are tested in pairs versus all others. Finally, there can be an order effect if very good products are tested against very poor ones. The second product can seem unusually good or bad when compared with the product used first. Or there can be "wear-out"—if highly spiced products are tested, for example—which makes testing more than one product difficult.

Despite these problems, sequential product testing usually offers the best combination of clear design and low cost, which is why it is the most widely used form of product testing.

Repeat Pairs

This is a testing technique that helps elicit the "true preference" between two products. It helps avoid the dilemma of the 50/50 preference, where you wonder whether the market is truly segmented into two groups or whether consumers are just expressing random choices between the test products.

The test measures two things: Can consumers truly differentiate between the two products? To the extent that they can distinguish between the products, which do they prefer? The technique is based on the assumption that consumers should be able to pick the same product twice from a pair if they have a "true preference" for one of the products. If, however, the preferences they express are merely random choices rather than true ones, many are likely to make inconsistent choices—that is, pick one product the first time and the other product from the second pair.

Repeat-pairs testing can be conducted by using either in-home or central-location procedures, although central-location techniques work best. The procedure is simple. Two side-by-side paired-comparison tests are carried out, one following the other, on the same sample of respondents. First, they are given two code-labeled products and asked which they prefer. Then they are given another pair of differently coded products—which are actually the same two products again—and asked which they prefer. In both cases, they are required to express a preference.

If consumers in fact have no "true preference" between the products—that is, if all choices are merely random—the results will reflect this. On a purely random basis, one-fourth of the respondents would pick one product twice in a row by chance, an equal proportion would pick the other one twice by chance, and half the respondents would choose one product from the first pair and another from the second. In this respect, the distribution of random choices is the same as the odds of flipping a coin heads or tails twice in a row.

The "true preference" for each brand is measured by the extent to which the proportion of consumers expressing consistent preferences is greater than the 25 percent that would be expected to randomly choose each product twice in a row.

This technique is particularly appropriate for testing cost-improved products, where the goal often is to demonstrate that consumers *cannot* differentiate between the current and the lower-cost formulation. In this situation, being able to separate the "guessers" from the respondents with true preferences between the two products is important.

Because four products must be included in the test, the repeat-pairs technique can get unwieldy for in-home testing. Also, the procedure does not handle large numbers of products efficiently, since they must always be tested in pairs.

Nevertheless, where products are very similar and the extent of true "no preference" evaluations is important, repeat-pairs testing is the only technique that can produce reliable results.

BIB Designs

Testing even a few products in pairs can quickly become unwieldy. Among as few as six products, for example, even if order is ignored, there are still fifteen different pairs that would have to be tested against each other. BIB designs make this testing feasible and efficient.

BIB stands for "balanced incomplete block." In this type of design, a large number of products can be tested together, two or three at a time. The order of use as well as the products that are tested together are rotated in a balanced way. However, every product is *not* tested in every possible position against every other product, which is why the design is an "incomplete block." Nevertheless, this method represents a sound design, and analysis of variance can be used to produce results that are statistically very efficient. More important, the technique can incorporate almost any number of products into a test, including such esoteric designs as a "three out of nineteen" study.

Figure 15-1 is an example of an actual BIB plan for testing thirteen products, four at a time. God forbid that you should ever need to test that many products, but it illustrates how this approach can handle complex designs. This is referred to as a "4/13" test plan, which reads, "4 out of 13."

Unfortunately, this type of BIB design does not generate very many direct comparisons on each pair of products, so it is difficult to analyze specific products directly on a paired-comparison basis. Also, it can be difficult to control and execute a taste test if a very large number of products is involved.

The BIB design is very common and useful for taste testing. Test plans for virtually any number of test products can be computer-generated.

Guidelines for Product Testing

Finally, here are some tips for conducting reliable product tests.

- *Control for position and contrast bias.* BIB designs (balanced incomplete blocks) provide an efficient way of rotating products to control for position and contrast.

Figure 15-1. Standard 4/13 test plan.

RESPONDENT NUMBER	1st	2nd	3rd	4th	RESPONDENT NUMBER	1st	2nd	3rd	4th
1	1	2	4	10	29	8	9	11	4
2	2	10	1	4	30	9	4	8	11
3	4	1	10	2	31	11	8	4	9
4	10	4	2	1	32	4	11	9	8
5	2	3	5	11	33	9	10	12	5
6	3	11	2	5	34	10	5	9	12
7	5	2	11	3	35	12	9	5	10
8	11	5	3	2	36	5	12	10	9
9	3	4	6	12	37	10	11	13	6
10	4	12	3	6	38	11	6	10	13
11	6	3	12	4	39	13	10	6	11
12	12	6	4	3	40	6	13	11	10
13	4	5	7	13	41	11	12	1	7
14	5	13	4	7	42	12	7	11	1
15	7	4	13	5	43	1	11	7	12
16	13	7	5	4	44	7	1	12	11
17	5	6	8	1	45	12	13	2	8
18	6	1	5	8	46	13	8	12	2
19	8	5	1	6	47	2	12	8	13
20	1	8	6	5	48	8	2	13	12
21	6	7	9	2	49	13	1	3	9
22	7	2	6	9	50	1	9	13	3
23	9	6	2	7	51	3	13	9	1
24	2	9	7	6	52	9	3	1	13
25	7	8	10	3					
26	8	3	7	10					
27	10	7	3	8					
28	3	10	8	7					

- *Because all sensations are potentially biasing on others, structure the questionnaire to reduce this problem.* For example, ask appearance questions before respondents use or taste the product.
- *Because people don't always agree on what specific attributes mean, do "descriptive testing" first with trained R&D panels.* What's "tangy" to one person may be "sour" to another.
- *Remember, there are no reliable "absolute" measures in product testing.* So all products must be evaluated either against other products or against norms from previous testing history.
- *Use discriminant testing by R&D panels to help cut down on the number of products to be tested.* If products aren't perceived as different by trained panels, there's little use testing them among consumers.
- *In that consumers tend to shy away from the extremes on a scale, use scales with enough points to yield discrimination.*
- *Be sure to control the stimuli.* Don't create biases by differences in serving sizes of food products, serving containers, or coding of samples.
- *When testing more than one product, make sure the date codes on all products are similar.* Shelf life affects almost all types of products, not just food products.

16

New Product Research

Remember Hunt's flavored ketchups? Corn Crackos cereal? Heinz Happy Soup? You don't? That's not surprising; neither do most people. They're examples of the seemingly endless parade of new products introduced each year that fail.

It's a simple fact of business life that most new products fail. Of 5,000 new product introductions studied by the advertising agency Dancer Fitzgerald Sample, fewer than 100—only about 2 percent—achieved adequate sales volume to qualify as even minimal successes. And if the large number of embryonic ideas that never make it past the concept stage are considered, the failure rate is surely even higher than 98 percent. In addition, the new product development cycles have grown shorter and costs of new product introductions continue to escalate. All this makes better new product research especially important.

Why do new products fail? An article in *Advertising Age* a number of years ago on the reasons for the failure of seventy-five consumer products that had been withdrawn from the market found this pattern:

Vague consumer difference	36%
Poor product positioning	32
No point of difference	20
Bad timing	16
Poor product performance	12
Wrong market for company	8

All these reasons for failure (with the possible exceptions of "bad timing" and "wrong market for company") can often be avoided through marketing research in the new product development process.

In most companies the process of developing and introducing new products goes through these steps:

1. Opportunity identification
2. Concept screening
3. Product development
4. Simulated sales testing

New products often go from simulated sales testing to national roll-out. Test markets are rarely used because they take too much time and reveal too much information to competitors. In some cases a new product may be introduced in one region then quickly "rolled out" to others as a limited form of testing. These same steps are applicable both to the testing of new services and to the testing of tangible new products.

Step 1: Opportunity Identification

The first step in the new product process typically includes a secondary data search and qualitative research. The purpose of the secondary data search is to pull together all the background information available on the market being considered to help determine the size of the new business opportunity and the chances for success. The secondary data may include:

- Market size estimates
- Market size trends
- Market shares
- Profiles of leading companies
- Trade practices
- Advertising expenditures by competitors
- Technology developments in the category
- Consumer use patterns

This information may come from a variety of secondary sources, including industry magazines, trade associations, government publications, and securities brokers. In other cases, syndicated data may be purchased from suppliers such as A. C. Nielsen Co. or IRI.

The earliest type of survey research done in the development of new products is often group interviews. The purpose of qualitative research at this stage is to develop hypotheses about consumer needs not being adequately met by current products. This is done by conducting group interviews about a product category, focusing on wants, needs, problems, complaints, and wishes.

The result of these group interviews usually is a series of speculations about "holes" in the market that might offer opportunities for new products. These opportunities often have to be inferred by the researchers and marketers observing the groups. It is futile to expect consumers to invent products they'd like to have that no manufacturer has ever thought of. Rather, group interviews serve to give direction to developing product ideas.

The focus at this stage should be on generating as many ideas as possible, not on evaluating ideas. Since the odds of success for a new product idea are so slim, the purpose at the beginning is to come up with as many ideas as possible, which increases the chances that there may be one good idea in the batch.

Step 2: Concept Screening

After you have generated a large number of product ideas, the next step is to weed out the ideas with little potential and to identify the most promising concepts. While the basic technique used to screen new product ideas is quantitative testing, another round of group interviews is often conducted as a preliminary step.

The primary purpose of group interviews at this stage is to check the clarity of the concept statement: Do people understand what the product is and what it is supposed to do? At the same time, a few concept ideas may drop out at this point. Some research purists claim that no product idea should be screened out only on the basis of group interviews. Yet if all the respondents in two or three groups see a major flaw in a concept that eliminates all interest in buying it, it is difficult to maintain much enthusiasm for pursuing the concept further.

It is a fact that most new product ideas stimulate little or no consumer interest. But that's okay, as long as this is discovered early in the concept stage, when ideas are relatively inexpensive to screen, rather than later at the test market stage, when products are extremely expensive to screen. The purpose of concept screening is to answer two questions: (1) Which of these ideas are best? and (2) Are any of them any good? Concept screening essentially "horse-races" the concepts in a test against one another to identify the best ones, then compares concept test performance of the best ideas against historical data (successful products tested similarly) to gauge their absolute potential.

Key questions asked in a concept test usually probe the following factors:

- *Buying intent.* This is the most critical measure in a concept test and is usually the basis for ranking ideas.

- *Reasons for interest or lack of interest.* Answers to questions in this area determine the key appeals of good ideas and identify areas needing improvement in weak concepts.
- *Expected frequency of use or purchase.* This spots products that would be purchased too infrequently to generate the volume needed to make them successful.
- *Uniqueness.* This screens out generic or "me-too" products.
- *Price/value.* This determines whether the projected price (either too high or too low) is affecting acceptance of the concept.

Concept screening will be discussed in further detail later in this chapter.

Step 3: Product Development

Now that you have a concept or idea that seems to generate consumer interest, the next step in the new product process is to turn that concept into a physical product that can be marketed.

The product development cycle for a new product usually takes longer than any other step. It takes time to formulate or design the product, then more time to produce prototype samples for testing. Because this cycle is usually repeated several times while the product is being improved, it can be years before a product is ready to be marketed.

At this stage, the "product" takes on many dimensions besides the physical product itself. This is the last step before actual sales testing, so all the marketing elements that the product will incorporate have to be fine-tuned. The research techniques used at this stage are discussed in detail elsewhere in this book. The dimensions of the total "product" that need to be developed and researched include:

- Product
- Package
- Name, slogan, and logo
- Product positioning
- Advertising

Step 4: Simulated Sales Testing

Because of the high cost of test marketing, companies are increasingly using simulated sales testing as a final checkpoint before taking products to test market. This technique simulates the purchase process without the cost or time required for an actual market introduction. From this stage on, however, only products that appear to have a good chance of success are pursued. In addition, many concepts that generate strong consumer interest fail to reach the market because no physical product can be found to meet the expectations created by the concept.

Simulated sales testing is the first point at which the complete marketing mix for a product is pulled together and tested in finished form. This includes product, name, packaging, and advertising—all of which have probably been researched individually in step 3. The purpose of simulated sales testing is to produce an estimate of sales volume or market share.

Simulated sales testing will be discussed in greater detail later in this chapter.

Concept Screening

Creating new ideas and turning them into successful new products is a difficult, high-risk process. Thousands of new products are introduced each year. They represent the best of the ideas generated by companies. Yet most of those products fail and are gone within a year or two. That's where concept screening comes in: Its purpose is to help find the one idea in a thousand that could become a successful new product.

Principles Behind Concept Screening

We all know that people are usually attracted by the idea behind a product or service before they become interested in the physical product or actual service. They want a more convenient dessert, more beautiful hair, or cleaner floors; products are merely the vehicles for delivering those benefits.

Because the *idea* is the most critical element in a product, consumers can react to the new product idea without seeing the physical product; they can in fact react even before the physical product exists. If the idea of the product stimulates little interest among potential customers, it's unlikely that the physical product will do much better. On the other hand, if the idea does have appeal, the product has potential if it can deliver the benefits promised by the concept.

Today concept screening is widely used and accepted, particularly by marketers of packaged consumer products (food, household-care items, and health and beauty aids). In addition, concept testing is gaining acceptance among marketers of nonconsumable products such as housewares, sporting goods, and clothing. The techniques of concept screening are being adapted even to industrial and medical products.

Purpose of Concept Screening

When concept screening is done in the very early stages of the new product development process, it can have several important benefits:

- It can identify winners and losers while the concepts are no more than rudimentary ideas.
- It permits a company to set priorities and focus its development efforts on the concepts that have the greatest chance of becoming successful.
- It allows concepts to be evaluated before significant resources are committed to their development. In this way, marketing research can play an important role in helping companies make optimum use of their R&D laboratories, marketing budgets, and management time.
- Developing a low-risk screening system encourages the generation of concept ideas. Because any new product effort is dependent on the input of many new ideas, this stimulation can be very healthy for the development of new products.

Concept screening has been shown to work well for most kinds of products. The exceptions are radically innovative products that would require people to alter their behavior significantly. For example, it probably would have been difficult to adequately measure, before their introduction, the true potential impact of television, cake mixes, or instant coffee. These new products diffused slowly through the population, and people are poor predictors of their long-term behavior with regard to products that require substantial commitment and behavioral change. Fortunately for the marketing researcher, these dramatic, innovative new products are extremely rare. The kinds of ideas that most companies spend the bulk of their time screening are very testable with concept-screening techniques.

Because a primary purpose of concept screening is to sort beginning product ideas into winners and losers, it's important to test early, before substantial money is spent on development. If concept screening is used only as a disaster check before large-scale quantitative research or test marketing is begun, a great portion of the potential savings from concept screening will already have been lost. In addition, there is a higher emotional commitment to ideas that are further along in their development than there is to beginning ideas. It is easier to kill a weak concept while it's still at the idea stage than when it's about to go into test market.

Typical Results

Here's a real-life illustration of why screening many concepts early in the new product development process is critical. To put it simply, most new product ideas are bad ideas. They generate very little interest from consumers. Fortunately, that's easy to tell from the first test of a concept, which is why concept screening works.

Figure 16-1 shows the range of buying-intent scores on a typical batch of 120 new product ideas tested. As can be seen from the figure, only 12 percent of the concepts tested stimulated one-fourth or more of the consumers interviewed to say they'd "definitely buy" the product described. As a rule of thumb, a consumer product should receive a "definitely buy" score of at least 20 percent at the concept stage. These all too typical results show that a large proportion of all concepts tested don't even generate enough initial interest to justify taking them to the next step of development.

Figure 16-1. Buying-intent scores for a group of 120 new product ideas.

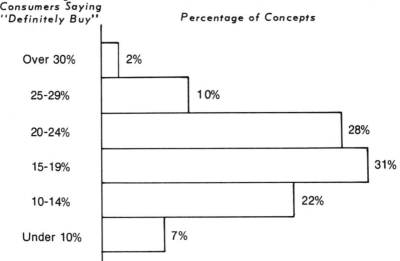

Presentation of Concepts

Fortunately, product descriptions used in testing need not be elaborate and expensive. In fact, simpler concept boards seem to work better. A fancy ad may inflate reactions to the product idea in the test. And if elaborate concept boards are used (including color photography, for example), production of the concept boards can become so expensive that it's impractical to test large numbers of new product ideas.

Only three elements are critical for inclusion in the concept statement:

1. *Copy describing the product, how it works, and what its benefits are.* The copy should not be full of puffery, exaggeration, and hard sell, but neither should it be too bland. A good guideline for preparing the copy is to try to write it as a newspaper reporter would: Make it interesting and informative, but stick to the facts.

2. *Some type of illustration, if only a simple line drawing.* This helps consumers in the test grasp the concept more quickly, and it makes the copy more interesting. For most products, drawings seem to be adequate. Photographs can be very expensive and are not necessary for most categories. The exception may be certain food products for which appearance, or "eye appeal," is expected to be a major factor in the product's success.

3. *Price and manufacturer's name.* This is information consumers usually want before making a purchase decision.

Most concept boards are 8½" × 11" in size and look something like Figure 16-2.

Interviewing Procedure

The fieldwork for concept-screening studies can be done in a number of different ways. However, because the purpose of concept screening is to efficiently evaluate a number of new product ideas, the following general procedure usually works best for consumer products:

1. Conduct the interviews using an "intercept" procedure in shopping malls, food stores, or other high-traffic locations. If the interview itself is relatively brief, this is the most efficient method of contact.
2. Divide the interviewing among several cities. This provides geo-

Figure 16-2. A typical concept board.

MOST cereal.

A COMBINATION NO OTHER CEREAL OFFERS.

This is a high-fiber multivitamin and iron-supplement cereal that teams up good nutrition with the honest flavor of wheat.

There's wheat germ for protein. Plus bran for the fiber many doctors say is important to good health. Plus vitamins and iron for good nutrition.

A 1-oz. serving of Most cereal gives you 100% of the U.S. Recommended Daily Allowance of vitamins A, C, D, E, B_6, B_{12}, thiamin, niacin, riboflavin, folic acid, and iron.

A 24-ounce package costs $1.95.

graphic representation where variations in concept reactions are expected in different parts of the country. Spreading the field-work over several markets also generally increases field efficiency.

3. Show each respondent no more than four concepts. This is important. Experience indicates that when consumers are given more concepts to evaluate, "wear-out" sets in and the quality of information deteriorates.

4. Rotate the order of concept presentation so that each concept appears an equal number of times in each position during the interviewing process.

5. Avoid showing the same consumers extremely similar concepts. It's usually better to mix up the types of concepts so that test respondents are exposed to a variety of product ideas.

Questions to Ask

Without doubt, the most critical question in any concept test is the one that measures buying intent. What you really want to know is: How many people will buy this product?

The most widely used question for evaluating buying interest is:
"Which of these statements best describes how you feel about buying this product?"

I definitely would buy it.   ☐
I probably would buy it.   ☐
I might or might not buy it.   ☐
I probably would not buy it.   ☐
I definitely would not buy it.   ☐

All the other questions that may be asked about a new product idea are for diagnostic purposes—to help explain why a concept has strong or weak appeal. These additional types of questions include:

1. *A follow-up, open-ended question probing why the respondent is or is not interested in buying the new product.* Typical wording: "Why do you say that?" Alternatively, a two-part question might ask: (1) "What's your main reason for saying that?" (2) "What other reasons do you have for saying that?" This helps uncover the relative importance of different concept appeals and benefits.

2. *Questions about the expected frequency of purchase.* Typical wording:

"Which statement best describes how often you think you would buy this product?"

Once a week or more often ☐
Once every two or three weeks ☐
Once a month ☐
Once every two or three months ☐
Once every four or six months ☐
Once or twice a year ☐
Less often than once a year ☐
Never ☐

Consumers are often inaccurate in estimating how often they will use a new product or in estimating how often they buy products they currently use. The frequency question can help screen out novelty or "birthday cake ideas"—products that are interesting to consumers but that they wouldn't buy often enough to make the product successful.

3. *Questions pertaining to the uniqueness of the concept.* These help identify "me-too" or generic ideas. Typical wording: "How different do you think this product is from other products now on the market?"

Extremely different ☐
Somewhat different ☐
Slightly different ☐
Not at all different ☐

4. *Questions relating to price/value reactions.* These are asked if the price is included in the description and is felt to be potentially either a positive or negative factor. Typical wording: "Which statement best describes how you feel about the value of this product?"

Very good value ☐
Fairly good value ☐
Average value ☐
Somewhat poor value ☐
Very poor value ☐

5. *Questions aimed at identifying current products the new product would replace.* These help identify the expected degree of cut-in or cannibalization of the company's existing products. For example, how much of a new product's volume will be taken from the company's other products and how much will come from competitors' products?

6. *Questions as to whether the product answers a need that isn't being satisfied by products now on the market.* These help to better clarify the product's appeal and uniqueness. Typical wording: "Do you feel this product might solve a problem or need that you or other members of your family have that isn't being satisfied by products now on the market?"

All these questions can of course be asked about new services as well as about new products. The same principles underlying testing product concepts apply equally to service concepts.

Analyzing Results

The buying-intent question is the key measure of concept interest. Standard ways of analyzing the buying-intent question are to look at either the "top box" ("definitely buy") score or the "top two boxes" ("definitely buy" plus "probably buy"). Both these measures identify the proportion of potential buyers who have a strong interest in the product, and they usually produce nearly the same ranking of concepts.

At the same time, some companies have moved beyond this simple "top box" system to a procedure that weights the buying-intent result to produce a number that seems to approximate penetration potential for a product. A weighting system often used is shown in the table in Figure 16-3. The weights in this case assume that only about three-fourths (.75) of the people who say they'll "definitely buy" the product will actually buy and only about one-fourth (.25) of those who say they'll "probably buy" will really buy, and so forth. In this example, the estimated potential trial purchase level for the hypothetical test product is 26.7 percent, which is then discounted for expected awareness and distribution.

Figure 16-3. A common weighting system for buying-intent responses.

Buying-Intent Scale	Test Responses		Weights		Weighted "Score"
Definitely will buy	21%	x	.75	=	15.8%
Probably will buy	29	x	.25	=	7.3
Might or might not buy	30	x	.10	=	3.0
Probably will not buy	15	x	.03	=	.5
Definitely will not buy	5	x	.02	=	.1
Total:	100%				26.7%

Simulated Sales Testing

Simulated sales testing techniques evaluate a new product in a way that reflects real-world behavior more accurately than does concept testing yet is faster and much less costly than full-scale test marketing. It also protects security more fully than test markets do.

Procedure

There are a number of research companies that offer different simulated sales testing techniques. These techniques vary in the underlying model or structure used to estimate sales potential, but all of them follow essentially the same general procedure for developing data. Five steps are involved:

1. *Exposure to advertising.* Some form of advertising, either print or TV, is used to expose consumers to the concept of the product. An ad, rather than a concept description, is used to get as close as possible to the type of exposure consumers will be subjected to in the real world.
2. *Opportunity to buy.* After seeing the ad, consumers are given an opportunity to purchase the test product, usually along with other products in the category. This is often accomplished through a small simulated store or store section—but sometimes a real store is used.
3. *Use period.* Consumers who buy the product take it home and use it as they normally would. In most cases, consumers are not told that they will be called back later and reinterviewed. This is done to make the use period as realistic as possible and to lessen the feeling among consumers that they are taking part in a test.
4. *Follow-up interviews.* After a normal use period, consumers are contacted and questioned about their satisfaction with the product and their intention to repurchase it.
5. *Repurchase opportunity.* Some techniques offer consumers an opportunity actually to repurchase the product. Again, this is an attempt to get a behavioral purchase measure rather than just a stated intention to repurchase.

The purpose of this procedure is to generate three consumer measures regarding the product:

1. *Trial rate*—the proportion of all consumers who try the product

2. *Repeat rate*—the proportion of onetime buyers (or triers) who purchase the product at least a second time
3. *Purchase frequency*—a measure of how often repeaters repurchase and how many units they purchase each time

The end objective of simulated sales testing is to produce an estimate of sales potential, usually expressed either as a measure of market share (if the product is in a well-defined category) or as an absolute dollar or unit volume estimate.

Strengths and Weaknesses

The primary strength of simulated sales testing as compared with concept screening is that it uses actual behavioral measures, so fewer assumptions about analogies to current consumer purchase behavior need to be made. Compared with full-scale test marketing, of course, simulated sales testing has the advantages of being quicker, less costly, more confidential, and better controlled.

At the same time, although simulated sales testing comes close to behavioral measures, it is still not completely realistic. Advertising exposures, simulated shopping experiences, and repurchase intentions all fall a little short of the real world. Another weakness of simulated sales testing is that it cannot measure the long-term adoption dynamics in a market—how ongoing repeat and frequency rates for the products are going to develop. Nevertheless, many companies believe that simulated sales testing is accurate enough to serve as a screening device instead of full-scale test marketing.

Suppliers

The most widely used simulated sales testing techniques and the companies that offer them are:

The *CRITIQUE*™ system from Custom Research Inc.
Litmus from Yankelovich Clancy Shulman.
The *BASES* service from Bases, Inc.
The *COMP* service of Elrick and Lavidge/Equifax.
The *Assessor* service of M/A/R/C.
ESP (Estimating Sales Potential) from NPD Research Inc.

Other models and procedures are offered by other research companies, but these are the best known.

17

Advertising Research

John Wanamaker, the famous retailer, is supposed to have complained, "I know half the dollars I spend on advertising are wasted—I just don't know which half." That was the problem many years ago, and it's still the problem today. Businesspeople intuitively know that some advertising is more effective than others, so it ought to be possible to research advertising. But nobody can agree on how to do it.

How Does Advertising Work?

Most of the problems with advertising research begin with the fundamental problem of advertising theory: Nobody knows for sure how advertising works. And if no one is sure how advertising works, it's difficult to measure how effective an advertisement is. For years it was assumed that advertising worked according to the following order:

1. Information
2. Attitudes
3. Action

In other words, advertising provides information, which creates positive attitudes toward a product, which eventually lead to a purchase. For many products this does seem to be the pattern, so this theory (which often includes a larger number of more finely defined steps) is useful in thinking about researching advertising for some kinds of products. Let's ignore, for the moment, what constitutes "information" or precisely how attitudes get created or changed.

Then it was found that for some types of products there is another order:

1. Information
2. Action
3. Attitudes

One of the clearest examples of this type of advertising is the billboard along the desert highway that says, "Last gas station for 100 miles." In that case, information often leads to action. Research indicates that many products bought on impulse also follow this pattern. Attitudes don't necessarily change prior to purchase; they may change *after* purchase as buyers justify their actions to themselves.

To make things even more confusing, it has been theorized that yet another pattern holds for some purchase decisions:

1. Action
2. Attitudes
3. Information

This appears to be the pattern for many expensive or ego-involving purchases. An example is the man who buys an expensive red sports car, gets a great ego boost from driving it, then seeks information about its features and performance to rationalize his action. Many major appliance purchases also seem to fall into this category.

These three theories of how advertising works—and there are many more—illustrate how difficult it is to define the precise role of advertising. In some cases its job is to change attitudes. In other cases its objective is to precipitate immediate action. And in other situations it may be used to justify actions that have already taken place.

Because it's difficult to come up with a simple definition of exactly what advertising is supposed to be doing, it is equally difficult to define how to measure its effectiveness.

Obstacles to Advertising Research

But maybe this is making the whole thing too difficult. The real purpose of advertising is to generate sales. Right? So why not just measure the sales effect of advertising directly? That would be better anyway.

Unfortunately, using sales information as a direct measure of advertising effectiveness has several drawbacks:

1. *Advertising is only one element in the marketing mix.* It is usually difficult to isolate the effect of advertising from that of distribution, sam-

pling, in-store promotions, shelf position, and all the other marketing variables that contribute to the success of a product.

2. *Competitive activities make sales measures difficult to interpret.* One competitor may increase its advertising or stop it altogether. Another may introduce a new product in the category. Yet another may run a high-value coupon program. How can the effect of these actions be separated from the effect of your advertising?

3. *Even where advertising has a direct effect on sales, the results often do not appear immediately.* There usually is a lag between the time an ad runs and the purchases that may result from it—and there may be an even longer lag before the manufacturer feels the effects in its shipments.

4. *Advertising has a cumulative effect.* For example, the sales results of a single ad for Kodak film are based, at least in part, on all the advertising that Kodak has run for its products over the years. So isolating the sales effect of a single ad, especially for a well-established brand, can be very difficult.

5. *Manufacturers' sales records can smooth out and hide sales responses.* Even if the sales effect of advertising were direct and immediate—which it usually is not—it would be difficult for most manufacturers to read relatively tiny, short-term bumps in retail sales. Most manufacturers do not sell directly to retailers. They may ship their products to regional chain store warehouses, which then distribute the products to individual stores. This "pipeline" can absorb small spurts in sales and make it difficult for the manufacturer to read anything except long-term sales results.

What Can Be Measured?

Since it is virtually impossible to measure the overall effect of a single ad or campaign on the sales of a product or service, research usually focuses on measuring the extent to which an advertisement achieves a specific, well-defined goal that has been set for it.

If it is assumed that a decision to purchase is made in stages—although admittedly those stages may take place in varying order—it's possible to measure the extent to which an ad or a campaign is successful in moving potential buyers through one stage or from one stage to the next. Examples of the actions or attitudes that advertising might be expected to generate include:

Product and/or brand awareness
Recognition of product benefits, features, or claims

Favorable attitudes
Predisposition to purchase
Motivation to purchase
Actual purchase
Reinforcement of satisfaction with purchase
Repeat buying

Most advertising research techniques focus on measuring the effectiveness of an ad in meeting one of these objectives. Does it create awareness? Does it really communicate the benefits of the product? Does it create a predisposition to purchase? (Examples of specific techniques designed to evaluate each of these dimensions are described later.)

Types of Advertising Research

The term *advertising research* is really misleading because it connotes a single type of research, when, in fact, many very different types of research fall under this heading.

Figure 17-1 shows some types of advertising research techniques and the types of decisions each technique is designed to help make. Many of these techniques either do not involve survey research or incorporate approaches, such as segmentation or positioning studies, that also have applications outside advertising research.

In the following section describing specific techniques, attention is focused on copy research and commercial tests that are designed to help in deciding "how to say it" and "how effective it was." These are the areas of advertising testing in which survey research is most often used.

Specific Advertising Testing Techniques

Techniques used to evaluate the effectiveness of advertising are too numerous to list. Here is an overview of some of the most widely used approaches to advertising research.

Qualitative research on copy. A first step in the early stages of development for many ads is qualitative research—involving either focus groups or one-on-one interviews—to get consumer feedback on the ad. The purpose here usually is to determine whether consumers find anything about these ads unclear or confusing, and whether they "take away" from the ad the main point intended by the advertiser. Because it

Figure 17-1. Types of advertising research.

To decide:	One must choose:	Using techniques known as:
What to say	Theme, copy, platform strategy	Concept tests, positioning studies, category studies
To whom to say it	Target audience	Market segmentation studies, category studies
How to say it	Copy, commercial execution	Copy research, some commercial tests
How often to say it	Frequency of exposure	Studies of repetition, fighting
Where to say it	Media plan	Media research, audience studies
How much to spend	Budget level	Sales analysis, test markets, single source tests, marketing models
How effective it was	Measure of results	Test markets, in-market ad tests, AAU studies, single source tests, some commercial tests

Source: Adapted from *Advertising Research: The State of the Art,* Charles Ramond, published by the Association of National Advertisers, 1976.

is qualitative research, it is necessarily imprecise; but it can be useful for revealing major problems early, while there is still time to find alternative approaches.

Some advertisers and advertising agencies have developed small-scale quantitative techniques to provide this same type of "early feedback" information. Typically, these techniques involve showing a test ad to consumers, then asking them to indicate on a series of scales or on a checklist their reactions to the ad. These reactions are tabulated and compared with profiles of other successful ads to indicate the extent to which the commercial is seen as believable, informative, humorous, and so on. This is another way of testing the copy in ads early in the development of a commercial.

On-air recall techniques. One of the best known of these techniques is "day-after recall." Respondents are recruited via telephone to watch a specific program in which a test ad is shown (usually on a cable station) in three or four test cities. The next day, telephone interviews are conducted with respondents who have watched the program on which the test commercial was telecast. These respondents are questioned, on an unaided and aided basis, about their recall of the ad. Those who remember seeing it are asked what they recall about the ad and what was said.

These results are then compared with a data bank of ads for other products in similar categories to provide a measure of the effectiveness of the test ad in generating recall. Audience Studies Institute (ASI) is the best-known company offering this technique.

Theater persuasion measures. Groups of consumers are invited to a theater setting, usually with the explanation that they will be shown pilot episodes of new television programs. Before the show, members of the audience are asked to indicate their preference among certain brands of products—including the test product category—usually under the pretense that a drawing will be held, with consumers awarded the products for which they have the strongest preference. Then some type of program film is shown with several commercials inserted in it. In this way it simulates the environment in which a commercial might actually be shown. After seeing the program and the commercials, viewers are again asked to express their relative interest in the products in the category. The measure of effectiveness used here is the change in purchase intention or preference for the test product between "before" and "after" an ad was shown. The best-known company offering this type of service is Research Systems Corporation.

Print ad tip-in. A test ad is inserted (tipped in) in copies of a magazine in which such ads would normally appear. A sample of respondents is recruited (usually in shopping malls) to take home the magazine and read it. A telephone callback is scheduled for the next day to get their reactions to the magazine. Then respondents are questioned on their recall of the test ad, in a manner similar to the on-air TV technique. Two of the best-known companies providing this service are Gallup & Robinson and Mapes & Ross.

Single-source ad tests. Some suppliers of single-source data have the capability to control and test the ads received via cable TV by recruiting panels of homes to participate in their systems. These households also identify themselves with ID cards when they purchase products in stores. Their purchases can then be linked to specific ads they have seen to get a behavioral measure of advertising effectiveness.

Portfolio testing of print ads. A portfolio is made up of six or eight ads, one of which is the test ad. Respondents are invited to look through the portfolio, taking as much time as they need. Then the interviewer takes back the portfolio and closes it. Next the interviewer asks the respondent to mention which products and brands he or she recalls seeing. If the test ad is mentioned, the interviewer asks what the respondent can remember about it. If the respondent does not mention the test ad, the interviewer asks about it on an aided basis. If there is still no recall, the interviewer may open the folder to the test ad and ask the respondent about the ad. This technique attempts to measure both recall and the communication effectiveness of the advertisement.

Preparing Commercials for Testing

Production of a commercial is often the most expensive part of testing finished television advertising. Producing a finished TV commercial can easily cost $150,000 or more, and the cost of buying media can run an equivalent amount.

Research shows that "roughly" executed commercials, particularly photo boards and live action, do an adequate job of providing copy testing material. So it may not always be necessary to go to final form to produce ads for testing. This makes testing a larger number of ads at the early stages of development much more feasible.

It used to be said jokingly that the motto of Mayor Richard J. Daley, the late political boss of Chicago, was, "Vote early and vote often." Most advertisers would be glad to be half as successful with their advertising as Mayor Daley was at getting himself and his fellow Chicago Democrats elected. So maybe his advice is good: "Test early and test often."

Studies of how advertising research is used indicate that it's most often used to make go/no-go decisions—often after considerable time and money have been spent producing finished ads for testing. To be most useful, however, research should be pushed forward in the process so that it can help plan and guide the development of the advertising, not just produce a score of "good" or "bad" at the end. Too often researchers serve as scorekeepers, when they would be more helpful as players on the team that's working to develop effective advertising.

18

Package Testing

Maybe you can't tell a book by its cover, but you can tell a product by its package. At least, many people think so. Decisions to buy a product, especially a new product, are often strongly influenced by whether the package attracts attention and makes the contents seem appealing.

A package is much more than just a container. It also plays the role of:

- Attention-getter
- Point-of-purchase advertising
- Reminder to current users
- Source of information about directions, ingredients, and cautions
- Announcer of special offers or deals
- Builder of expectations about what's inside

All in all, then, the package is one of the most important marketing tools for a product. The package is the only piece of communication about the product that every buyer sees.

This means that having a better package can make a difference for a product, particularly a new product. Research can help select the best package for a product and ensure that what the package communicates is consistent with the overall strategy for the product.

When to Test

Most packaging research is done on new products. At that point it's still easy to explore alternatives, even to consider "far-out" package designs.

But once a package is on the market, major changes are infrequent. There's always a fear that regular buyers won't be able to find a redesigned package, so changes are made only for good reason. Some of the major considerations that could justify changing an existing package are:

An improvement in the physical package (new package material, new closure, new shape, and so on)
"Improved," reformulated, or redesigned product
Eroding market or other competitive activity
Major product repositioning
More contemporary graphics or a more modern look

It's important to test as early as possible, preferably before the final packaging is developed. Even mock-ups are expensive to make, and if large numbers of four-color packages are required for testing, it simply becomes too costly for most companies to test.

For this reason, photographs and slides are useful for testing in the early stages of development. In a photograph, a mock-up often cannot be distinguished from a finished package. So using photographs of mock-ups (and often only one or two sides of the package need to be mocked up for a photograph) makes it practical to test packages early, before package production costs are incurred.

It is easiest to test alternatives for new products. That way the alternatives can be "horse-raced" against each other and the best alternative selected. It is difficult to test existing packages directly against alternative new packages. The familiarity of a package that has been on the market for years usually makes it easier for consumers in the test to recognize the existing package. In addition, the associations that have been built up in consumers' minds make it difficult for them to separate the image of the brand from the connotations of the current package.

What to Test

Make sure there is a measurable difference among the alternative packages being tested. Among the differences that are usually significant enough to be measurable in a test are:

- Product name
- Principal color
- Illustrations or photos
- Logo
- Type of package (bottle versus box)
- Shape
- Size
- Main panel elements

But you can't and shouldn't test everything. Although there may be important changes—maybe even legally required ones—not every package revision is measurable. The effect on the package of temporary deals or premium offers can rarely be tested. Neither can revisions in secondary panel elements (preparation directions, ingredient listings, and cautions).

Because a package has to perform many roles, it stands to reason that a package cannot be adequately evaluated on just one dimension. That is the primary weakness of many single-measure package testing techniques.

There are three principal components of a package's effectiveness: visibility, image, and function.

Visibility

One of the most important jobs a package performs is to stand out and call attention to the product on the shelf, then tell consumers who notice it what's inside. The visibility element is made up of three components:

1. *Display visibility.* Does the package stand out in an array of competitive products to consumers who are *not* specifically looking for it? In other words, does it demand to be noticed? Does it "jump off" the shelf?
2. *"Findability."* How readily can the package be found on the shelf by people who *are* looking specifically for it? Can people who have seen the package in an ad find it easily? Do repeat buyers have trouble finding the product again?
3. *Readability.* How quickly and easily are elements of the package perceived? Once consumers notice it, how easy is the package to read?

Each of these components must be measured to get a complete evaluation of the visibility of a package. The visibility measures are usually the most important in researching a new product. Among the methods used to research visibility are:

• *Tachistoscope.* The classic version of the "T-scope" uses a darkened box in which the package is placed. The box is illuminated for the respondent under controlled intensity and duration of lighting. Although this method offers considerable control, the setting is somewhat unrealistic.

• *Eye cameras or pupil meters.* These are devices for recording the pattern traced by the eyes as they look at a package or display. They have the advantage of offering a very quantified measure of what respondents look at. The drawback is that analysis and interpretation can be difficult.

• *Find-time.* This type of test is usually conducted in an actual store or a large simulated display section. Each respondent is told to find a specified product and pick it up as quickly as possible. The lapsed time required to find the product is measured from the point where the respondent enters a marked-off area near the display. This method has the advantage of realism—it's done in an actual store or real section— but the problems of carefully controlling the mechanics of the test can make it difficult to find significant and consistent differences between alternative test packages.

• *35mm slides.* This approach uses timed exposures of actual shelf displays or individual packages. After each exposure, respondents are asked to report everything they saw or read. Because it uses photographs as stimuli, it can show the test package within a competitive category display. And mock-ups of packages are adequate for making slides. The timed slides offer a combination of the realism of "find-time" and the control of the tachistoscope.

Image

A package communicates much more than just the objective information printed on it. It can make the product look interesting or dull, appetizing or unappealing, different or run-of-the-mill. Good research should measure the connotations of a package too. If visibility alone were important, every package would be fluorescent orange.

Any method of showing the package can also be used to measure its image—actual packages, mock-ups, or slides. Among the techniques that can be used to evaluate a package's image or connotations are these:

• *Probes.* These are open-ended questions asked to determine what consumers like and don't like about the packages. They may uncover a weakness or "turnoff."

• *Profiles.* Rating scales can be used to obtain an overall picture of the image created for the product by each package.

• *Projective techniques.* Associations with types of consumers or product characteristics can indicate the strengths and weaknesses of alternative designs. Especially on new products, if respondents have only the package to go on, the results can be a good measure of package connotations.

• *Perceptions.* Mapping techniques or other questions can be used to reveal how consumers see the brand fitting into the product category.

• *Preferences.* At the end of the interview, it's sometimes useful to ask consumers to express a direct preference among the alternatives. (A buying-intent question is another way of measuring this.) Although preference measures should not be allowed to override evaluations of visibility and readability, a strong preference result can increase confidence in selecting a new package alternative that is only marginally better on visibility and readability measures than others.

But use preference measures with caution. Consumers tend to prefer the familiar and the usual. In other words, they'll usually prefer the cereal package that looks like other cereal packages, the soap package that looks like other soap packages, and so forth. As a result, relying heavily on preference measures is likely to lead to choosing a "me-too" package even when a dramatic or innovative package alternative would be more successful.

Function

Of course the package must work. Often this doesn't have to be tested, since most packages are simply graphic variations of boxes, bottles, or bags that are already in widespread use. But if the package is a new design and there are questions about whether it will work or not, this dimension should be included in the research.

Among the functional elements that can be tested are ease of:

• Reading and following directions and usage instructions
• Grasping, holding, or gripping
• Opening
• Closing or resealing
• Removing or emptying contents
• Storing unused product

These measures can be especially critical for industrial or medical products, areas where package functionality is often more important than visibility.

Guidelines on Testing

To be useful, package research should have three characteristics:

1. *It should show products in a realistic setting of competitive products.* Often a package that looks attractive and attention-getting by itself loses impact among competitive products on the shelf. This may be the case when many products in a category use similar colors in their packaging. The only way to determine this is by testing the product in its real-life competitive environment.

2. *It should be comprehensive.* Testing must provide a complete, objective evaluation of the strengths and weaknesses of a package. It should measure all the elements of a package's performance—at least all those about which there is any question or concern.

3. *It should be controlled.* Exposure to the package and measurement of its visibility or image need to be carefully controlled. One way to do this is through the use of slides rather than actual displays, because exposure to the shelf display presented in a slide is more easily controlled. The other device for ensuring maximum control is the use of some type of tachistoscope, which can be used to control light intensity and exposure duration.

Packages, theoretically, can also be tested under actual sales conditions, in either test markets or simulated sales tests. In practice, however, this rarely happens. There are substantial practical and cost problems involved in producing large quantities of a product in two or more different packages. As a result, most companies do their package testing before proceeding to sales testing.

Although these testing techniques are used primarily for evaluating packages, they can be adapted to other research problems in which visual impact and connotations need to be evaluated—such as point-of-purchase materials, special store display units, or billboard advertising.

19

Name Research

"What shall we name the baby?" every parent-to-be asks. Jane? No, that's too ordinary. Humphrey? No, I never liked Humphrey Bogart in the movies. Charlene? I had an Aunt Charlene who was a shrew, and I wouldn't want the baby to be like that.

Names are powerful because they convey so much information—not directly, necessarily, but through all the associations a name carries for each of us.

Product Names

Companies, too, take a lot of care in naming their "babies." The name of a new product, for example, is one of the most important ways of communicating to potential customers what the product is like. Marketing research can play an important role in selecting names for products.

Types of Product Names

Companies follow many different strategies in naming their products. The approaches include:

• *Company names.* Many companies attach their corporate names prominently to the products they market. Scott Paper, Pillsbury, Kraft, and Libby are examples. Other corporations—General Foods and Procter & Gamble are prominent examples—subordinate their company names to individual product brand names.

• *Line names.* Betty Crocker and Aunt Jemima are examples of line names assigned to a variety of specific products manufactured by a company.

• *Descriptive names.* These names are meant to describe, in a literal yet appealing way, the physical product. Examples are Minute Rice, Rice Krispies, Light 'n Lively, Stir 'n Frost, and Buc-Wheats.

• *Imagery names.* These types of names, which are very common, do not literally describe the product, yet they are intended to suggest indirectly characteristics about the product. Examples include Log Cabin, Mrs. Butterworth, Mazola, A-1 Steak Sauce, Roman Meal Bread, Tasters Choice, and Pampers.

• *Manufactured meanings.* In recent years, as products have proliferated and the list of legally available product names has shrunk, a new type of brand name has begun to appear. These names usually have no literal meaning associated with the category, although they may have indirect meanings that the manufacturer hopes will reflect favorably on the product. Two categories, health and beauty aids and cigarettes, seem to be the most active users of this type of name. Examples include Aim, Scope, Fact, and True.

Dimensions of Product Name Research

Research on new product names typically involves five dimensions: connotations, suitability, pronunciation, memorability, and familiarity.

Connotations. A key concept in most name research is the distinction between the "denotation" and the "connotation" of a name. The denotation is the literal, explicit meaning of a name. It usually is unnecessary to conduct research to determine this. The connotations of a name, on the other hand, are its associated implications, beyond the literal, explicit meaning of the name.

The difference between connotations and denotations is often dramatic. For example, the name Adolf literally means "noble hero." Yet how many people know that? It's a fair guess that the first association most people would make with the name Adolf is with Adolf Hitler—an association that is quite opposite to "noble hero."

Connotations are often stronger than denotations in giving meaning to names. As a result, understanding the connotations that potential names have for consumers is often the focus of name research.

One way to study the connotations of new names, which works particularly well with products, is to research the *types of people* consumers think would use a product with the name. For example, consumers might be asked by interviewers—using either a checklist or some type of agree/disagree scale—which of the following types of people they would expect to be users of a product called such-and-such:

Banker
Factory worker
Scientist
Student
Poor credit risk
Artist
Teacher
Person like me

The list of types of people used in the research should include the kinds of people the brand wants to attract as well as those the brand is not intended to appeal to.

Connotations of product names can also be evaluated by measuring the *characteristics* associated with the name. For example, respondents might be asked what type of product they would expect each potential name to represent, if the product were available. The list of characteristics might include:

High quality
Low price
Unique and different
Flavorful
Smooth and creamy

With both approaches—studying types of users or characteristics associated with the names—the purpose is to draw a profile of the connotations associated with alternative new names. When these profiles are compared, it is usually possible to see the strengths and weaknesses of each name and to identify the one that is most appropriate.

Suitability. After the general connotations of a name have been researched, it may be useful to measure whether consumers see the name as fitting with the company that is considering using it.

For example, consumers might be asked, toward the end of the interview: "Which of these products would you most expect to see marketed by a company like Johnson & Johnson?" For corporations with very strong company images—which would include companies that use their names as a prominent part of product brand names—this can be important information in selecting among alternative brand names.

Pronunciation. Most product names aren't difficult to pronounce, so this issue rarely needs to be researched. But if the list of name candidates includes any highly unusual names—and coined names or very technological-sounding names often fall in this category—including a measure of the ease of pronunciation of the alternatives is a good idea.

This is done toward the beginning of the interview, before the interviewer has uttered any of the names, by giving the respondent a list of the names and asking him or her to read them aloud. The interviewer then simply marks the pronunciation as correct or incorrect, according to the pronunciation indicated on the copy of the questionnaire. Remember to give the interviewer a phonetic spelling of any difficult names, even if pronunciation isn't being tested, so that the name will be pronounced correctly during the interview.

Memorability. Being easy to remember is an important characteristic of a name, although it is difficult to measure accurately in an interview situation.

However, clues about which names may be unusually easy or difficult to remember can sometimes be developed in this way: At the end of the interview, after asking any demographic questions, the interviewer asks, "By the way, which of the names that we talked about during the interview do you happen to remember?" This can indicate any names that are particularly easy or difficult to remember.

Another way to measure memorability is to conduct a callback interview a couple of days later and ask which, if any, names the respondent remembers from the interview. This is much more expensive, of course, than simply asking the question at the end of the interview, but it gives a better indication of long-term memorability.

Familiarity. A name generally shouldn't seem too familiar, or it may be difficult for a company to communicate that the product is new and different. One way to measure this is to ask, early in the interview, whether respondents think they have heard of a product with this name before. To make this question more credible, mix the alternative new names with several actual brand names from the category.

If a name generates a significant degree of claimed recognition, it may suggest that the brand name is confusingly similar to existing brands or so ordinary that it sounds as if it ought to exist already. Both situations are clearly undesirable, for a brand shouldn't sound too familiar before it reaches the market.

Company Names

According to anthropologists, elderly Eskimos used to take new names, believing that they would thereby be enabled to start a new life. Many companies seem to have a similar belief in the revitalizing power of a new name.

Companies most often select new names to overcome a weakness or limitation in an existing one. For example, Standard Oil of New Jersey changed its name to Exxon when it concluded that the name Standard Oil wasn't adequate to describe the company's diversified businesses.

Two types of research can be undertaken to help management evaluate whether a company name change should be considered:

1. Studying a company's existing image will indicate the potentially valuable associations of a current name.
2. Testing the types of products or markets associated with an existing name will show whether that name has the breadth to be associated with the variety of businesses in which the company is now involved or may become involved in the future.

Types of Company Names

Companies take many different kinds of names. Some company names are literally descriptive of their products, while others bear no direct relationship to the business the companies are in.

- *Descriptive names.* These include many well-known companies, such as General Motors, General Electric, U.S. Steel, and Control Data.
- *Alphabetical names.* These initials may be developed as the name of a company, or they may simply represent a company adopting as its official name an abbreviation already in widespread use. IBM, 3M, ITT, RCA, and LTV are examples.
- *Coined names.* These names may be adopted because they have no literal meaning, or they may represent combinations of old, longer company names into single, shorter names. Many company name changes in recent years have been moves in this direction. Examples include Xerox, Exxon, Uniroyal, Alcoa, and Airco.
- *Location names.* Many companies originally took names reflecting their locations. Ashland Oil, Cincinnati Milicron, Texas Instruments, and Minnesota Mining & Manufacturing are a few examples.

- *Family names.* The founders of companies gave their names to such companies as Chrysler, DuPont, Kaiser Industries, and Litton Industries.
- *Traditional names.* A common practice is to couple an industry or product category name with such words as Allied, United, General, American, Continental, or International.
- *Combination names.* Companies with more than one founder, or businesses born through the merging of two companies, have spawned such names as Allis-Chalmers, Gulf + Western, Borg-Warner, and Hewlett-Packard.

The same research dimensions that apply to product names apply equally to company names: connotations, suitability, pronunciation, and memorability. The same basic research approaches that work for products also work for company names.

In addition, for company names, the associations between alternative names and specific characteristics can be researched. For example, respondents can be asked which characteristics they would expect a company called such-and-such to have:

Industry leader
Large
Reliable
Old-fashioned
Undependable
Technological leader

Analyzing Name Research

It is important for those who are to make the decision on the basis of name research to think about how they will interpret the results *before* the results are available.

You should sit down with the questions asked in the research and develop a "profile" of the connotations you hope the new name will have—which desirable connotations you hope will be strong and which undesirable associations you hope the final name will *not* have.

Most of the individuals involved in name research have their favorite candidates. And if a discussion of decision rules is postponed until after the results are available, there is a natural tendency for each person to look for ways to justify the selection of his or her favorite candidate.

Discussing decision rules beforehand helps make the analysis more objective and increases the odds that the research will lead to a better name choice.

Other Considerations

Availability

An astonishing number of names, even many not currently in use, have been registered and are therefore unavailable for use. In addition, laws in foreign countries make certain types of names unprotectable by registration there, which may be an important consideration in selecting a product name for a multinational company.

For this reason, the legal availability of all alternatives included in the research should be checked before the research is conducted. Otherwise, there is a risk of finding, at the conclusion of the research, that the "winner" isn't available.

Creativity

This is the element that sometimes overrides all the logic behind name research. Occasionally a name that doesn't seem to fit a product can be successful precisely *because* it doesn't fit the product. An example is Charlie perfume, introduced a number of years ago by Revlon. Before the product was introduced, the name Charlie probably had no connotations that made it suitable for a new perfume. But the name formed the basis of a marketing campaign that sold the product as something different and unconventional—and made it the world's top-selling fragrance for a time.

These exceptions to the rule are sometimes used to show that name research isn't necessary. But most examples of this type come from the cosmetics field, where the difficulty of achieving demonstrable product differentiation makes the use of unusual product names more common.

Also, most people forget that Charles Revson, the founder of Revlon, named Charlie after himself. Who could argue with the boss?

For most products in most categories, however, finding a name that has desirable connotations is important. A name with strong positive associations can be a powerful marketing tool.

20

Image and Identity Research

Reputation, reputation, reputation!
O! I have lost my reputation.

—William Shakespeare, *Othello*

The "image" of a company is sometimes mistakenly thought to be nothing more than the puffery resulting from a public relations campaign. The stereotyped advertising man of books and movies is always telling the client that his company needs to "fix its image"—which usually requires only a quick dose of advertising.

We all enjoy being with people whom we like, respect, and trust. Similarly, we generally like to buy the products of companies we feel positive toward. But think of a company's image as its reputation or the overall impression that people have of it, and it's easier to see why image is important.

So image research is really a matter of measuring the overall impression that people have of a company or product. In this sense, image is a very real, very important thing.

Although the terms *image* and *identity* are often used interchangeably, they actually have different meanings. *Identity* refers to all the ways in which a company identifies itself to the outside world. This includes advertising, packaging, trucks, stationery—easily dozens of things for most companies. A company's *image*, on the other hand, is the result of this identity. It is the perception of the company by all its publics.

Identity is cause; image is effect.

When to Do Research

Image research can be precipitated by a number of things. Companies most often conduct image research when they are considering a name change or a logo/symbol change. Determining what impression consumers have of the company is an important first step in deciding how to identify the company.

Image research can also be an important first step in planning corporate advertising efforts, since it helps identify areas of the company's reputation or operations that consumers may be unaware of or confused about. These often become the focus of corporate communication programs.

Finally, image research is often done as part of acquisition or merger evaluations. When one company purchases another, a large share of what it is buying is the reputation and goodwill of the new company. If the company to be acquired is in a field with which the acquiring company is unfamiliar, an image study may help determine the quality of the reputation—and, therefore, part of the value—of the company being acquired.

Steps in Image Research

The typical image study involves two basic steps: (1) determining what characteristics are important to consumers and (2) measuring how the company or product is viewed on these characteristics. For example, it's important to know whether "availability and delivery" as a characteristic is more important than the "technical knowledge of sales representatives." Once this is determined, you need to know how company A is viewed on these characteristics compared with its competitors.

But another step is also important: *identifying the characteristics on which the companies being evaluated differ the most.* Overlooking this can limit the usefulness of the research. A classic example of this is the airline industry. Any air traveler would agree that safety is a critical element in the reputation of any airline—if it's absent. At the same time, however, most travelers probably believe that all airlines are about equal on safety. No one airline is really much safer than another. Airlines are seen to differ most on such things as schedule convenience and quality of meals. Consequently, these characteristics, rather than safety, are more logical subjects for advertising.

In summary, then, it's necessary to measure which characteristics are important, but it is also critical to measure which characteristics are "discriminators." It's these discriminating attributes that become critical in turning research results into action.

An Example

The easiest way to illustrate how image research works is to describe an example. The hypothetical company doing this image study is Acme Chemical Co.

Step 1

The first step is to determine how Acme and its competitors are viewed overall by the market. Let's suppose that Acme's key competitor is Universal Chemical Co. Respondents could first be asked to indicate their overall opinion of each company on a scale such as this one:

Entirely favorable	☐
Mostly favorable	☐
Mixed—about equally favorable and unfavorable	☐
Mostly unfavorable	☐
Entirely unfavorable	☐

This might be followed by a "why do you feel that way?" question to determine, on an unaided basis, the most important top-of-mind impressions of each company.

This overall opinion scale serves two purposes. First, it gives a summary profile of each company (what proportion of people feel positive, neutral, or negative about the companies). Second, this scale can be the basis for later cross-tabulations and analysis. For example, it might be useful to look at how the specific attitudes of customers who have favorable opinions of Acme differ from those who have generally unfavorable opinions. This could help isolate the characteristics that are problems for Acme.

Step 2

The second step is to have respondents indicate their opinions of the importance of a list of company or product characteristics. This list is usually developed through exploratory research, such as group interviews. The results might resemble those in Figure 20-1.

A word of caution: "Product quality" almost always comes out on top on a list like this. But that can be deceptive, because quality alone is rarely the key factor in a market. To understand what people mean by "quality," it's usually helpful to know: (1) whether there are other characteristics that go together with quality to form a package; and (2) whether respondents really mean that some "threshold" of quality, rather than absolute quality, is important. Obviously, no one wants a poor product, but neither do most people want the best product possible regardless of price. People usually have a threshold of quality in mind, a minimum quality level that's acceptable. A product mustn't fall below this level, but neither should it necessarily be too far above it—or it risks being priced out of the market. Adding quality usually adds cost too.

In short, then, don't accept an overly simplified, naive definition of quality. Make sure you understand exactly what quality means in that market before you begin an image study, then build measures of the complete quality definition into the study.

After these importance ratings are obtained, respondents should be questioned about the characteristics on which they think companies in this industry differ most. Perhaps in Acme's market, buyers believe that suppliers differ most on prompt delivery and technical service. This would suggest that product quality and prices are important—and Acme must remain competitive in those areas—but that they aren't seen as characteristics that differentiate suppliers.

Figure 20-1. Hypothetical ranking of company and product characteristics by customers.

Company or Product Characteristics	Percentage Rating Characteristic as "Extremely Important"
1. Product quality	92%
2. Competitive prices	86
3. Prompt delivery	81
4. Salesmen's knowledge	73
5. Technical service	70
6. Innovative research and development	65
7. Company size	40
8. Industry leadership	29
9. Effective management	23

Step 3

The third step is to have respondents rate each of the companies on the list of more important characteristics. In our example, the results might look like Figure 20-2.

In this example, it appears that one reason for Acme's better overall reputation, compared with Universal's, is that Acme is more highly regarded on delivery and technical service—two of the characteristics that buyers earlier said were differentiating attributes among suppliers. On the other hand, Universal is seen as having more innovative R&D and being an industry leader, but these are much less important characteristics. In other words, Universal's strengths are in the less important areas, while Acme is strong in the areas that are most important to the market.

Figure 20-2. Hypothetical rating of two companies on characteristics deemed important.

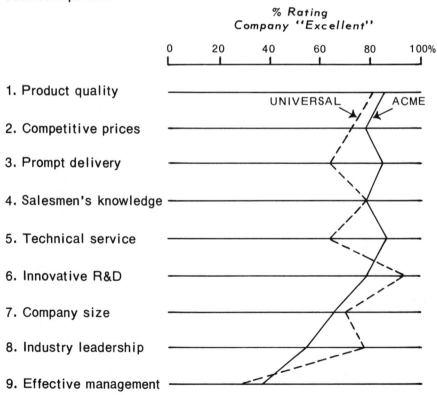

Whom to Interview

The two most important "publics" to include in any image research are customers and prospective customers. Customers are important, of course, because any company wants to understand why it is successful with the people who are buying from it. Prospective customers or competitors' customers are important because they are the people you hope to turn into future buyers.

In some cases, stockholders and representatives of the financial community are important to study too. Top management often believes, usually correctly, that a company's image can have a strong effect on its stock price.

Finally, don't forget to evaluate the image of a company among its employees and management. Any effort to change the image of a company must be consistent with the way people within the company think about it and want it to be seen. So understanding the attitudes and perceptions of employees, especially at the middle-management level and above, should usually be part of an image study.

21

Business-to-Business Research

Business-to-business research is just like consumer research—only different. Most of the principles and techniques of consumer research can be applied to business products and services. The difference is that the structure of commercial markets and the types of respondents to be interviewed make it necessary to revise and adapt consumer research techniques. *But many of the basic approaches are the same.*

The term *business-to-business* is used to refer to marketing to companies or institutions rather than to individual consumers. Examples of these markets would be:

- Business computers
- Hospital supplies
- Heavy machinery
- Building components
- Office equipment
- Corporate financial services
- Institutional food service supplies

Differences From Consumer Research

Business-to-business research is different from consumer research in some important ways. These differences must be understood so that the appropriate adjustments can be made in the consumer research techniques used.

Market Concentration

Many commercial markets are extremely concentrated, usually much more so than consumer product markets. One household may be twice as big, maybe even five times as big, as another household. But a large company can be at least a thousand times as big as a smaller company, which can create high market concentrations compared with consumer product markets.

In some cases, only a handful of companies make up the entire market. (The commercial aircraft market would be an extreme example.) A more typical market is the hospital market, where 18 percent of the hospitals (those with over 300 beds) account for 53 percent of all hospital beds. So those few large hospitals represent more than half the potential for many hospital products. At the other end of the scale, the hospitals with fewer than 100 beds account for nearly half the hospitals, but only 13 percent of the total beds.

The problem of market concentration is usually dealt with through stratified sampling. Sampling is carried out according to the market volume represented by each size category, not the number of businesses or institutions in that category. So in the hospital example, 53 percent of the interviews would be done in the hospitals with over 300 beds; alternatively, the responses of those hospitals would be weighted to account for 53 percent of the total survey result.

Universe Identification

In business-to-business research it is first necessary to define the universe of the types of establishments you want to include in your studies. A common method for doing this uses the government's Standard Industrial Classification (SIC) Coding System. The SIC System is organized much like the Dewey Decimal System used in libraries. Each commercial establishment is categorized into a broad industry group and assigned a two-digit SIC code. The broad industry groups and their two-digit SIC code ranges are as follows:

SIC	*Industry Group*
01–09	Agriculture, Forestry, and Fishing
10–14	Mining
15–19	Construction
20–39	Manufacturing

40–49	Transportation, Communications, Utilities
50–51	Wholesale Trade
52–59	Retail Trade
60–69	Finance, Insurance, and Real Estate
70–89	Services
90–98	Public Administration

The first two digits of the SIC code describe the nature of the business activity very broadly. Each establishment is assigned codes with additional digits (up to as many as eight) to describe the activity of the business more specifically. For example, in the manufacturing group, the code numbers would look like this:

SIC 35	Industrial Machinery and Equipment Manufacturers
SIC 354	Metalworking Machinery
SIC 3546	Power-Driven Hand Tools
SIC 354602	Saws and Sawing Equipment

Samples can be drawn from various sources that usually include SIC codes and employee size classifications. The kinds of sampling sources most often used in business-to-business research include:

General directories, such as Moody's, Thomas Register, and Dun & Bradstreet
Trade associations
Mailing list houses
Magazine subscription lists
Specialized list companies (i.e., Computer Intelligence for computer owners or R. L. Polk for vehicle registrations)
Telephone directory Yellow Pages
Internal customer lists

Multiple Purchase Influences

With consumer products, the purchaser and the user are usually the same person (the homemaker). By contrast, business products are often used by one person but actually purchased by someone else. In many cases, several people may be involved in the purchase decision.

This often means doing multiple interviews to cover all the purchase influences. It can mean doing different types of interviews with different people in the purchase process. For example, the end user of a personal computer may be the appropriate respondent for a product test, while the MIS director might be the right person to interview in a new product concept study.

Respondent Accessibility

Business executives, architects, and doctors are difficult to reach, and they generally don't have a lot of time to talk when you do finally reach them. This doesn't mean that they can't be interviewed, but it does mean that you have to work your schedule around theirs and be briefer than you would be with most consumer research. You may have to split the interview into a brief telephone chat followed by a mail survey.

Terminology

Most business-to-business markets have languages all their own, which must be incorporated into questionnaires. You have to use the technical terminology of the respondent to be taken seriously by the person you are interviewing. This doesn't mean you can't be conversational. But you must deal with the subject of the interview in the respondent's own terms. For example, the person who operates the heart-lung machine is called a "perfusionist" or "pump tech," so that's the term you should use.

The special terminology is usually not as mysterious, extensive, or difficult to learn as it seems at first. A quick vocabulary cram session with someone familiar with the market is often enough to get you by.

Special Interviewers

Even the most assertive consumer interviewer is usually self-conscious about going into an operating-room suite or a company president's office to conduct an interview. This generally means that you need special interviewers to conduct business-to-business research. We've found that former nurses, trained in research techniques, work best as interviewers in the hospital environment and that interviewers who are themselves computer hackers are best for interviewing data processing executives. It is important that you use interviewing services with trained, experienced "executive interviewers" on their staffs.

These are mostly differences of degree, not kind. Business-to-business research can use most of the techniques used for consumer research, but the differences must be recognized so that the research techniques can be adapted to overcome the problems.

Similarities With Consumer Research

Although the customers in business-to-business markets are technically companies and institutions, the purchasing decisions are still made by people. And people are not all that different on the job from the way they are at home. Their job may require them to be somewhat more rational and objective in their business decisions than in their personal decisions, but even this is not always the case. It's really true that "people are people."

In business-to-business research, you still have someone asking questions of someone else, so many of the proven techniques of consumer research interviewing can be applied to these fields too. The same principles of questionnaire design and scale construction also apply.

Everybody likes to give an opinion, and this includes business executives, purchasing agents, and doctors—as well as homemakers. This form of flattery ("Your opinion is important to us") is basic to all types of marketing research. And it gets cooperation from most people, whether they are being interviewed as businesspeople or individual consumers.

As mentioned earlier in this chapter, sampling can be a problem if you cannot define the universe. In some fields, such as the medical supply market, drawing a good sample is often easier than it is in consumer research. For example, a complete list of virtually every hospital in the United States, including bed size and numerous other characteristics, is readily available. The same is true of product categories sold mainly to single SICs. Having this complete list is a sampler's dream, one that usually isn't available in the consumer research world.

So business-to-business research isn't as different from consumer research as is often thought. The basic components—respondent, questionnaire, and interviewer—are there whether the topic is cake mixes, machine tools, or surgical instruments.

Research Techniques

There are five basic methods used in business-to-business research.

Group Interviews

It's easier than you'd think to get businesspeople to attend a focus group. Getting business respondents to participate in focus groups is a mystery to many researchers. Yet there is a simple secret: money. Obviously you can't buy business executives; you can't pay them enough to make it really worth their time. But you can easily insult them by asking them to give you an hour or two of their time for nothing or a mere token. You have to ante up.

Beyond offering an adequate fee, appeal to the respondents' professional interest. Most people like to keep up with new things that are happening in their field. Then try to keep the session businesslike but informal. (Forget about trying to serve cocktails or managing a sit-down formal dinner. They're not worth the trouble.)

Another key to business-to-business focus groups is good scheduling. Set up sessions when it is easiest for your respondents to come. Many operating-room supervisors, for example, prefer a 4:30 P.M. session (right after they leave the hospital) to an evening group. Businesspeople may prefer a 6:00 P.M. group, with a box lunch or light snack offered, so that they can be home by 7:30 or 8:00 P.M.

Telephone Research

Businesspeople and doctors usually answer the phone—even when there is an interviewer on the other end. In other words, telephone research works surprisingly well with these groups.

Telephone interviewing has replaced door-to-door contacts for many kinds of consumer research. Similarly, telephone interviewing is now more common in business-to-business studies. For example, most doctors prefer patients to phone in with their questions. The same is true of research. Where the telephone is suitable, most business respondents seem to prefer a telephone interview to a personal interview.

We've done telephone studies ranging from five-minute interviews with office managers to twenty-minute interviews with cardiovascular surgeons. And surprisingly, refusal rates often tend to be lower on business-to-business studies than on consumer projects. Telephone research offers an opportunity to get a larger, more geographically dispersed sample at a fraction of the cost of personal interviews. So in many cases in business-to-business research, not only is telephone interviewing an acceptable alternative, it's actually a *better* alternative.

Personal Interviewing

When all else fails, interview the business executive or doctor in person at his or her office, or invite the person to a central-location interviewing facility. Telephone interviews are usually faster and cheaper, but sometimes, when you have a product to show or questions that involve lengthy rating scales, a personal interview is necessary. Personal interviews take time, and you have to set up an appointment. Be direct about what you want and why you're there. Doctors usually expect to be paid for their time during an office interview, whereas this generally is not the case with businesspeople.

Product Testing

Most consumer product companies wouldn't dream of introducing a product that hadn't been successfully tested among potential users. Yet careful, well-designed product testing still seems to be the exception in business markets.

Business products *can* be tested. With companies, it usually demands perseverance to get the testing cleared through all channels. But it can be done.

Product tests requiring rotated order of use, paired comparisons, and most of the other techniques of consumer research can be carried out on most business products. In the medical field, for example, we have successfully completed product tests on a variety of products, including many operating-room supplies, casting materials, tapes, sponges, and dental products.

Mail Research

An almost forgotten technique of consumer research—the mail survey—can often be effective in business-to-business studies. We've found that well-designed mail surveys sent with a token incentive can get up to a 70 percent response rate in the medical field (50 percent is our rule of thumb, and we regularly achieve it). This rate of return is unheard of in consumer research, where a return rate of 10 percent is generally considered good.

The key here is to use mail only on certain types of simple, straightforward, high-interest subjects. Then take the time to design the cover letter and questionnaire carefully. Another effective approach is to recruit business respondents by telephone to participate in a follow-up mail survey.

22

Research for Service Companies

We hear every day that the economy of the United States has become a service economy. By all measures, both the size of the service sector and the number of service businesses have grown dramatically in recent years and continue to grow steadily. With that growth has come a surge in the use of marketing research by service businesses.

What Is a Service Business?

A service business is usually described as a company that sells *intangibles*. That seems simple and straightforward enough. Banks, hospitals, and airlines differ from product (*tangible*) companies in that they all market only intangible services. Or do they?

Banks differ from one another in the facilities and services they offer. One hospital may be equipped to provide a type of surgery that another does not. And airlines have different types of aircraft, different seat sizes, and different meals—all very tangible. So the fact that a company markets intangibles or tangibles is not a reliable indication of whether it is in a product or service business.

Given the problems of identifying tangibles and intangibles, perhaps the best definition of a service business is this: *A service business is one that controls the distribution of the product or service to the end user in addition to providing or producing the product or service.* The product or service may be tangible or intangible.

By this definition, an example of a service business would be a fast-food restaurant chain, which has control over the distribution of its products in a way that a manufacturer of packaged food products does not. Similarly, a hospital deals directly with patients, while a manufacturer of medical equipment and supplies does not. The actual delivery of health care, then, is the service that makes a hospital a service industry.

Examples of Service Businesses

The following types of commercial businesses are generally considered service businesses:

- *Health care*
  - —Hospitals, clinics, and nursing homes
  - —Freestanding health care providers
- *Finance*
  - —Banks
  - —Savings and loan associations
  - —Loan companies
  - —Securities brokers
- *Insurance*
- *Real estate*
- *Travel*
  - —Hotels and motels
  - —Airlines
  - —Ship lines
  - —Travel agents
  - —Rental car companies
- *Retailers*
  - —Merchandise retailers
  - —Restaurants
  - —Dry cleaners, repair shops
- *Entertainment*
  - —Television and radio broadcasting companies
  - —Motion picture companies
  - —Cable TV and videotape companies
- *Professionals*
  - —Attorneys
  - —Accountants
  - —Physicians, dentists, social workers, and counselors
- *Management services*
  - —Consultants

—Advertising agencies
—Computer-service bureaus
—Marketing research companies

There are also many noncommercial and nonprofit institutions that provide services:

• Government (federal, state, county, and local)
• Churches
• Colleges and private schools
• Foundations
• Charities
• Museums, orchestras, and theaters

The growing interest among these noncommercial institutions in marketing (finding how they can meet the needs of users) has brought an accompanying increase in their use of marketing research. While this chapter focuses on commercial applications, the research principles apply equally to noncommercial and nonprofit institutions.

Why Research Is Important to Service Businesses

Up until a few years ago, marketers of packaged goods were far and away the heaviest users of marketing research. These included, in particular, manufacturers of food products, health and beauty aids, and household-care products. Why? The reasons seem tied to their use of another mass marketing tool: advertising. Advertising is a form of non-personal—although not impersonal—selling. Just as packaged goods companies used advertising rather than face-to-face selling to market their products, it was also natural for them to use research when personal contact with individual consumers was no longer feasible.

Why didn't service businesses go in for research until relatively recently? Primarily because most service businesses were still small, locally owned and operated enterprises and because they felt that they had enough face-to-face contact with customers to know what those customers wanted. Look at the list of service businesses: hospitals, banks, real estate brokers, restaurants. In the past, these businesses were almost all local operations. Today the opposite is true; they are almost all part of larger, multiunit organizations—usually national chains.

As service businesses have grown and developed into national chains, most have also developed into large-scale mass marketers. And marketing research has naturally evolved as a tool to help manage these businesses.

Services and Products Research: Similarities and Differences

Service businesses differ in one critical respect from product businesses: It is usually difficult, if not impossible, to simulate or pretest the use of a service. This can have a major impact on the types of marketing research that are feasible in service industries.

For example, it is obviously impossible for a potential user to pretest a new type of service that a hospital is considering providing. There is no practical way for banks to test with prototypes, as is often done with products in other categories. They must fully develop the software for a new service before customers can use it, even on a test basis. Finally, even where physical products might be tested—as in fast-food restaurants—it is extremely difficult to test against competitors because their products are available only in their own outlets. As a result, it is much tougher to conduct a side-by-side test between McDonald's and Burger King than it would be between two competing packaged food products sold in the supermarket.

These limitations do not mean that a wide range of research is not possible with service businesses. It just means that some kinds of research—especially product or service development research—are more difficult in service industries.

All things considered, the similarities in research between service and product industries are much more important and dramatic than the differences. Almost all the principles and many of the research procedures that apply to marketing research on products also apply to research on services. That is one reason why marketing research in service industries, particularly health care and finance, has progressed so far in such a short time. Researchers in these industries have been able to learn from the experience, both good and bad, of their associates in packaged goods markets. In fact, many service companies have recruited professionals for their research departments from packaged goods companies for precisely that reason.

The problems that service companies face in testing "finished products" create one important shift in their research emphasis: They attach relatively more importance to overall studies of the market and to studies of new service concepts in order to help compensate for the difficulties involved in testing anything like prototype products.

Research on the Market

Basic studies of a market or category are the core of many companies' research programs. And as service companies have begun to use marketing research, market studies have become a critical part of their research plans too. The following types of market studies are made by service companies.

Qualitative Research

Qualitative research can be conducted on a one-on-one basis through individual in-depth interviews or through focus groups, which are sometimes also called group discussions. A focus group typically involves six to ten recruited respondents who meet predefined specifications. As the name suggests, the results are *qualitative*; they are helpful for suggesting ideas and developing hypotheses. For this reason, they are a common and useful first step in many research programs. Marketers in service companies find them insightful as a way of hearing real people (both customers and prospects) talk about issues in a category.

Some of the purposes for which service companies use qualitative research include:

- Getting an overview of a service or market category
- Orienting new service teams
- Suggesting hypotheses for further quantitative testing
- Gaining an understanding of consumer language and terminology
- Roughly evaluating new service concepts
- Generating ideas for revitalizing old, established services
- Suggesting new communication and advertising approaches

Category Studies

This type of study is meant to give a picture of a category—a snapshot at a point in time—by measuring quantitatively:

- What proportion of consumers are users of a service
- Which services they are using
- Why consumers use the services of one company instead of another
- What the personal and household characteristics of users are

This information is collected through large-scale surveys, usually conducted by telephone but occasionally by personal interviewing.

Market Segmentation Studies

As service markets have become more competitive, companies have begun looking at market segments within larger markets. A market segment is simply a subgroup within the overall market where members have similar demographic or attitudinal characteristics, which it is thought should make them more receptive to a particular service or advertising approach.

The information collected on attitudes or demographic characteristics is analyzed by one or more multivariate techniques—cluster analysis, discriminate analysis, or factor analysis, for example—to identify the segments within the overall market. New service concepts or advertising strategies may then be tested against these segments to see if a segmented marketing approach is more effective than a generalized strategy.

Tracking or Trend Studies

The category study is just a snapshot in time. But service companies often want a series of pictures over time to help them identify changes and trends in the market. One way to accomplish this is to repeat category studies over time. When comparable (preferably identical) sampling and questioning procedures are used, the results show what changes have occurred and whether there is a trend in the market for a service.

These types of tracking studies are often called awareness, attitude, and usage (AAU) studies. This is the type of information that is most often tracked and trended over time:

- *Awareness of*
  —Companies in the market (unaided and aided)
  —Services these companies provide
  —Advertising by companies in the market
  —Advertising messages or main points
- *Attitude toward*
  —The overall market or category of services
  —Companies in the market

     —Individual services these companies provide
     —Advertising of individual companies
- *Usage of*
     —Individual services in the category
     —Companies in the market

This information is usually collected by a combination of closed-ended (multiple-answer or scale-type) questions and open-ended, discussion-type questions. In addition to the subjects listed, demographic information is also usually collected.

    The results of awareness, attitude, and usage tracking studies can be used to identify:

- Market shares
- Changes in market shares over time
- Companies' strengths to be built on
- Companies' weaknesses that need correcting
- Competitive strengths and vulnerabilities
- Characteristics of customers and competitors' customers

These types of tracking studies are typically conducted once or twice a year. As mentioned before, careful matching of samples and questioning procedures over time is crucial if results are to be comparable from one period to the next.

Customer Satisfaction Research

Because the service component of this type of business is so important, it is difficult to measure objectively the quality of the "product." That makes measuring customer satisfaction an especially important research task among service companies. (Chapter 23 deals with this topic in greater detail.) In fact, this type of research is sometimes called service quality research, reflecting its importance to service companies.

New Product and Service Positioning Research

New products and services are the lifeblood of service companies, just as they are of product marketers. This means that a solid, continuing program for researching new services and their positioning is critical for service businesses.

New Service Concept Testing

This is one of the most common types of research undertaken by companies in service industries. All concept testing is based on a simple, logical premise: People are usually attracted by the idea behind a product or service before they become interested in the product or service itself. They want a convenient way to handle their finances or a carefree vacation; banks and travel services are merely the vehicles that deliver those benefits.

Because the idea is the most crucial element in a new service, consumers can usually react to the new service idea without experiencing the service itself. That is what makes concept testing for services work. And because it is often impractical—or impossible—to develop a prototype service for research purposes, concept testing is particularly valuable in service industries.

Concept testing for services usually works like this. Researchers develop a *concept board* that gives a description in a few paragraphs (usually a hundred words or so) of the service, its benefits, and how it works. An illustration is often helpful too. Consumers who might be prospects for the service are then given an opportunity to read the concept board and are next asked a series of questions on a number of topics, including:

- What is your buying intent or buying interest?
- What are your reasons for interest or lack of interest [open-ended]?
- Do you see a uniqueness in the service idea?
- Is the service sold at a reasonable price? Does it represent good value?
- How frequently would you use the service?
- Would you use the service instead of or in addition to services already on the market?

In addition to testing totally new concepts, service companies also sometimes test *line extensions,* which are new services that could be added to existing services and sold to current customers. This is done because service companies recognize that current customers represent their best prospects for new services. A person who already has a checking account at a bank, for example, is much more likely to use that same bank for additional financial services. And the more services a company can sell an individual consumer, the more solid its relationship with that customer will be. So most service companies are careful to research their new services among current customers as well as among prospects.

Service Positioning Research

The *position* of a product or service is used as a way of describing how it fits into a category relative to the competition. It can also be used as a way of planning how to compete more effectively. To the degree that service businesses have intangible—along with tangible—dimensions, positioning research can be useful in helping to understand what image and perception consumers have of a company's services.

A position could be defined as the mental space a company's service occupies in consumers' minds relative to the competition. Positioning research usually involves answering the following questions:

1. *Where are we now in consumers' minds?*
   —What dimensions define the category for consumers?
   —Which dimensions are most important?
   —Where are we positioned by consumers on each dimension?
   —Where are our key competitors positioned?
2. *Where would we like to be positioned?*
   —Where are the gaps or unfilled needs in the market?
   —What strengths do we have that could be exploited?
   —What vulnerabilities do our competitors have?
3. *How do we get from where we are to where we want to be?*
   —What new services can we create?
   —How can we communicate the new position to consumers?

Communication Research

Because consumers' perceptions are especially important in service markets, advertising is a critical marketing tool owing to the role it plays in creating images and perceptions.

The decision to purchase any service or product is usually made in stages, so service advertising is most often developed to move potential customers from one stage to the next. As a result, advertising research in service industries usually focuses on tracking the effectiveness of an ad or campaign in accomplishing one of the following specific objectives:

- Service, brand, or name awareness
- Recognition of the benefits, features, or claims of a service

- Favorable attitude toward a service
- Predisposition or intention to purchase a service
- Motivation to take action to purchase
- Actual purchase or use of the service
- Reinforcement of satisfaction with use of the service
- Repeat use or purchase of the service

To be most useful, advertising research should be used to help develop, focus, and improve a service company's advertising, not just to produce a score that indicates whether the advertising that has been developed is good or bad. In addition to the advertising tracking research outlined, two other types of advertising research can be useful to service businesses:

1. *Copy testing to help determine*
   —What to say
   —How to say it
2. *Media research to help determine*
   —Where to say it (which media)
   —How often to say it (what frequency)

As the structure of service industries has changed and service businesses have become dominated by national chains, research by service companies has boomed as a tool to help plan marketing efforts.

The primary difference between service and product companies is that it is frequently impractical for service companies to have consumers actually test services before they are introduced. It is usually impossible to provide prototypes of services. Service industries, therefore, attach greater importance to market studies and new service concept testing.

Despite this difference, however, the research needs of service and product marketers are generally very similar. This makes it possible for service companies to borrow and learn from the experience of product marketers.

23

Customer Satisfaction Research

Customer satisfaction research is a rapidly growing type of marketing research. It is closely tied to the quality revolution in America, which has made U.S. companies realize that they need to deliver world-class products and services to compete in today's marketplace. A key component of world-class quality is measuring, through research, what customers expect and whether you are at least meeting (and preferably exceeding) their expectations.

Customer satisfaction has become an umbrella term for many companies' marketing efforts. In fact, one definition of the purpose of business is *to develop a satisfied customer*. As more companies adopt this approach, the research to measure satisfaction becomes a central part of their decision-making process.

One way to go about measuring customer satisfaction is to try to map out each customer's mental report card. Experience shows that customers rate a company on three important dimensions: (1) what is important to them as individuals; (2) what they expect of the company; and (3) how the company is performing. These dimensions in turn require you to:

1. Understand priorities from the customer's perspective
2. Determine the level of performance the customer expects from an excellent supplier of the product or service
3. Measure how your performance matches up to customers' expectations

Key Questions for Measuring Satisfaction

The three types of questions typically used to measure satisfaction are geared to learning:

1. The customer's expectations of an "excellent supplier" on each of several performance dimensions
2. The customer's overall satisfaction level with each major company
3. The customer's satisfaction on individual performance dimensions (the same dimensions on which expectations are measured)

A good way to measure expectations and performance is to use the same wording on questions evaluating expectations as you do on questions evaluating performance so the two can be compared.* For example:

- *Expectations:* "An excellent bank shows sincere interest in me."

Agree Completely   Disagree Completely
        1   2   3   4   5   6   7

- *Performance:* "The First National Bank shows a sincere interest in me."

Agree Completely   Disagree Completely
        1   2   3   4   5   6   7

What Is Important to Customers?

One way to measure importance is simply to ask customers to rank or rate the importance of certain performance dimensions on a list. This gets at top-of-mind issues, which are "must haves" in most businesses.

A second way to measure importance is to look at the dimensions that score highest on expectations. It is logical to assume that the things that are most important are the ones most strongly associated with an excellent supplier.

---

*The approach described here for measuring expectations and performance is adapted from research done by Leonard L. Berry, Valarie A. Zeithaml, and A. Parasuraman, most of which has been published by the Marketing Science Institute, Cambridge, Massachusetts.

A third way to measure importance is through regression analysis, identifying the attributes most highly correlated with overall satisfaction. (Overall satisfaction is the dependent variable; individual performance attributes are the independent variables.)

Regression trees are powerful and insightful analytical tools for this purpose. They make results easy for nonresearchers to understand and act on. The example from the health care field shown in Figure 23-1 is interesting because essentially it documents the phenomenon of "bedside manner."

The case history presented in the figure shows that the most important attributes affecting satisfaction with a health care supplier are "soft" dimensions like attitude of physician, time spent waiting, the way the physician communicates, and the willingness of the physician to spend time with the patient. (These important dimensions show up on the right side of the regression tree.) In this example, we see a wide range of overall satisfaction in the regression tree using only a few attributes out of a much larger set measured in the study. (The overall satisfaction numbers for each ending segment are shown in the numbers in the bottom row of boxes. They are measured on a seven-point scale where seven means "extremely satisfied.")

What Do Customers Expect?

There are three alternatives for measuring customer expectations: (1) asking directly for a rating of an "ideal" supplier; (2) asking for a rating of "importance"; or (3) asking about ratings of an "excellent" supplier.

Experience indicates that:

- *Using an "ideal" supplier as a target is unrealistic.* The definition of "ideal" is too open to overstatement and exaggeration. It sets up a target of perfection—a worthy goal, but probably not a realistic one for most companies.
- *Asking "importance" directly can be misleading.* Because asking for this measure gives respondents the option of saying that everything is "extremely important," discrimination among attributes can be masked. And it makes it more difficult to compare actual performance with expectations.
- *Creating the profile of an "excellent company" sets a high, but reachable, goal.* This measure is discriminating: Respondents do *not* rate everything at the most positive point on the scale. And the ratings create a worthy, though still reachable, standard for delivery of customer satisfaction.

Figure 23-1. Health care regression tree.

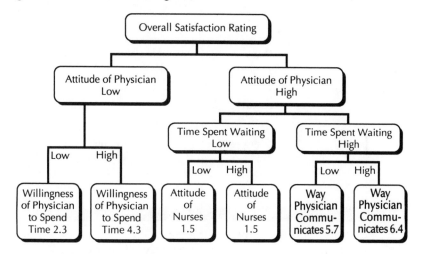

Analyzing and Presenting Results

Clear and insightful analysis is especially important in customer satisfaction research because the results usually have application across the entire organization. Because many of the people who need to understand and act on the findings have little experience with marketing research reports, it is important to find a simple way of presenting the results. Here are two approaches that can be helpful.

Service Leverage Grid

This provides a way to display satisfaction survey results by combining the measures of "excellence" and "performance" to give a graphic picture of how you're doing and where improvement is needed (see Figure 23-2). A Service Leverage Grid puts each dimension of your performance into a quadrant. The meanings of these are as follows:

1. *Possible points of leverage.* These dimensions are important and you perform well. Keep up the good work. Feature and promote these dimensions.
2. *Work on these.* The dimensions that fall here are important, but you perform below customers' expectations. These should be the focus of your efforts to improve.

Figure 23-2. Service leverage grid.

Work on These (Concentrate Here)	**Possible Points of Leverage** (Keep Up the Good Work)
Let These Ride (Low Priority)	**More Than You Need** (Possible Overkill)

(y-axis label) EXCELLENT COMPANY (IMPORTANCE)

PERFORMANCE

3. *Let these ride.* These dimensions are less important to customers and your performance is not particularly strong. But they don't warrant much attention.

4. *More than you need.* Your performance is excellent on these dimensions, but they aren't terribly important to customers. So there is a risk of overkill, and you should consider shifting resources to other areas that better justify attention.

"Gap Analysis": Comparison With Expectations

Another way to measure satisfaction and identify areas for improvement is to directly compare the ratings of your performance with the target profile of an "excellent supplier" by means of a graph, like that pictured in Figure 23-3. The gaps revealed between the two are obvious areas for improvement. In this example, the company falls short of customers' expectations in every dimension except "appealing facilities."

What About Competition?

Measuring customers' satisfaction with the competition and then comparing it with their level of satisfaction with you can also be important, but this is not as critical as comparing your performance against customers' expectations. If you are performing at a high level against expectations, it hardly matters what the competition is doing.

Figure 23-3. A comparison revealing the gaps between excellence and your performance.

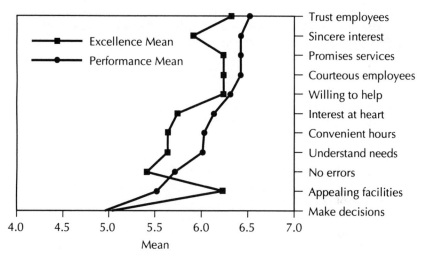

Figure 23.4. An index of comparisons between a bank's performance and its competitors' performance.

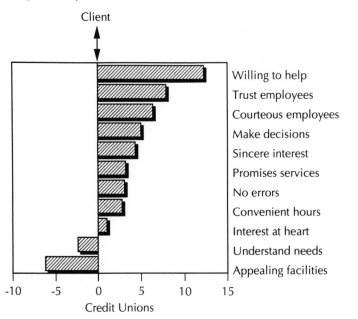

Yet most companies *are* interested in knowing how their competitors are doing. Adding competitor ratings to the gap analysis shown in Figure 23-3 could make the chart complicated and confusing. One way to show competitive satisfaction data simply is to *index comparisons.* The chart in Figure 23-4 shows competitor performance compared with your performance. That's usually how companies want to think about it anyway: "Where are we beating competition?" "Where is competition beating us?" Figure 23-3 shows how one bank compared its performance with local credit unions. It was performing worse on all the dimensions shown, especially those at the top, which were related to friendly, helpful service.

There is a saying in quality management circles that "customer loyalty is the lack of a better alternative." In other words, if customers can find a better product or service, they'll buy it. The only way to stay competitive in this sort of marketplace is to know your customers—what they think is important, what they expect, and how they feel you are performing. The increased focus on measuring these things from the customer's perspective is what is creating the growth in customer satisfaction research.

24

International Marketing Research

We all know that people in different countries behave differently, even with respect to the most common, day-to-day activities. You can bargain with shopkeepers in some countries, but not in others. You can trust taxi drivers in some countries, but you'd better count your change in other places. And business negotiations in Japan are quite different from those in the United States—and both are very different from negotiations in the Middle East.

So we shouldn't be surprised that cultural and economic differences affect marketing research. And they do in several important ways that determine how research must be done outside the United States. Let's look at some of the chief differences.

Willingness to Cooperate

Compared with people in most other countries, Americans tend to be unusually helpful and friendly. This is reflected in their general willingness to cooperate in marketing research surveys. Americans will answer the questions of a total stranger—the interviewer—regarding almost any aspect of their personal lives, up to and including their sexual habits. And Americans will agree to be interviewed anywhere: over the telephone, in a shopping mall, or at their place of business.

This climate of general cooperation and openness can spoil Americans for doing research elsewhere in the world. Individual consumers in many other countries are less ready to answer any questions posed by an interviewer, let alone delicate or personal ones. Businesspeople in many parts of the world have a more closed attitude than Americans have toward taking part in surveys.

In Korea, for example, businesspeople are reluctant to answer survey questions about their company; they consider it disloyal to divulge any type of information to "outsiders." And most Japanese businesspeople are hesitant to take part in surveys during business hours; taking time away from your work for a survey is considered tantamount to stealing from your employer. This all means that to do marketing research in countries other than the United States, you must first understand what is the same and what is different—what works and what does not work—in the nation being studied.

Research Costs

The cost of doing exactly the same research can vary dramatically from country to country, depending on the cost of living. Japan is generally regarded as the most expensive research market in the world, with projects there usually costing several times what the same studies would cost in the United States.

But even within a single region, such as the European Community (EC), costs can vary dramatically from country to country. ESOMAR, the European Society for Opinion and Marketing Research (the European equivalent of a combined American Marketing Association and Advertising Research Foundation), periodically studies differences in research costs from country to country within Europe. Figure 24-1 gives examples of some of the cost differences ESOMAR found in its most recent study.

Method of Interviewing

The telephone has become the preferred and most efficient method for doing almost all types of survey research in the United States. It has made virtually all types of respondents—not just individual consumers, but executives and business-to-business people as well—accessible to large-scale interviewing.

But telephone research is not common in most other countries. In some regions of the world, the incidence of telephones is not high enough to make them a useful method of contact. Elsewhere, in Japan for example, it is not culturally acceptable to answer the questions of strangers over the telephone.

Figure 24-1. Examples of EC research cost indices.

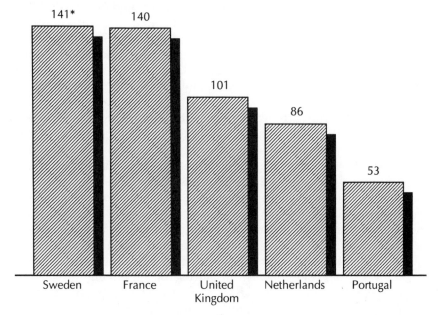

*100 = average for 16 EC countries
These are the average scores for 6 types of projects

Source: European Society for Opinion and Marketing Research (ESOMAR) 1991 prices study. Used with permission.

In some countries, other methods of data collection are sufficiently acceptable as to make telephone studies unnecessary. In the United Kingdom, for example, door-to-door interviewing is still widely used. And in Sweden, a high proportion of people will respond to a mail questionnaire; with government lists of every Swedish household available as a mail sampling frame, mail studies become much more feasible there than they are in the United States. You should consult a research company in any country where you are planning to do research to get its recommendation as to the most appropriate interviewing method.

Use of Scales and Questions

One of the most important and dramatic ways culture impacts multi-country research is in the different ways people in various countries respond to survey questions and use questionnaire scales. In a carefully controlled experiment, Custom Research Inc. explored the use of different kinds of scales in new product research among eighteen countries. The result: Extraordinary differences are to be found from country to country in the way respondents use common survey scales. For example, survey respondents in the Philippines and Italy are four times more likely to use the top box of a buying-intent scale than respondents in Hong Kong or Japan.

These differences are clearly the result of culture, not economic levels. Japan and the United States, two of the most affluent countries in the world, are dramatically different on these measures. These differences must be understood and taken into account in analyzing multi-country studies. Figure 24-2 shows a few of the differences that CRI found on use of the buying-intent scale. But the effect of cultural differences on scale use is even more complex: Differences exist even within the same country from one scale to another. This is illustrated by a comparison between Figure 24-3, showing use of the uniqueness scale, and Figure 24-2 on buying intent. Italians are less bullish in their use of the uniqueness scale, compared with their use of the buying-intent scale, while respondents in the United Kingdom are more aggressive in using the uniqueness scale than in stating buying intent.

Figure 24-2. Examples of buying-intent indices.

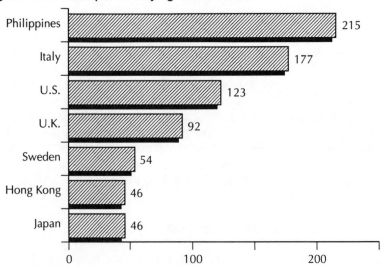

Source: Custom Research Inc. Used with permission.

Figure 24-3. Examples of uniqueness indices.

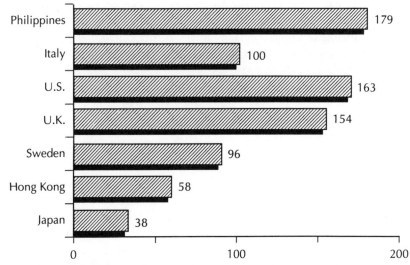

Source: Custom Research Inc. Used with permission.

All this means that there is no single, simple way of adjusting for country-to-country differences. It requires experience across countries and a thorough understanding of how each separate scale is used in each country.

Other Differences

Finally, there are some other differences that must be allowed for in doing research around the world. They're not necessarily the result of cultural differences alone, but they're very important nonetheless.

Pace of Business

Things move quickly in American business. We pride ourselves on our ability to get things done—fast. That's not true everywhere in the world. So if you want something "soon" from people in another country, you'd be well advised to tell them exactly when you expect it. To them "soon" may be the end of next week.

In addition, differences in time zones make it very easy to get behind in a hurry. By the time you get an expected fax from Japan when you arrive at the office in the morning, the people in Japan have already gone home for the day. This time difference can be helpful, in that it means that the people you're working with in the Far East are essentially working during the night (by U.S. time). But because it also means that there is no overlap between your workday here and normal office hours in Japan, getting a simple message back and forth across the Pacific can take a full day or two. So, as a rule of thumb, always allow more time for getting international research done than you would allow for a similar study in the United States.

Language

Marketing research organizations around the world that do research for international clients always have someone on staff who speaks English, usually reasonably well. But most people who have learned English as a second language are more comfortable with written English than with spoken English. So it's advisable to put all requests, inquiries, and confirmations in writing. That helps eliminate any possibility of confusion.

Mailing and Faxing

The U.S. postal system, for all its faults, is still one of the most efficient in the world—when compared with postal systems in most other countries. So if you have important documents or information that you want to send abroad, always send it by air express, never by conventional mail. There are horror stories about packages sent by conventional mail being delayed for months in some countries.

Fortunately, the fax offers yet another alternative to mail for smaller documents. And faxing has become the standard form of communication around the world; in fact, faxes were widely used in international business even before they became popular in the United States.

The Basics of International Marketing Research

Concentrating on some of the differences to be found from country to country may make it seem as if international research were burdened with so many differences that it isn't worth the effort. In fact, we've found just the opposite: *Our experience shows that the principles of good marketing research are similar worldwide.*

For example, in new product research, we've demonstrated that what drives interest in new food products (perceived taste) is the same in the United States, Malaysia, Italy, and Latin America. Similarly, we've proved that what drives interest in nonedible new products (perceived ability of the new product to solve a problem) is the same worldwide. Of course, exactly what constitutes "good taste" may be very different in the United States, Malaysia, and Italy. And research must be sensitive to these important differences. But it is good to know that at the root of everything are principles of marketing that are surprisingly similar around the world.

The bottom line of all the points made in this chapter is that there is a large, active marketing research community around the world. But navigating through it isn't as simple as it may look at first. Often you don't see the pitfalls until it's too late.

The best answer to this problem is to work with an experienced worldwide research organization to coordinate your multicountry work. The advantages include:

- Making certain that your objectives are understood and acted on in a consistent way across all countries
- Shortening and simplifying the reporting and authority chain between you and the places in which the work is being done, especially if several countries are involved
- Standardizing, or at least making comparable, the research questions, techniques, and methodologies that are used to implement the research
- Creating the opportunity for more comparable, unified analysis and presentation of the results
- Achieving economies of scale by focusing responsibility for budget control

As the business world becomes more global, marketing research is sure to follow the same pattern. So international research is certain to become a more important part of every researcher's role.

25

Single-Source Data

Marketing researchers love to experiment. In fact the whole nature of marketing research is to experiment: Set up an in-store display and see if sales increase; increase the price and see if sales stay the same or drop; introduce a new product and measure how many people buy it. All these efforts involve experiments, which are simply situations in which one or more variables are changed and the result is measured, after which a conclusion is drawn and a principle developed about it.

In the past, researchers have unfortunately had to assemble these experiments on a makeshift basis. It was not possible to track among the same consumers (and that is the key: *the same consumers*) the effect of marketing variables like price changes and in-store displays on purchase behavior. Researchers had to conduct separate pieces of research, then link them together through logic and assumptions.

Having single-source data has changed all that for products sold through mass marketers—typically food products, household-care products, and health and beauty aids. These products are tracked simultaneously through three types of data coming from a single source: (1) retail store sales; (2) consumer behavior; and (3) degree of exposure to advertising. ("Single source" means all these types of data are supplied by a single research organization and are collected from the same group of stores.)

Retail Store Sales

The core of single-source data is the measurement of sales through universal product code scanning at the checkout counter. This is now the basic way mass marketers track their sales and market share. But the information goes far beyond category and brand tracking. It also identifies which products are sold with displays, price deals, display ads, and all the other promotional techniques a company (or its competitors) may use.

Scanner data make it possible to track category and brand information at a level of precision and detail that wasn't possible before this form of research became available. A further advantage of scanner data is that of shortened turnaround time: What used to take weeks or months to track and report is now available almost instantly, because scanner data from stores are collected electronically on a daily basis.

This speed and level of detail, ironically, have also become the primary drawbacks of scanner data. It is possible, even easy, to get buried in detail. Information is available down almost to individual store level for every brand in every size for every combination of price deal, in-store display, and feature ad—and more.

With all this information, it can be difficult to draw conclusions about which marketing tools are working and which are not. That's why the two major suppliers of scanner data, A. C. Nielsen and Information Resources, Inc. (IRI), have also developed an array of programs and services to help clients analyze and report scanner data.

Consumer Behavior

The in-store scanner data show product movement at the aggregate level. They don't tell the marketer whether the thousand packages sold last week came from one shopper buying a thousand packages or a thousand shoppers buying one package. That is why Nielsen and IRI have developed a measure of consumer behavior linked to the in-store data.

IRI measures consumer behavior at the checkout counter by recruiting panels of cooperating households who agree to present a special card each time they check out at a store. The household's identification number is read off the card into the scanner, and the purchases scanned at the checkout counter are linked back to other data already known about that household (demographics, previous purchases, and advertising exposure, which is described later in this chapter).

Nielsen measures consumer behavior slightly differently by recruiting shoppers in their homes. Nielsen's cooperating households are given a handheld computer with a scanning device, which they use to scan everything they purchase from grocery, discount, and drug stores. Then these households periodically feed the data to a central Nielsen computer via a toll-free phone number.

The consumer behavior data can be used to measure not only which brands are bought this week but which were bought last week, last month, or last year. That makes possible the analysis of brand loyalty along with responsiveness to displays, price deals, and advertising—all the same marketing tools that are also tracked in-store.

Exposure to Advertising

The third leg of single-source data is a measurement of what advertising consumers have been exposed to. Both Nielsen and IRI get their cooperating panels of households to agree to have their TV viewing monitored in their homes.

IRI took this a step further by pioneering the concept of setting up the capability of controlling the advertising that goes into a panel member's home. Via cable TV hookups, IRI is able to split its panels into matched subgroups, then substitute test commercials for half the panel and use a control ad for the other half. Because panel members' purchases can then be tracked, for the first time it becomes possible unobtrusively to track the effect of exposure to advertising on actual purchase behavior.

Advantages of the Single-Source Methodology

The primary advantage of the single-source method is inherent in its design: It creates a real-life, ongoing marketing experiment. It makes it possible to test simultaneously an almost unlimited combination of advertising, promotion, and product variables and then to measure the results largely without consumers being conscious that they are taking part in a test.

Beyond one-shot experiments, the single-source method makes possible longer-term learning by marketers. Today's experiments can be combined with the results of last month's or last year's experiments to develop underlying principles and guidelines about marketing effectiveness. And experiments across different companies and product categories put IRI and Nielsen in the position of running continuing experiments representing almost the full range of consumer products marketing. The potential learning from this is almost unlimited.

Drawbacks of the Single-Source Method

Single-source research really began in 1979. So it is still a relatively new field, especially given the complexity and sophistication of the information being developed. Most of the weaknesses of single-source data are related to the relative infancy of the method and will likely be ironed out over time.

One drawback is the potential complexity of the data. Because such a large array of detail is available at the store, brand, and promotion levels, there can be an overwhelming amount of raw data from which it is difficult to draw clear conclusions.

A second limitation to scanner data is that it is restricted largely to food items in scanner stores. That is where coverage is most complete. It is less applicable to products that are sold through other types of outlets. Scanner coverage in other types of retailers, such as drug stores, convenience stores, and warehouse clubs, is still developing.

Related to this limitation is the fact that single-source data are now available primarily for mass market consumer products. Other types of products have not yet been able to take advantage of this revolution in research.

Finally, the TV measurement link will remain weak until researchers find a foolproof way of measuring actual TV exposure, as opposed to measuring simply what channel the TV set is tuned to. It isn't possible currently to know whether the whole family is watching TV or whether the set has just been left on in an empty room. This weakens the link between ad exposure and purchase data.

For all its weaknesses, the single-source data method is clearly a key marketing research tool for the future. In concept, it represents the dream of researchers of being able to link store sales, consumer behavior, and advertising exposure. While the mechanics of these systems are still evolving (and probably will always be undergoing improvement), the systems have already proved their worth as an invaluable tool for conducting in-market experiments.

26

Product Positioning Research

The concept of position is important in most sports. In football, defensive backs are careful to be aware of their position so that they can defend the portion of the field for which they're responsible. Tennis players are told by teaching pros to watch their own position on the court as well as the position of their opponent. Basketball coaches discuss the importance of having strong players at each position.

In sports, positioning is an effective way to compete and win. It's also important in marketing, where the position of a product is used as a way of describing how a product fits into a category relative to competition—and how it can exploit its location to compete more effectively.

What Is a Position?

For the manufacturer, a position might be defined as the mental space a product occupies in consumers' minds. Put another way, a position is the product's address on the mental map consumers construct to think about a category.

From the consumer's viewpoint, a position is a device people use to structure the world and simplify it. Most consumers have heard of literally thousands of products. Individuals are bombarded with hundreds of advertising messages every day. All this is too much for the brain to handle. Some scientists believe that the brain can focus on no more than seven items at a time. If true, this means that the mind has to find a simplified structure to represent reality. It simply cannot retain all the information presented about every product. One way it seems to do this is to summarize its impression of products into a few key concepts, which become the product's position.

In other words, a product has a position whether that's intended or not. Marketing and advertising people talk about "creating a position," as if there won't be a position unless they create one. Wrong. You can create a position—or try to—but even if you don't, the product will have one anyway. Consumers form impressions and images about the product and create a position for it in their mental picture of the category. They don't need your permission to do it.

It's true that the position many products have is as "one of the bunch," but this is simply an undifferentiated position. That's not the same as having *no* position.

So when marketing people talk about creating a position, they usually mean trying to influence where consumers position a product. A position is built by communicating to consumers—through advertising, brand name, and packaging—a consistent message about the product and where it fits into the market.

A classic example of positioning is the Avis campaign: "We're number two. We have to try harder." The 7-Up "Uncola" effort is another example. Still another is the well-established association of Marlboro cigarettes with rugged, outdoor men. Most well-known, successful brands have a clear position in their markets. That's one of the reasons they're successful.

From the manufacturer's standpoint, there are two key elements of a product's position: (1) things that *describe* the product; and (2) things that *differentiate* the product from competition. Much of the wasted effort in thinking about positioning probably results from focusing largely on the descriptive issues, when it's the differentiating characteristics that are key.

The critical thing in finding a successful position is to identify characteristics that are both differentiating and important to consumers. A primary task of research in positioning work is to measure whether positioning characteristics are both differentiating and meaningful.

The Role of Research in Positioning

Figure 26-1 shows a conceptual framework for thinking about the research steps connected with a new product. At the top of the pyramid, when a product is in the rough-concept stage, you're looking for clues about positioning. Where does it fit? What need does it fill? Where do the opportunities seem to be? And so on. As you move toward the bot-

Figure 26-1. Conceptual framework for the research steps on a new product.

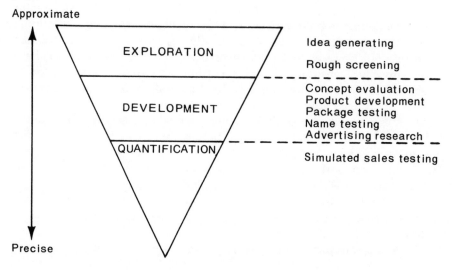

tom, you're looking for product definition. Once you complete simulated sales testing, the position you'll be using for a product must be finalized before you introduce it to the market.

So the role of research during the major stages along the way can be seen as:

- *Early qualitative research*—looking for positioning clues and opportunities
- *Refining the product*—identifying the position dimensions that are both differentiating and meaningful
- *Final quantitative testing*—making sure the position is effective

The best opportunities for research to make a contribution to positioning are in the early stages, particularly in the exploration and development stages. By the time the product gets to simulated sales testing, there's not much you can do to affect what happens.

This "model" of the research process—the approximate/precise dimension—also applies to repositioning research on established products. In looking for new positions for existing products, you have to go back and start with the search for positioning opportunities, using very "approximate" research, then move toward refining those opportunities.

Research Issues

Here are the three positioning questions that need to be addressed in the early stages of the development of a product or in the first stages of a product's repositioning:

1. *Where are we now?* As mentioned before, every product has some sort of position, whether it was intended or not. So the first step is to find out what that is—either the established position of an ongoing product or the likely "natural" position of a new product. This includes specific issues such as:

- What does the "space" look like? What are the most important dimensions in the category?
- Where is our product in that space on each of the key dimensions?
- What are the other products in that space and where are they?
- What are the gaps, unfilled positions, or holes in the category?
- What are the primary attitude dimensions in the category?
- Which dimensions are most important?
- How do these attitudes differ by market segment?

2. *Where do we want to be?* Maybe right where we are, or maybe just slightly ahead on one or two dimensions. Or maybe in a completely different position. Ideally, research can help find a key dimension that, if you could move on it, would produce a new position that was both differentiating and meaningful for the product.

How do you decide where you want to be? Some of the positioning opportunities for a product include:

- Finding an *unmet consumer need* or at least one that's not being adequately met by the competition
- Identifying a *product strength* that is both unique and important
- Determining how to *correct a product weakness* and thereby enhance a product's appeal (the legitimate "new and improved" products reflect this type of positioning move)
- Changing *consumer usage patterns* to include different or additional uses for the product
- Identifying *market segments* that represent the best targets for a product

3. *How do we get from here to there?* This is where reality becomes a constraint. "Getting there" could come from one or both of two sources: (1) physical product differences and (2) communication.

Some positions are based strongly on physical product differences. Duncan Hines cake mix maintained leadership of that category for years by stressing that it was moister than other brands—a claim it could back up. Years later, Pillsbury added pudding to its cake mix, changed the name to Pillsbury Plus, and rejuvenated its sales by claiming even greater moistness than Duncan Hines. That's an example of positioning on the basis of product differences.

On the other hand, some positions are based almost solely on communication—finding a memorable and meaningful way of describing the product. Nothing about Avis really changed after it began describing itself as "number two." Calling 7-Up the "Uncola" did not involve any product changes. Creativity can be the key component of a position change.

The main point here is *not* to talk about a physical product difference that can't be backed up with performance. The product must be able to fulfill the expectations created by its position.

Strategy Issues in Positioning

Selecting a strategy isn't simple, and some of the problems encountered are the same in almost any category. For example:

- Is going for a large segment already being served by other brands better than trying for a smaller segment that isn't being addressed by anyone? Should you hit-'em-where-they-are or hit-'em-where-they-ain't?
- Should you focus on one product characteristic at a time or attack several simultaneously? Should you try specialization or offer something for everyone?
- Is it more effective to emphasize product strengths or to try to overcome perceived weaknesses? The former strategy could seem naive; the latter may come across as negative.
- Can one product occupy several positions, perhaps in different market segments? Can you mean different things to different people?
- What's the value of a creative gimmick? Some positions lend themselves more easily than others to clever names, packages, or advertising campaigns. What is this worth?

Research can provide information to help make all these decisions. Yet rarely will the information clearly indicate the decision or strategy that's best. In the end, it's people—not computers or research techniques—who must select and develop a position. And in that process, experience and judgment—often disguised as hunches or intuition—usually play a crucial role. That's what makes positioning one of the most interesting facets of marketing.

Research Techniques

Positioning research is an approach, not a technique. Clues about the best positioning for a product or service can come out of many types of research. Qualitative research, using focus groups or one-on-one interviews, is a place to begin because it often stimulates ideas and generates hypotheses. A basic study of the usage of products in the same category and of attitudes toward them, conducted in person or by phone, usually gives an indication of the current positions of products.

Beyond this, multivariate techniques can be used to get a more quantified fix on current or possible positions. The most commonly used multivariate techniques for this purpose are:

- *Multidimensional scaling*—to provide a map of the market's perceptions of products' positions
- *Cluster analysis*—to show either groups of products that are perceived as similar (if the products are clustered) or groups of consumers who behave or feel similarly (if the clustering is applied to people rather than products)

Getting the right positioning for a product is a critical step in its introduction. Research, paired with creative insight, can select a position that will create a unique niche for a product in the marketplace.

27

Group Interviews

A good listener is not only popular everywhere, but after a while he gets to know something.

—Wilson Mizner

Most of us, if we have a normal amount of curiosity, like to overhear conversations about things we're interested in. That's the basic purpose of a group interview: to listen to real people—customers or prospects—talk about a marketing issue that's important to us, and, in the process, to learn something.

A group interview is a unique opportunity to experience "the market" firsthand. Most marketing research studies reduce people to numbers and percentages, but in a group interview the people are alive and right there. For this reason, the group interview provides a special opportunity to get a picture of person-by-person behavior and attitudes rather than of the aggregate patterns that are the output of most large-scale studies.

Many of the concepts and techniques used in group interviews originated in clinical psychology. Group therapists discovered years ago that some people could talk more freely in a group and could benefit by listening to others. This approach, adapted to marketing problems, formed the basis for developing group interviewing techniques.

Today group interviews are one of the most widely used types of marketing research. There are many names used—focus groups, group discussions, qualitative research, and group depth interviews—but they all refer to the same approach.

What Is a Group Interview?

There is no precise definition of a group interview, because the term describes a general approach, not a specific technique. Generally, however, a group interview involves eight to ten people recruited to meet predefined characteristics (age, usage of a certain product, interest in a new product idea, and so on). The interview is usually held in a relaxed, informal atmosphere, either conference-room or living-room style, to encourage conversation. The session typically lasts between one and two hours.

Group interviews are led by experienced moderators, who work from a topic discussion outline.

The sessions usually are arranged so that representatives from the client organization can observe the session, either through a one-way mirror or by closed-circuit TV. The interview is usually recorded on either audio- or videotape.

Because the dynamics of an individual group can make any single session misleading, it is usually desirable to conduct more than one session per subject; two or three per topic is best. It is common to spread out the interviews geographically to get an indication of regional differences. Finally, it is best to have similar respondents in the same group. If young homemakers are mixed in a session with older women to talk about beauty products, for example, the differences among respondents in the group may make it difficult to see any trends or patterns. It would be better to have one session composed of young women and another group made up of older women.

Group interviews can be conducted with almost any type of consumers: women, men, children (minimum age is about six), and people in business or the professions (physicians, lawyers, or accountants).

Uses of Group Interviews

For many types of marketing problems, group interviews are a typical first step in research. They are a logical way to begin because they are relatively inexpensive and flexible and can be adapted to a variety of problems and issues.

Although group interviews can be conducted on almost any subject, most are concentrated in two subject areas: new products and advertising.

Appropriate use of group interviews requires an understanding of the differences between group interviews and large-scale quantitative research. The differences can be summarized in this way:

Group interviews are . . .	*Quantitative research is . . .*
Descriptive	Diagnostic
Subjective	Objective
Exploratory	Definitive
Approximate	Precise

The specific uses of group interviews usually fall into the following categories:

1. *Suggesting hypotheses for further testing.* Groups are a common means of generating ideas to be tested in large-scale quantitative studies. These hypotheses may be about attitudes toward a product category, reasons for using a brand or type of product, or factors that are responsible for the structure of a market.

2. *Helping structure questionnaires.* A major use of group interviews is to hear how respondents talk about a category or the products in it. Knowing the words consumers use can help in phrasing questions in the language of respondents. It can also help suggest the range of answers that should be listed for a closed-ended question.

3. *Looking at categories.* Group interviews can be a useful way to get a quick overview of, or orientation to, a new business or product category. This can be helpful for new product teams looking at unfamiliar categories. It also can help companies explore markets in which they are considering acquisitions.

4. *Evaluating new product concepts.* Although group interviews are not appropriate for ranking new product concepts, they can be useful in indicating the major strengths and weaknesses of a new product idea. Often consumers are able to identify drawbacks to a new product idea that have been overlooked by the marketing people working on the new product. Groups can also be useful for checking whether the uses and benefits of a new product are clearly communicated in concept statements. This can be a valuable check before large-scale concept tests are conducted.

5. *Generating new ideas about older products.* Marketing teams can sometimes be stimulated to recognize new, alternative uses for established products by listening to consumers talk about ways they have discovered to use a product.

6. *Suggesting new creative approaches.* Advertising agencies often use group interviews to provide input for creative teams. Listening to consumers talk about exactly how they use a product or the things they like about it—or even the problems they have with a product—can generate ideas for advertising.

7. *Interpreting quantitative research results.* Sometimes group interviews are used as a last step in research. If the results of a large-scale study raise questions about why respondents answered one question as they did, group interviews can be used to probe in detail for the reasons behind quantitative test results.

8. *Preventing disasters.* Sometimes groups are used simply as a "disaster check" for products, promotions, or advertising, to make sure that some glaring problem or communications gap has not been overlooked.

Why Group Interviews Work

Group interviews are an effective way of developing information from respondents because the dynamics of the group lead to:

- *Interaction.* Consumers hear each other talk and are stimulated by the ideas and comments of others in the session. This usually generates a more lively conversation among participants in a group than can be expected from a one-on-one interview.
- *Synergy.* Because of the group interaction, respondents are often able to be more creative, interesting, and thoughtful in their comments than they would be if interviewed individually. In this respect, a group can generate more ideas and information than would result if the participants were interviewed individually.
- *A sense of commonality.* It's important that group respondents have basic similarities in their attitudes and/or life-styles. This creates a feeling of sharing and understanding, which helps stimulate discussion.
- *Feelings of security and freedom.* On some types of sensitive subjects, the group can help respondents feel free to share unorthodox ideas and opinions. Hearing other respondents say that they don't understand or don't like something about an ad, for example, may help respondents feel comfortable in admitting that they share the same view.
- *Enjoyment.* Most respondents enjoy taking part in a well-con-

ducted group interview. It's usually fun and stimulating. As a result, participants want to make the session productive.

In addition to the factors that make group interviews productive, there are several reasons why groups are effective from the client or user standpoint:

- *Flexibility.* With the clients or users viewing, it is relatively easy to revise the questions or the structure of the research, if necessary, from one group to the next. If a question isn't working well, for example, it can be revised for the next session.
- *Speed.* Results are virtually instantaneous, at least for those viewing the session. So where time pressures are heavy, group interviews can be a way to develop a preliminary understanding of a topic within a matter of days.
- *Firsthand experience.* Hearing real live people talk about a product or category provides very valuable firsthand experience for the viewers. Hearing how respondents actually talk about a product and the way they use it, for example, is important for a marketing team.
- *Stimulation.* Group interviews are useful not only because of what happens in the group session but also because of the ideas that they can stimulate in the minds of the people who are watching the session. For this reason, it is valuable if the end users of the research can attend and view the session.

Dangers and Drawbacks

Although group interviews have many strengths, they are by no means foolproof. Group interviews can fail for any one of a number of reasons:

- *A dominant individual.* Probably the most common reason for a group interview to fail is one person dominating the interview. The moderator can try to encourage others to speak, but an outspoken person is often difficult to suppress.
- *Questioning, not discussion.* Inexperienced moderators sometimes conduct a group interview by going around the group and asking a question of each individual, one at a time. This precludes the interaction that makes group interviews valuable.
- *Reliance on isolated comments.* Sometimes viewers of groups pick up

a chance comment by one of the respondents that supports their ideas or position on a question. In the course of most group interviews, almost any position can be supported by selecting isolated comments out of context. Basing conclusions on verbatim comments rather than on the general tone of the group is a common misuse of group interviews.

• *Order effect.* Reactions to ads or products can be affected by the order in which they are shown. This, of course, is the reason that order is rotated in quantitative tests. If only one or two group interviews are conducted on a subject, however, completely rotating the order of exhibits or questions is impossible. This is another reason why holding more than one group interview on a subject is desirable. At the least, the possible biasing effect of the order in which questions were asked should be kept in mind during the analysis.

• *Group dynamics.* Groups develop personalities, just as individuals do. The dynamics of a group can be either positive or negative. One group can, for some reason, be unusually positive about a new product concept, while the next group will turn sour on it. The moderator can attempt to balance the direction of the group through his or her questions and comments, but group dynamics can sometimes be nearly impossible to control. This is another argument for doing multiple group interviews on a subject.

• *Inappropriate purpose.* Clients can use groups for the wrong reasons—either as a definitive measure or as "quick and dirty" research to avoid a quantitative study. Counting noses in a group interview and projecting these numbers as a representative sample of the population would seem an obvious misuse, but it is done all too often.

Planning the Group Interview

A "discussion guide" is usually prepared as a way of planning the group interview and allocating time among all the topics to be covered. The guide should be detailed enough to suggest all the issues to be covered, yet flexible enough to permit adjustments as the group progresses. *It is a guide, not a questionnaire.* A good moderator will sound as if he or she is conversing with participants in the group, not working from a prepared outline.

Moderators should also understand that the flow of a successful group interview is from general to specific. The interview should usually begin with a general discussion of the product category, then move toward a discussion of a specific product or perhaps even specific characteristics of a product. But the general topics should come first; comments will be biased if discussion of a specific product or brand precedes the general discussion.

Ways to Improve Group Interviews

Research projects—especially those undertaken by ad agencies—probably involve focus groups more than any other single technique. Yet on no other type of research is there such a "formula" approach, almost regardless of the type of problem being studied. Strangely, most group moderators get excited about whether the table should be round or square, whether there should be a table at all, or whether a one-way mirror is better than closed-circuit TV. Who cares? What difference does it make whether you're watching through a mirror or on a TV screen if nothing is happening that's worth seeing?

Here are some ways to get out of the rut. They've been developed over several years through research on many products among all types of respondents, from physicians to six-year-old kids. Not all are suitable for every study, but one of them could probably add a dimension to your next qualitative research project.

• *Dual moderating.* This approach is especially useful on highly technical subjects, where it's virtually impossible to give an outside moderator all the detailed background information he or she might need. We've had good results in these cases from using two moderators: our own moderator plus a second moderator from the client. The client moderator is often an R&D expert or someone else familiar with the technical details of the product. Our moderator is responsible for the flow of the session and the basic probing, while the expert moderator follows up on technical issues that might otherwise be overlooked. The approach is particularly useful on projects studying new product applications for basic technologies. On less technical subjects, the client moderator can even be a product manager or account executive. But be careful: Some clients come on like F. Lee Bailey if the respondents say anything negative.

• *Minigroups.* Why is a group interview almost always made up of eight to ten respondents? Several studies of group dynamics have shown that people have difficulty interacting with more than six other people. And, at best, a ninety-minute session allows an average respondent only nine minutes of conversation.

We've found that fewer respondents produce better results on many types of subjects, especially where there is a lot of personal variation in opinion or behavior. Minigroups of four or five people are ideal for exploring new categories in depth. They're also helpful for interviewing professionals, such as doctors or nurses. And they're almost imperative for children.

• *Life-style groups.* Marketers and advertisers believe in segmentation. Yet we often make no attempt to segment people in focus group sessions. Consumers are *not* all the same. Having young, new-values consumers in the same groups with older, traditional consumers can be disastrous. Try screening respondents and putting them into different basic life-style groups. You'll find that the contrast from group to group is often amazing. This approach is particularly useful in "needs" exploration for new products.

• *Respondent + client groups.* Have you ever felt excited observing a focus group session, then been unable to remember a few days later what had you so worked up? Group sessions are strong stimuli to clients, yet even hot ideas tend to cool off quickly.

Consider thinking of groups in pairs: a respondent session to provide input, then a formal review session with the client team. Use the review session to recapture the ideas from the group, and then try to build on them toward complete problem solutions.

• *Helping respondent creativity.* This is the most underutilized area of focus group research. The purpose of groups is to find out what's in people's heads—yet we rarely do much to help them tell us. Here are three ideas:

1. Encourage respondents to be wishful, unrealistic, playful, and childlike. This is very effective in helping consumers break away from the constraints of reality and talk about real needs they have. The ideas that come out are often ones the client knows how to realize—although not always in the way the respondent would have expected.
2. Have respondents focus on feelings rather than just ideas. We ask questions like: How does cleaning the bathroom make you feel? How do you feel when you fix breakfast in the morning? How do you feel when the bank tells you you're overdrawn? We all live in a world where feelings are often the only real thing to us. Why not use this approach in conducting qualitative research?
3. Help respondents in a group to keep score. A group interview is

a task-oriented activity, even if the task is only to generate ideas. We often use large flip-sheet pads of paper to jot down the ideas that consumers mention in the groups. As the sheets fill up, we tape them to the walls of the room. Writing down the ideas lets every respondent know that his or her idea has been heard and valued. And as the walls of the room become filled with sheets of ideas, the energy level of the group really accelerates when it might otherwise be lagging. (This idea runs counter to all the conventional wisdom of many qualitative research gurus. But it works!)

• *Groups "plus."* Think about having respondents do something before they come to a session. You might ask them to try a new product, shop at a certain kind of store, or even just think about a question related to the subject the group is discussing. This gives the group a common experience to talk about. It also helps respondents to focus on the subject of the session, so you can move more quickly into the discussion.

Because groups are largely unstructured, they lend themselves to experimentation. If something doesn't work, you can quickly drop it and go on to something else. So the risk is low, and the payoff can be high.

Finally, it is important to point out that group interviews, although they are the most popular kind of qualitative research, are not the only kind. One-on-one depth interviews are an alternative that should be considered in some cases. Individual interviews can be useful for exploring subjects on which personal differences are so great that the interaction in a group interview may be more destructive than useful. One-on-one interviews are often better, for example, for exploring political issues or some types of financial questions.

28

Research
in the Courtroom

"The first thing we do, let's kill all the lawyers." Dick the butcher said it in Shakespeare's *King Henry VI, Part II,* but many researchers have thought it while working on projects designed to be used as evidence in legal cases.

Actually, the association between marketing research and the legal profession is a recent one. Before the 1950s, the Hearsay Rule prevented marketing research results from being admitted as evidence. "Hearsay," in legal terminology, is the reported statement of someone who is not available to be sworn in under oath and cross-examined. To protect the rights of the parties in litigation, judges have historically ruled such evidence inadmissible. Since it is obviously impractical for every respondent in a survey to be available to testify, this precedent effectively excluded research from legal proceedings.

That has changed, however, as the courts have come to recognize that a sample of opinion is often the only accurate and practical means of measuring public attitudes. In addition, the government, primarily the Federal Trade Commission (FTC), has promoted the use of research in some types of legal proceedings by using research as a basis for filing complaints against advertisers.

Today research, if properly done, is well accepted as evidence in many types of legal proceedings, especially those involving advertising claims.

Legal Applications of Research

What types of projects might become evidence in legal cases? Every type. Even projects not designed with any legal application in mind may become involved in litigation. For example, if a product becomes the subject of a government complaint or a competitor's lawsuit, any research done on that product might be subpoenaed. Similarly, even qualitative research done in the course of developing advertising messages could be subpoenaed if it is later claimed that the advertising is false or misleading.

There are two types of legal proceedings in which marketing research might be used:

1. *Judicial processes,* where one company sues another over some issue.
2. *Administrative procedures* involving a government agency, most often the FTC. This type has grown rapidly with the increase in consumer protection and advertising regulation by government agencies. Today most of the research that is done for use in legal proceedings has to do with such administrative cases.

Here are specific examples of some of the kinds of cases in which research might be conducted by one of the parties for use as evidence:

• *Antitrust cases.* Research could be used to help define the relevant market for a product, which is often a key issue in antitrust proceedings. What do consumers consider the relevant market, or relative alternatives, for a riding lawn mower? a cola? a ballpoint pen?

• *Trademark infringement.* To what extent are consumers confused by brands with similar names? This is often the issue on which trademark infringement cases hinge.

• *Unfair competition.* Research is sometimes used in this type of case to help define a geographic trading area.

• *Change of venue.* Although unusual, this type of case often gets publicity in the newspapers. In sensational murder cases, for example, the defendant may use a survey to support his claim that the trial should be moved to another city (a change of venue) because so many people in the home city are already convinced of his guilt that it would be impossible to select an impartial jury there.

• *False or misleading advertising.* One company may challenge a competitor's ad, claiming that it is misleading or disparaging. This type of complaint may also be brought by the FTC. An advertisement may be determined to be misleading, even when every word of it is true, if the overall impression or effect created by the ad is misleading. This may be deliberate, but it need not be. Regardless of the intent, it is the result or effect of the ad that counts in determining whether it is misleading.

• *Substantiation of advertising claims.* This is a growing area of research, boosted by the FTC policy that advertisers must be able to substantiate, usually through research, every claim made in every advertisement. Advertising substantiation cases probably account for the largest volume of research involved in legal proceedings today.

For example, Swift's Peter Pan peanut butter made the claim: "In a survey, kids with a preference preferred Peter Pan's taste over Jif or Skippy." The National Advertising Division (NAD) of the Council of Better Business Bureaus (another organization that monitors advertising) asked Peter Pan to substantiate this claim. Swift submitted the results of blind product tests between Peter Pan and Skippy and between Peter Pan and Jif. Each panel of children, eight to fifteen years of age, included regular peanut butter users. The users of creamy peanut butter tested the creamy varieties, and users of crunchy peanut butter tested the crunchy varieties. The findings indicated that the children tested had a greater preference for the flavor of Peter Pan over Jif or Skippy at a 99 percent confidence level. After reviewing the data presented, NAD closed its file on the basis that the claim had been substantiated.

General Guidelines

Most legal processes are adversary proceedings, which means that each side tries to present its case as forcefully as possible, with an impartial party (or parties) reaching a verdict on the basis of the information given. The implication of this for researchers is that unfriendly attorneys may be examining their research files looking for ways to discredit the results. If they find something suggesting that the research was not done properly, they will try to use it to have the research ruled inadmissible or at least to raise a question about the credibility of the research before the judge or the jury.

Therefore, research that may find its way into court has to be done with extra care. Here are some things to consider while you are setting up and conducting your study.

• *Study design.* Be particularly specific and precise in stating the objectives of the study and why it was conducted as it was.
• *Sample.* Include a detailed description of the sample and how it was selected, along with a statement of limitations of the sample,

if that is necessary. Sampling is one of the most vulnerable areas of a study in that it is one of the easiest to raise questions about. Be sure to define the universe or population from which the sample was drawn.

- *Questionnaire.* Ask only questions that are related to the purpose of the research. Otherwise you may be collecting information that could later be used against you by the other side.
- *Coding.* Be as narrow and specific as possible in developing codes and doing the coding. Try not to link together in a single code more than one idea or to imply cause and effect.
- *Conclusions and implications.* Keep these direct, narrow, and data-based. Stick to the findings that are supported by the figures. Be especially careful here to separate ideas and speculations from statements of findings. Better yet, avoid speculations altogether on this type of project.

There are plenty of other things to keep in mind if you think there might be a courtroom in your future. Here are the most important ones:

Some Do's and Don'ts

- *Keep the research as simple and straightforward as possible.* The people making the decision on the basis of the research will not be researchers or even marketers. Instead, they will be judges, with legal backgrounds, or laypeople, in the case of a jury trial. Either way, they are not likely to be familiar with research techniques or terminology. In advertising substantiation research, for example, be as straightforward and specific as possible in the way you measure opinions of the claim. Otherwise, you may end up with a chain of elegant, indirect logic that substantiates the claim but that you cannot possibly explain to someone untrained in research.

- *Get the lawyers involved early.* Accepted definitions of what constitutes misleading advertising, for example, are constantly changing. The decisions finally reached will be legal ones rather than marketing decisions. While you must do good, sound research, you must also be certain that the results will be acceptable from a legal standpoint before you proceed. So talk with the lawyers early.

- *Keep your objectivity in mind.* The lawyers probably won't. Remember, lawyers are trained to play an adversary role. This means that the lawyer you are working with is trying to prove something and probably will want to push as hard as possible to get the research to come out advantageously. Protect your objectivity, particularly if you have any responsibility for analyzing or reporting the findings. Otherwise, you may later be asked to explain and defend a procedure you never believed in.

• *Maintain complete records and documentation.* Good files are extremely important. You need a record of exactly what you did at each step of the way. You may be required to explain details of the sampling procedure, for example, and you will need complete records in your files to do this. It's possible that you will be asked to provide the names and addresses of every interviewer who worked on the study, along with a statement of their training and experience in interviewing. You can't keep all this in your files, of course, but you need records complete enough to form the basis for creating the very detailed information that you may be asked to supply.

• *Remember that everything in your files can be subpoenaed as evidence by the other side.* This is the flip side of keeping complete records—you don't want them to be *too* complete. The FTC can and routinely does subpoena everything on an issue before it issues a complaint. In addition, in a judiciary proceeding, one side in a lawsuit can usually obtain access to everything in the research files of the other side. That includes every memo, letter, and report—even notes scribbled on scraps of paper, if they are in the files. So keep written documents to a minimum, and don't keep anything you would mind someone outside your company seeing.

• *Limit the number of people involved.* This will make the project easier to control. It also will allow you to say, with more assurance, exactly what was done, by whom, and why. To maintain objectivity, let as few people as possible know the purpose of this type of research. Interviewers, of course, should never be told why it is being done.

• *Select interviewers carefully.* Although respondents will probably never be called to testify, it's possible that some interviewers will be questioned. So the interviewers assigned to these types of projects should be the best available.

• *Beware of "fishing expeditions."* You may end up being the one caught! Every question asked in a survey becomes part of the record. So the extra question tacked on to the end of a study could come back to haunt you. For example, suppose you decided to add this question to the end of some type of advertising research: "Is there anything about this ad that you find unclear or confusing?" The answers could end up as evidence if a competitor were to claim that the ad under investigation was false or misleading. Even a very small share of people saying the ad was misleading could be damaging to you. Extra questions run the risk of providing evidence for the other side, so be careful. Stick to the specific objectives of the study.

• *Keep in mind that decision rules are not the same as for commercial research.* For example, advertising has been found to be misleading on the basis of as few as 5 percent of the consumers being confused or misled. In research done to aid in a company's own decision making, a 5 percent level would rarely cause concern. But the rules are different—and often very unclear—in legal proceedings. That's another reason why the early involvement of a lawyer is helpful in designing these types of studies.

• *If you are called to testify, answer questions concisely.* Never volunteer anything. If you don't know the answer to a question, say so. Don't speculate. Be careful of every answer you give so that it cannot be used against you later.

• *Don't be paranoid but do be careful.* That is really the overriding guideline for doing this type of research. The rules of good research are basically the same for all types of studies; they're just enforced more strictly when there are legal implications than when the research affects only decision making within the company. As a result, you have to pay special attention to the details of design, execution, and record keeping on projects that may be involved in legal proceedings.

Part V
Research
Tools

29

Sampling Simplified

By a small sample we may judge the whole piece.

—Cervantes, *Don Quixote de la Mancha*

We all believe in sampling, whether we realize it or not. Every cook determines whether the soup has enough salt by taking a spoonful (a sample) and forming an opinion; there's no need to eat the whole kettle. No one needs to drink a whole glass of spoiled milk to tell that it has gone bad; one swallow (a sample) is enough. Even the U.S. Census uses a sample to collect some types of information about the population.

Sampling is cheaper and faster than conducting a census of the entire market. And in most cases, of course, sampling is the only feasible research alternative; it simply isn't practical even to think about surveying the entire population. But if the sample is developed properly, it can provide more than enough accuracy for decision-making purposes.

Sampling in marketing research has two dimensions:

1. Selecting the units in the population to be included in the study
2. Interpreting the results of the study in order to estimate parameters of the population from sample data and to test hypotheses, usually about the differences between two samples or between a sample and an "expected" result

There are entire books devoted to sampling, so it isn't necessary to describe every sampling concept in detail here. The purpose of this chapter is to serve as an introductory guide to the various types of samples and to discuss the practical strengths and weaknesses of each kind.

Definitions

Sampling has its own terminology, and if you want to make sense of discussions about sampling, it's important to understand these key terms.

- *Population*—all the units about which information is sought. For example, this could be all U.S. households, men between eighteen and fifty-five, companies that own computers, or short-term hospitals. The first step in drawing any type of sample should always be to define the population to be studied with precision.
- *Sample*—a proportion of the population selected for a particular research study.
- *Sampling unit*—one unit (a household, a teenager, a hospital, or whatever) of the population selected for inclusion in the study.
- *Sampling frame*—a physical listing of all units in a population or a procedure for producing a result comparable to a complete listing.

Basic Sampling Methods

There are two broad categories of sampling methods: probability sampling and nonprobability sampling. Every sampling technique falls into one category or the other.

Probability samples are also called random samples. Probability sampling methods involve essentially selecting respondents by chance, with no interviewer judgment or screening involved in the choice. Probability samples are theoretically soundest and most representative; they are also the most expensive. In fact, for many studies they are prohibitively expensive.

Nonprobability samples are all other kinds of samples—anything that is not completely random. Interviewing women in a shopping mall and calling men from telephone book listings are examples of nonprobability sampling.

Most research textbooks give primary attention to probability sampling. But this doesn't really reflect what goes on in the real world, where most studies use nonprobability samples because of budget constraints.

Both probability and nonprobability sampling have their appropriate uses. The trick is to identify the situations in which only probability sampling will suffice and to determine the steps that can be taken to improve the quality of nonprobability samples when that's the only economically feasible alternative.

Probability Sampling

This is the most objective and scientific type of sampling. A requirement for probability sampling is that every unit in the population (in consumer studies these units would typically be either households or individual consumers) have an equal and known probability of being selected in the sample. There must be no interviewer judgment involved in the selection of respondents. There are several different forms of probability sampling.

Simple random sampling is the most basic type. It involves simply selecting respondents completely at random, much as you might draw names out of a hat. Obviously, this requires a perfect sampling frame, that is, a complete listing of every unit in the universe.

Stratified random sampling involves first grouping the population into homogeneous segments (or strata) and then sampling within each stratum. In probability samples of the United States, for example, it is common to stratify by region and/or degree of urbanization. Stratification prevents the disproportionate representation of some parts of the population that can result by chance with simple random sampling.

Cluster sampling involves sampling groups of respondents as a unit rather than as individual elements. For purposes of efficiency in door-to-door interviewing, for example, it is common to interview several households (a "cluster") in a neighborhood that has been selected to be part of the sample.

Systematic sampling includes every *n*th element from the population in the sample. This is a common procedure, which can be combined with both cluster and stratified sampling. For example, either clusters or individuals can be selected in this systematic way, or a systematic sampling can be done within a stratified sample.

The primary advantage of probability sampling is its accuracy. It is the best approach for developing a sample that is perfectly representative of the population. At the same time, probability sampling has several important drawbacks that keep it from being widely used:

• *To select a probability sample, it is necessary to have a list, or sampling frame, for the entire population.* In the case of personal interviews with households, this means having a list of all dwelling units in the United States. For some areas of the country, where new homes are being built and the population is rapidly growing, this can be a serious problem, particularly when the most recent census data are eight or nine years old. Regardless of the adequacy of the sampling frame, drawing a probability sample—especially for door-to-door interviewing—is a very detailed, time-consuming task.

• *Despite the best attempt at sampling, "nonresponse errors" can affect the accuracy of the results.* Some respondents simply are not at home when the interviewer calls; others refuse to begin the interview; and still others may terminate the interview before completion. So a probability sample doesn't necessarily guarantee an accurate survey result.

• *Probability sampling is extremely costly to execute, especially for door-to-door studies.* For this reason alone, its use is usually limited to studies for which a higher degree of accuracy is worth the additional cost. Also for cost reasons, national telephone studies are replacing door-to-door probability studies wherever the information can be collected by telephone.

Sampling Error and Nonsampling Error

While good sampling methods can produce very accurate results, no sample is absolutely precise. For example, suppose a national probability sample showed that 40 percent of the households interviewed owned a dog. It's unlikely that a census of every household in the United States would find that *exactly* 40 percent of all households owned dogs. If the original sample was well drawn, well executed, and large enough, there's a good chance that the "true" ownership revealed by the census would be close to 40 percent, but it probably wouldn't be *exactly* that figure.

These "errors"—or differences between the survey results and the comparable population figures—come from two sources: *sampling* and *nonsampling* factors. Sampling factors (or "sampling errors") usually get the most attention. Yet other types of problems ("nonsampling errors") probably have greater impact on the results of projects. Both types of errors are important and must be controlled.

Sampling Error

In the dog ownership example, it would be possible to measure the sampling error in the study and attach a "confidence limit" to the survey figure in order to estimate the population figure—and in most research projects you're interested in using the survey results to estimate total population data.

Suppose the dog ownership study had used a probability sample of 1,000 households. In that case the 40 percent ownership figure would have a range of ± 3 percent at the 95 percent confidence level. In other words, the chances are 95 out of 100 that the confidence range—37 percent to 43 percent (40 percent ± 3 percent)—includes the true percentage of dog ownership for the entire population.

That's what sampling error is: the range (expressed as "plus or minus X percent") that has to be attached to any survey result because it came from a sample. This range reflects the commonsense assumption that no sample is likely to mirror exactly the characteristics of the total population.

Large samples have less sampling error (and therefore tighter confidence ranges) than small samples. In our dog study example, the 95 percent confidence ranges at different sample sizes—assuming each study measured ownership at 40 percent—would be:

Sample Size	Confidence Range	
50	26–54%	(± 14%)
100	30–50%	(± 10%)
200	33–47%	(± 7%)
400	35–45%	(± 5%)
1,000	37–43%	(± 3%)
2,000	38–42%	(± 2%)
4,000	38.5–41.5%	(± 1.5%)

These ranges at different sample sizes illustrate two principles about sampling error:

1. The sample size must be quadrupled (50 to 200, 100 to 400, and so on) to cut the sampling error in half. This means that tight confidence ranges are relatively expensive to achieve: You only get *half* of what you pay for.

2. The rate of improvement in sampling error slows down as sample size increases, and sampling error never disappears completely (unless you conduct a census or something very close to it). In the example, the confidence range with a sample size of 4,000 is actually 1.5 percent (half the range at 1,000). But it's difficult to imagine the circumstances in which it would be worth the cost of 3,000 additional interviews (going from a sample of 1,000 to 4,000) to gain only 1.5 percent of precision in the results.

This trade-off of cost (in sample size) and precision (in confidence ranges) is the reason most marketing research studies use samples of between 200 and 1,000—and often toward the lower half of that range. This level accuracy is adequate for most business decisions. Even television ratings services and political polls—where more precision is desirable—rarely use samples larger than 1,200 people. It just isn't worth it.

A final word about sampling error: Confidence ranges are applicable, strictly speaking, only to probability, or random, samples, which is a primary advantage of that type of sampling.

Technically speaking, it's not possible to make any statements about the sampling error in a nonprobability sample. From a practical standpoint, of course, researchers nevertheless make inferences about population data from nonprobability samples. If 600 respondents in a mall intercept study taste two products and prefer product A to product B by a two-to-one margin, most researchers will conclude that the population—or a probability sample—would prefer A, too. But those inferences cannot really be supported by statistical theory, even though the findings may be perfectly adequate for decision making.

Nonsampling Error

The importance and impact of nonsampling error are generally underestimated by researchers. Most textbooks devote at least a full chapter, and often more, to lengthy technical discussions of probability sampling theory, sampling error, and related statistics. Then all the other potential sources of error are dismissed in a short paragraph. In fact, the emphasis should often be exactly reversed!

Other sources of error are critical because there are so many of them. Despite their number, they're often controllable—but only if you appreciate their importance.

What is nonsampling error? As the name suggests, it's *everything else*—besides sampling error—that can introduce bias, inaccuracies, or uncertainty into the results of a study. Nonsampling error includes, but isn't limited to:

1. Inability to locate correct respondents (resulting from poor instructions, poor maps, nonexistent addresses, and so on)
2. Refusal by respondents to begin the interview
3. Terminations by respondents during the interview because it is felt to be too long, too boring, or too threatening or personal
4. Intentional lying by respondents
5. Poor recall, biased guesses, inaccurate memory

6. Misunderstanding of questions due to unclear wording
7. Leading by the interviewer
8. Nonverbal clues or biasing by the interviewer
9. Recording errors by interviewers
10. Coding errors
11. Editing errors

In other words, the accuracy of the best probability sampling methods can be negated by a problem in just one of these areas. Yet the impact of these potential nonsampling errors is largely ignored by most theory-based textbooks on sampling.

What's the solution to the nonsampling error problem? It's basically careful planning and close attention to the details of project execution. Don't stop at the theoretical level of sampling (although your sampling method must be conceptually sound), but carry through with:

• Thorough interviewer training
• Complete, clear instructions to interviewers
• Precisely worded questionnaires
• Pretesting
• Easy-to-follow questionnaire formats
• Careful coding and editing
• Respect for the respondent's cooperation and goodwill

Nonprobability Sampling

The second type of sampling is called *nonprobability sampling*. Although this category includes everything except probability sampling, there are three basic types of nonprobability sampling methods:

1. *Convenience sampling*. This leaves the selection of respondents primarily up to the interviewer. For example, a hundred women might be interviewed in a shopping center, with no quotas or qualifications for participation in the study.

2. *Judgment sampling*. This involves selecting certain respondents—perhaps category users or residents of certain communities or neighborhoods—for participation in a study. In many cases, significant costs can be saved by focusing a study on only a few subsegments of the population.

3. *Quota sampling*. This structures the sample to include specified numbers of respondents having characteristics that are known or be-

lieved to affect the subject of the research. For example, it's common to set quotas on interviews by age, income, or employment. Quotas are used in this way to help limit the possible bias in nonprobability sampling and to make the end sample of respondents as similar as possible to the total population.

Obviously, most types of studies—product tests, shopping center interviews, group discussions, and most projects not done on a nationwide basis—have to use nonprobability sampling methods. So often there's not really a choice between doing probability sampling and nonprobability sampling. Nevertheless, steps can be taken to ensure that nonprobability samples are as representative as possible and to minimize nonsampling error. These steps include:

- Conducting a study in as many cities as possible to lessen the potential effect of regionality
- Spreading interviews within a city across different areas to provide a broad representation of different socioeconomic groups
- Giving attention to question design, then pretesting the questionnaire, to make communication with the respondent as clear as possible
- Writing detailed interviewer instructions covering the questionnaire and sampling procedures to cut interviewer errors

Telephone Sampling

As use of the telephone has grown for conducting many types of national studies, more sophisticated methods have been developed for drawing telephone samples.

Telephone Book Sampling

The most straightforward type of telephone sampling is telephone book sampling. This approach takes a systematic sampling of the numbers listed in telephone books covering the area being studied and selects every nth number for contact. This is a very simple and efficient way of sampling for telephone research.

The drawback is that even the most recent telephone book is not a complete listing of households that have telephones. Some new households have moved into the area since the book was printed; others have moved out of town; still others have chosen to have unlisted numbers. To overcome these problems, other methods of sampling for telephone studies have been developed, and these are described in the next section of this chapter.

Despite the theoretical problems with telephone book sampling, however, the survey studies using this method often produce remarkably accurate results. Many studies that have examined the differences between listed and unlisted samples have concluded that samples drawn from telephone directories produce virtually the same survey results as samples that include unpublished numbers.

For many types of studies, telephone book sampling is quite adequate, and its lower cost makes it attractive. But it is always theoretically better to use a sampling technique that includes households with unlisted numbers.

Random Digit Dialing and "Plus One" Sampling

Random digit dialing is a sampling method developed to reach households with unlisted telephone numbers. It involves randomly generating telephone numbers so that unlisted numbers will be included by chance, along with listed ones. These numbers can be generated in a number of different ways to help minimize the likelihood of generating numbers that have not been assigned to households. For example, sometimes only the last four digits are randomized, using prefixes that are known to have been assigned. In other cases, all seven digits may be generated, but following a pattern determined to reflect the prefixes that are in use. A significant proportion of all households have unlisted numbers, either because these numbers are too new to be listed or because they are unlisted by request. The proportion of unlisted numbers is greater than 20 percent of all households and is higher yet in large metropolitan areas, particularly in the Northeast or on the West Coast.

While the research results from random digit dialing may not be substantially different from those obtained by telephone book sampling, random digit dialing nevertheless comes closest to being a probability sample; it's the only telephone sampling method that allows you to reach virtually every household with a telephone. For this reason, it is the surest way to obtain a sample that is as representative as possible of the total population.

"Plus one" sampling is a method of telephone sampling that incorporates some of the characteristics of random digit dialing but avoids some of the inefficiencies of that technique. "Plus one" sampling involves simply adding one to every listed telephone number; thus, 853-

1414 becomes 853-1415. Because telephone numbers are generally assigned in blocks, this technique maximizes the likelihood of generating a telephone number that has been assigned. Studies comparing "plus one" and random digit dialing confirm that "plus one" sampling is more efficient than random digit dialing. Its drawback is that it does not include numbers that are not adjacent to listed numbers. For this reason, not every household has an opportunity of being included. But it represents a compromise between telephone book sampling and random digit dialing that includes some of the advantages of randomness while still being cost-efficient.

Telephone Interviewing vs. Personal Interviewing

As telephone interviewing grows, the question is often asked: "Does telephone interviewing really produce results that are comparable to those obtained from personal interviewing?"

One study, done by Chilton Research Services, indicates that results from telephone interviewing are very comparable to—and in some cases better than—the results from personal interviewing. A study was done using two interviewing techniques—personal contacts and random digit dialing telephone interviews. A comparison of the demographic characteristics of the respondents showed that the samples were virtually identical in most respects. There was one difference: More interviews were obtained with individuals in elevator apartments on the telephone than through personal interviews. The reason for this difference is that it is often extremely difficult for personal interviewers to gain entrance to apartment buildings for face-to-face interviews.

This study produced another interesting result. It is commonly believed that telephone interviews are not as effective as personal interviews for obtaining information from scale questions. On this project, however, respondents were asked to indicate their interest in becoming involved in several selected activities on a six-point scale. (The wording was slightly different for the two approaches.) The results from the two approaches indicate that the telephone is very comparable to personal interviews in obtaining even subtle attitude information.

Real-World Sampling

With all the pros and cons of probability and nonprobability sampling, what method of sampling is used most frequently? Here are some rules of thumb:

Probability Sampling

- Probability sampling methods are most often reserved for use on large, national category studies—particularly category awareness, attitude, and usage studies (AAUs)—in which precision is a major concern and the ability to compare data from wave to wave is an advantage.
- Telephone interviewing is replacing personal interviewing on many types of studies, and this is certainly the trend in probability sampling. Telephone studies allow random respondent selection and facilitate multiple callback attempts—both important requirements of probability sampling.
- Typical sample sizes are 500 to 1,000—perhaps up to 2,000 if subgroups are to be analyzed separately.

Nonprobability Sampling

- The majority of real-world research projects employ some form of nonprobability sampling, most often either shopping mall intercept studies or prerecruited central-location tests.
- Cost is the primary advantage of nonprobability sampling. If additional controls (such as quotas) are used, the results are usually entirely adequate for most day-to-day decision making.
- Although sample sizes vary with the purpose and type of test, 200 to 500 respondents is a typical range for most product tests, attitude studies, and the like.

30

Basic Statistics— All You'll Usually Need

Today's high temperature of 83 and low of 68 were above the normal high of 78 and low of 65. The current temperature is 73; the relative humidity is 54 percent; and the pollen count is 106.

Our lives sometimes seem controlled by statistics. From weather reports to stock market averages and blood pressure readings, we all deal routinely with a wide array of statistical measures.

Statistical analysis is useful to researchers because it's a tool to help summarize and interpret the large volume of numbers collected as part of even the smallest survey. The statistical principles used in marketing research borrow heavily from the behavioral and physical sciences. As a result, there are many entire books on statistics, probably more than on any other facet of research.

The purpose of this chapter is to give you an overview of the most important types of statistical measures used in marketing research. If you want more technical or detailed information, refer to one of the many good statistics books available. These are basic statistics, but they're all you'll usually need.

Although there are literally hundreds of different statistical measures and tests that can be used by researchers, the most common ones all serve one of these three purposes:

1. *Measuring central tendencies*—summarizing data in terms of a typical or average case
2. *Estimating population parameters*—drawing inferences from survey samples about the characteristics of the total population

3. *Determining significant differences*—determining whether two subgroups within a sample are different, or whether this sample is different from the population

Measuring Central Tendencies

The purpose—or at least one of the purposes—of almost every research project is to describe the typical or average customer or prospect in the market. The three statistical tools most commonly used for doing this are the mean, the median, and the mode.

Arithmetic Mean

This is usually called the mean or simply the average. (The term *average* isn't technically correct or precise, but where it's used, it usually refers to the arithmetic mean. In any case, it's better to say "mean" than "average.") This is simply the sum of a series divided by the number of figures in the series.

The mean is appropriate to use when the results are symmetrical and normally distributed. But the mean can be very misleading as a summary statistic in other cases. For example, the table in Figure 30-1 shows the scores of three products on a product test using a scale question. All three products tested have the same mean. The mean of 3.0 on this scale is quite descriptive of the normal distribution of product 1, but it would be misleading if used to describe either product 2 or product 3. Most research results are normally distributed (that is, bell-shaped around a midpoint), but other distributions are common enough that you should always check, before using the mean, that it is in fact descriptive.

Figure 30-1. Scores of three products on a scale question (spice level).

Spice Level		Product 1 "Normal"	Product 2 "Flat"	Product 3 "Bimodal"
Much too spicy	(5)	5%	20%	50%
Somewhat too spicy	(4)	10	20	0
Just about right	(3)	70	20	0
Somewhat too bland	(2)	10	20	0
Much too bland	(1)	5	20	50
Mean:		3.0	3.0	3.0

The mean has one other weakness to watch out for: It is affected by extreme observations. For example, if the incomes of two millionaires were averaged with the incomes of ten laborers, the average income for all twelve would be more than $200,000, which obviously is a misleading figure for the group's average income. Nevertheless, if you avoid using the mean for abnormally distributed data or data including extreme observations, it's the most useful statistic for describing the average. In any case, if you are planning to use the mean, always check the distribution to be sure that the mean is really descriptive of the data set.

Median

This is simply the middle case in a series. Half the observations fall above the median; half fall below. It has the advantage of being unaffected by extreme cases. So it is often used instead of the mean for describing "average income," "average sales," or any type of data that may include a few extreme cases that would distort the mean. To avoid confusion, always identify it as the "median"; don't call it the "average."

Mode

This is the most frequent observation. It's the plurality, or the most commonly given response. If no one response occurs more frequently than any other, there is no mode (as for product 2 in the spicy/bland example). If two different responses occur with the same frequency, then the distribution is bimodal (as for product 3 in the spicy/bland example). Because of these limitations, the mode is rarely used.

Estimating Population Parameters

Another thing researchers are often trying to do is make inferences about the population on the basis of results from a survey sample. In fact, that's what researchers are *always* trying to do. The fact that the 300 people in your test prefer product X to product Y by a two-to-one margin is important only in that it allows you to conclude—actually, infer—that the population as a whole also prefers product X. This is called inferential statistics, which involves making a decision about the entire population on the basis of the characteristics of a subgroup or sample.

Survey results are often expressed as percentages—percent aware, percent preferring a product, or percent giving a certain response. To make an inference about the population, you must apply a *confidence limit* or *confidence range* to the percentage result you found in the study. For example, if your telephone study found 30 percent of the respondents aware of product A, it's unlikely that exactly 30 percent of the entire population is aware of product A, but the population figure should be close to 30 percent if your sample is large enough and well drawn. This difference between your sample results and the population is sometimes called the *sampling error*. The range attached to the survey result to estimate or infer the population figure is called the *confidence range*.

A chart of confidence ranges is shown in Figure 30-2. It is read this way: In a sample of 400 interviews, if an observed percentage result is 50 percent, the chances are approximately 95 in 100 that a range of ± 5 percent (45 percent to 55 percent) includes the true percentage in the entire population.

Two points should be kept in mind when reading this chart:

Figure 30-2. Chart of 95 percent confidence range (two standard deviations).

	Percentage Result Obtained						
Sample Size	50%	40% or 60%	30% or 70%	20% or 80%	10% or 90%	5% or 95%	1% or 99%
25	±19.6	±19.2	±18.0	±15.7	±11.8	±8.5	±3.9
50	13.9	13.6	12.7	11.1	8.3	6.0	2.8
75	11.3	11.1	10.4	9.1	6.8	4.9	2.3
100	9.8	9.6	9.0	7.8	5.9	4.3	2.0
150	8.2	8.0	7.5	6.6	4.9	3.6	1.6
200	7.1	7.0	6.5	5.7	4.3	3.1	1.4
250	6.3	6.2	5.8	5.0	3.9	2.7	1.2
300	5.8	5.7	5.3	4.6	3.5	2.5	1.1
400	5.0	4.9	4.6	4.0	3.0	2.2	1.0
500	4.5	4.4	4.1	3.6	2.7	2.0	.9
600	4.1	4.0	3.8	3.3	2.5	1.8	.8
800	3.5	3.4	3.2	2.8	2.1	1.5	.7
1,000	3.2	3.1	2.9	2.6	1.9	1.4	.6
1,200	2.8	2.8	2.7	2.3	1.7	1.3	.6
1,500	2.5	2.5	2.4	2.1	1.6	1.1	.5
2,000	2.2	2.2	2.0	1.8	1.3	1.0	.4
2,500	2.0	2.0	1.8	1.6	1.2	.9	.4
3,000	1.8	1.8	1.7	1.5	1.1	.8	.4
4,000	1.6	1.5	1.4	1.3	1.0	.7	.3
5,000	1.4	1.4	1.2	1.1	.9	.6	.3

1. For technical reasons, the confidence range around a result is larger the closer the result is to 50 percent. So there's no single confidence range for a sample of 1,000, for example. It depends on whether the result (awareness, preference, or whatever) measured in the sample of 1,000 is closer to 50 percent or to 5 percent.

2. Strictly speaking, these statistics apply only to normally distributed data developed from probability samples. Unless a survey is drawn from a probability sample, technically it isn't possible to make inferences about the population. In practice, however, researchers commonly use these confidence ranges to provide guidelines for interpreting other types of survey results too.

Determining Significant Differences

Often a research project is designed to compare results between two samples or subgroups. The most common comparisons are between:

1. *Two or more subgroups within the same sample.* Do people with incomes exceeding $25,000 have different opinions from those held by people with incomes lower than $25,000? Are men's evaluations of the product different from women's?
2. *Samples drawn at different points in time.* Has awareness of the product increased in the past year? Is market share higher than it was three years ago?

The first thing you do, of course, is take a simple, straightforward look at the results. If responses of men and women are the same, you don't need a statistical test to tell you any more. If market share is unchanged from three years ago, you've got your answer.

But if the results differ among any of your subgroups, as they almost always do, then you're faced with two basic questions: *Is the difference in results so small as to suggest it probably occurred by chance?* (That is, if you did the test again, is there a good chance that it would come out the other way?) *Or is the result large enough that it is probably the result of a "true" difference?* (That is, if you repeated the test again and again, is it very likely to come out the same way every time?) There are a number of statistical tests that help you to answer these questions.

Before you can run a statistical test, you must have a *hypothesis*. This is simply a statement or relationship you would like to prove either true or false. In statistics, it's usually assumed that two populations or two subgroups are equal until proved otherwise. This is called a *null hypothesis*.

Starting with the null hypothesis, if the difference between two samples is small enough that it could easily have occurred by chance, then the null hypothesis cannot be rejected and you must conclude that the difference between the two samples "is not statistically significant at the 95 percent confidence level" (or whatever confidence level you choose). On the other hand, if the difference in survey results is so large that it would not be likely to occur by chance, you reject the null hypothesis and conclude that the difference between the samples "is statistically significant at the 95 percent confidence level."

How big must a difference be to be statistically significant? That depends on two things:

1. *The size of the two samples being compared.* The bigger the samples, of course, the smaller the difference needed to be statistically significant. Or, put another way, you will be able to read smaller differences with larger samples.
2. *The level of percentage being compared.* Assuming it's a percentage that is being compared, the closer the percentage is to 50 percent, the larger the difference required to be statistically significant.

The table in Figure 30-3 gives guidelines for determining the statistical significance of differences between survey results from two samples. The chart is read this way: In two separate samples of 500, if two observed percentages near the 50 percent level differ by 8 percent or more—46 percent versus 54 percent, for example—the chances are 95 in 100 that it is a true difference and not due to chance alone.

As with confidence ranges around a single percentage point, these differences apply, strictly speaking, only to results from probability samples. But in practice they're often used as indicators of the statistical significance of other types of survey results as well.

In addition to this measure of the difference between percentages in two samples, there are other, more specialized statistical tests that are useful for evaluating some kinds of research results. Here are the most frequently conducted tests (look them up in any statistics book if they appear to apply to your problem):

Chi-square test. This test can be used to compare survey results with theoretical or expected frequencies in the population. There are many versions of the chi-square test, which apply to a wide range of marketing research problems. The test can be used whenever the results, responses, or respondents can be arrayed in various categories.

Figure 30-3. Chart of significant differences between two sample percentages (95 percent confidence level).

Sample Sizes Being Compared		Approximate Percentage Result Obtained				
		50%	40% or 60%	30% or 70%	20% or 80%	10% or 90%
2,000 and 2,000		4%	4%	4%	3%	2%
	1,000	5	5	4	4	3
	500	6	6	6	5	4
	100	13	12	11	10	7
1,500 and 1,500		4	4	4	4	3
	750	5	5	5	4	3
	500	6	6	6	5	4
	100	13	12	12	10	8
1,000 and 1,000		6	5	5	4	3
	750	6	6	5	5	4
	500	7	7	6	5	4
	100	13	13	12	10	8
750 and	750	6	6	6	5	4
	500	7	7	6	6	4
	100	13	13	12	10	8
500 and	500	8	8	7	6	5
	100	14	14	13	11	8
250 and	250	11	11	10	8	7
	100	14	14	13	12	9
100 and	100	17	17	16	14	10

Analysis of variance. This test divides the variance found among test data into parts, assigning each part to some source or factor. You can then evaluate these variations and see if any are greater than would be expected by chance. This technique is often used to test the significance of differences among products in a product test. It is a very efficient and powerful way to analyze balanced test plans. One of the most common methods of analysis of variance (or ANOVA) is called Scheffe; it is used in testing for differences in one-way scales, such as hedonic ratings.

Student's t-test. Unlike analysis of variance, which compares ratings across products, this test compares ratings of each product to an optimum. It is especially useful in evaluating ratings on bipolar scales, where the midpoint is optimum and either end is undesirable.

There are far too many other statistical tests even to list here, but those just mentioned are some of the most basic and most frequently used ones.

"Significant Differences": A Warning

Perhaps as important as, or more important than, knowing how to use statistical measures is knowing how *not* to use them and how to accurately represent what the statistics mean.

Be careful about saying that something is "not significantly different" when what you really mean—and all you can truly say—is that two numbers are *"statistically* not significantly different." For example, market shares of 32 percent and 37 percent might not be statistically significantly different as measured in a test, but that difference could be very significant in the real world. Or suppose an opinion poll found a sample of people split 49 percent versus 51 percent on an issue and concluded that the difference wasn't statistically significant. That 49 percent/51 percent split would make all the difference in the world if it held up in an election or referendum.

Also be aware that some statistically significant differences are spurious and not meaningful from a marketing standpoint. For example, you may find that people with some college education rate a new product as significantly more appealing than do either people with no college education or those with advanced degrees. The finding may be statistically significant but nothing that is really meaningful or actionable.

So be precise and accurate in using the term *significant* and get in the habit of always modifying it with the word *statistically*. All that researchers can usually talk about is *statistical significance*. What's really significant and what's not is often a much bigger, broader topic, usually far outside the scope of a simple research project.

Sample Size

Also keep this in mind about statistical differences: Because the difference needed for statistical significance is related directly to sample size, another way of saying that something isn't statistically significant is to say that the *sample size is too small!* Virtually any difference between two percentages would become statistically significant if the sample size were large enough. Especially when survey sample sizes are small, it's often difficult to find differences that are large enough to be statistically significant. But be careful about saying that they "aren't significant" — you're usually going further than the research results justify. (It's not necessarily that the differences aren't big enough, but rather that your sample size isn't big enough to make the differences statistically significant.)

These last points boil down to keeping statistics in perspective. Do tests of significance on key measures and important subgroups, but don't go overboard on searching and searching through your data just because there might be some statistically significant difference.

31

Multivariate Analytical Techniques

Statistics are no substitute for judgment.

—Henry Clay

Despite dramatic improvements in the techniques and equipment available to marketers, research often remains more of an art than a science. There really is no substitute for creativity, insight, and judgment.

Nevertheless, there are many computer-based analytical procedures that can be valuable aids to judgment. A good researcher should be familiar with their applications and know when to use them.

When several variables are analyzed together, the procedure is called multivariate analysis.

The first analytical step in most research projects is—or should be—a straightforward cross-tabulation of the results. This is a form of multivariate analysis, albeit a simple form, that often identifies the most significant variables and almost always eliminates a few as obviously not significant. But beyond compiling these cross-tabs, it's often desirable to look for more complex relationships that may not be apparent from the data tables.

The multivariate techniques most often used for analyzing marketing research results are:

- Multiple regression analysis—linear and regression trees
- Factor analysis
- Cluster analysis
- Multidimensional scaling (perceptual MAPPing)
- Conjoint analysis

The first technique—multiple regression analysis—measures *dependence* between variables. This method deals with two types of variables, and it's important to understand the distinction between them:

1. *Dependent or criterion variables.* These are the variables you are trying to predict or explain. A typical example is volume of product or brand usage, or overall satisfaction with a product or company.
2. *Independent or predictor variables.* These are the variables that explain or predict differences in the dependent variables. Demographic characteristics or attitude data are typical independent variables.

The other techniques—factor and cluster analysis, multidimensional scaling, and conjoint analysis—are designed to measure *interdependence* among all the variables. With these methods there are no dependent and independent variables.

Regression Analysis

This approach develops a prediction equation relating a dependent (or criterion) variable and a set of independent (or predictor) variables. This is one of the most straightforward, basic multivariate techniques. It is most useful for predicting a single metric (or interval) criterion variable, such as volume of usage, income, or price.

The procedure provides an equation that defines a line that gives the best fit to the data. The equation for this line can then be used as the prediction equation. For example, suppose a frozen-pizza manufacturer wanted to predict annual household frozen-pizza consumption, using income and family size. The prediction equation might be:

No. of pizzas $= 5.1 + 6.5$ (no. in household) $+ 1.1$ (household income)

The numbers 5.1, 6.5, and 1.1 are values that are derived from the analysis.

Because this equation is developed by a procedure known as "least squares" and defines a straight line, it is not appropriate for situations where the relationship between the dependent and independent variables is not linear. Also, the predictor equation applies only within the range of data used to develop the equation and should not be extrapolated beyond those limits.

Regression Trees

A common use of multiple regressions is to determine which attributes or characteristics (independent variables) drive, or have the most impact on, some overall measure (dependent variable), such as buying intent or overall satisfaction. This is particularly common in customer satisfaction work, where a regression analysis can help a company zero in on those performance elements that would have the greatest impact on raising customer satisfaction.

A newer variation on multiple regressions is a technique called regression trees, which divides people into segments based on some dependent measure. Using customer satisfaction work as an example, in a typical study, each respondent provides an overall satisfaction rating for a company. All these ratings are aggregated into one average overall score. We know, however, that this average score is made up of a wide range of ratings, from the low ratings given by respondents who are not very satisfied to the high ratings given by those who are very satisfied. A regression tree is a multivariate technique for dividing people into satisfaction segments varying from low to high, and helping us explain what is impacting those low or high satisfaction ratings.

The tree begins with everyone in one segment. The technique splits this beginning segment into two, with the most satisfied people going into one group and the least satisfied people going into another group. The analysis tells us which other variable in the study has the greatest impact on overall satisfaction and provides us with the best split, that is, the greatest difference in satisfaction *between* the two groups, and the greatest consistency *within* each group. Both of the two resulting segments are split using the same process. The analysis continues splitting and funneling until the sample sizes become too small and the tree becomes unstable.

The final tree consists of from two to ten segments, varying from low satisfaction to high satisfaction. The analysis does not attempt to control the size of the segments; rather, the differences in scores and the variation around those scores determine the segments and their size. This technique is highly sensitive, with the ability to identify even very small segments. Each segment is highly consistent in terms of overall satisfaction, and the series of splits in the tree helps us to explain why a segment is satisfied or dissatisfied. One key advantage of this technique is that it can include nominal and ordinal data as well. The segments identified in a regression tree can be used as banner points for cross-tabs to further analyze what impacts customer satisfaction.

Figure 31-1 shows an example of a regression tree used for an airline, with overall satisfaction as the dependent variable. The tree shows seven segments at the bottom, ranging from the least satisfied (mean of 2.2 on the far left of the tree) to the most satisfied (mean of 6.5 at the right of the tree). Following down the right side of the tree to see what is impacting or driving the high satisfaction ratings, we can see that for this segment high ratings on convenient schedules and frequent flyer programs are making the difference.

Factor Analysis

This is a general term for techniques that analyze interrelationships among variables and attempt to reduce them to a smaller set of under-lying variables, or factors.

In marketing research, it's common to measure a large number of product attributes or ideal characteristics and of consumer behaviors or attitudes. Yet it's reasonable to believe that in most cases all these vari-

Figure 31-1. Regression tree showing ratings of an airline by satisfaction segments.

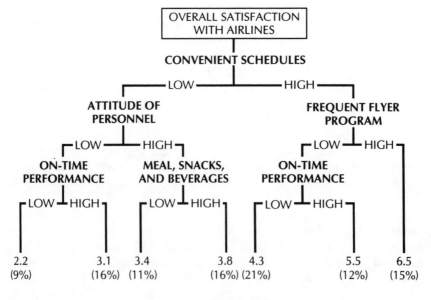

% OF MARKET

Note: Ratings are based on a scale of 1 (lowest) to 7 (highest).

ables are facets of a smaller number of underlying variables. The purpose of factor analysis is to ascertain the basic dimensions—factors—that underlie the larger number of variables.

For example, a manufacturer of health care products might want to have nurses evaluate the importance of a skin lotion for patients, using a list of nine product attributes. A factor analysis of these ratings would produce a series of factor loadings, ranging from $+1$ to -1, that show the degree of positive or negative association of each attribute with underlying factors. The resulting table of factor loadings might look like Figure 31-2. (Only the factor loadings of .5 or more have been included in the table.)

Factor analysis is a purely mathematical procedure. The computer produces values for the relationships or factors, but it doesn't identify or name them. Looking at the attributes with high loadings on factor 1, you might conclude that it should be named "convenience." Perhaps you'd call factor 2 "efficacy" or "effectiveness" and factor 3 "price."

The next step often is to reduce respondents' ratings to factor scores, which represent summary ratings for each underlying factor, then to work with this reduced set of data for further analysis. Generally, the greater the number and variety of attributes measured, the more useful this procedure can be for reducing the data for analysis.

Cluster Analysis

This approach attempts to define the natural groups of people or products within a total population that are similar. Cluster analysis creates

Figure 31-2. Factor loadings in a hypothetical study testing nine product attributes.

Product Attribute	Factor1	Factor 2	Factor 3
Easy-to-use container	.81		
Perfumed scent		.71	
Expensive			−.83
Easy to apply	.62		
Absorbs quickly		.53	
Good all over body	.53		
Not sticky		.51	
Soothes rough skin		.83	
Well-known manufacturer			−.69

subsamples containing units that are more like each other than they are like the members of any other subsample. In other words, it identifies clusters of essentially (or ideally) homogeneous units.

Cluster analysis is often used to identify people with similar attitudes. For example, a financial services company wanted to determine whether there were groups of people with similar attitudes about investing. Respondents rated a series of attitudinal statements about investing on an agree/disagree scale. The cluster analysis then examined the ratings and identified groups of respondents who were alike in their ratings/attitudes and, at the same time, were different from other groups of respondents. For example, one cluster included "experienced investors" who already had a variety of investments and who felt confident in their own ability to make investment decisions. This cluster was markedly different from others, for example, "dabblers," who were interested in investing and had a few investments but who felt that they needed professional advice to make investment decisions.

Typically, a cluster analysis provides a number of different solutions. For example, one solution may find three distinct clusters, another four, and so on. To determine which solution to use, you examine a cluster against the average of all other clusters in the solution to determine what makes the cluster different from the others. If two or more segments are fairly similar to one another, you examine just these two in a pairwise comparison to isolate the differences. The goal is to choose the solution that gives the minimum number of clusters, while still providing the best explanation of each. Generally, each cluster is given a descriptive name and the clusters are often used as banner points for cross-tabs against other data.

Cluster analysis is an analytical method frequently used as part of market segmentation projects and life-style or psychographic studies (see Chapter 32).

Multidimensional Scaling (Perceptual MAPPing)

MAPPing (Mathematical Analysis of Perception and Preference) is another name for multidimensional scaling, and it's a good one, because the objective of the technique is to represent consumers' product perceptions and preferences as points in a space. The results usually take the form of a map or graph.

The following example will illustrate how MAPPing works. A candy manufacturer wanted to develop an understanding of the market for eight leading candy bars. Consumers judged the perceived similarity of each pair of products and also gave preference ratings for each of the candy bars. Finally, other information on the reasons for similarity ratings was used to identify the dimensions of the perceptual map. The results are shown in Figure 31-3.

The results show the positioning of each brand in consumers' minds, which allows manufacturers to determine if they have the position they want. The analysis also identifies the most important product attributes. Finally, the map shows opportunities for new or improved products—"holes" in the market.

The map in Figure 31-3 considers just two product factors at a time, chocolate and nuts. Other perceptual maps show brand performance across many attributes or measures. Such maps can be generated in a variety of ways. One technique uses the matrix from an analysis of variance as the basis for the map, with the advantage that this technique maintains the rank order of significant differences in the data. Figure 31-4 is an example of this type of map, showing perceptions of several airlines on a number of performance dimensions. Each vector or arrow represents a performance dimension that differentiates the airlines, that is, where there are significant differences in how they are regarded.

Conjoint Analysis

This technique separates respondents' overall judgments about complex alternatives, such as product characteristics, into their components.

Conjoint analysis is often used for studying purchasing behavior in real-world contexts. The classic application is for products that are still being put together by the manufacturer. Conjoint helps to identify how much each of the constituent elements of the product contributes to its appeal. The analysis produces utility values for each item that help both in analyzing consumers' judgments and in building the best possible product.

A pharmaceutical company wanted to determine the best combination of features for a new over-the-counter medication. The elements under consideration and the utility values developed were:

Time	
3 hours	−3.285
6 hours	+0.215
13 hours	+3.070

Figure 31-3. Perceptual map showing the position of eight candy products on two dimensions.

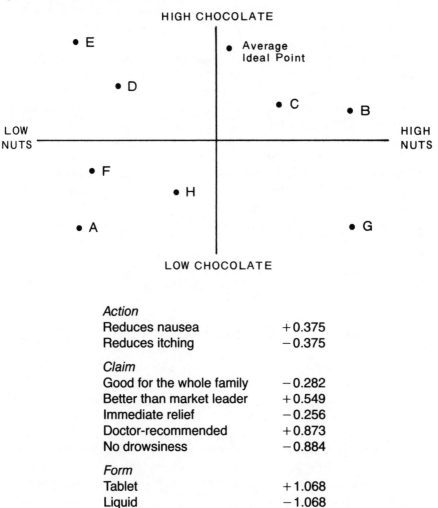

Action	
Reduces nausea	+0.375
Reduces itching	−0.375
Claim	
Good for the whole family	−0.282
Better than market leader	+0.549
Immediate relief	−0.256
Doctor-recommended	+0.873
No drowsiness	−0.884
Form	
Tablet	+1.068
Liquid	−1.068

The conjoint exercise for the respondents may be conducted in a number of ways. In a trade-off, just two elements are considered at a time, for example action versus form; the respondents rank the four possible products that result from the combinations of these two items, and then go on to evaluate two other elements. In a full-profile, all the elements are considered at once. This method has the advantage of being more real-world, because consumers typically consider the entire prod-

Figure 31-4. Perceptual map showing the position of six airlines on multiple performance dimensions.

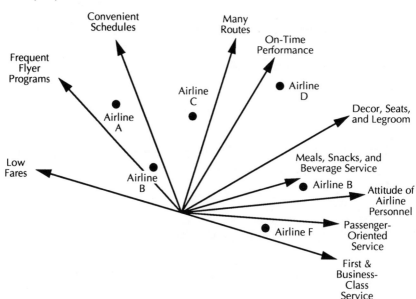

uct, not just two elements at a time. In this method, the combinations of the various elements and levels result in a total of sixty products to be evaluated. Because this is too many, an experimental design is used to cut down the number of alternatives a respondent has to evaluate. The respondents are presented with sets of attribute combinations and asked to rank them from most to least preferred.

Two types of results are provided by the conjoint analysis:

1. *Utility values, showing the relative appeal of each item.* The higher the utility score, the greater the appeal the item has.
2. *Span, a measure of the importance of each attribute in relation to the others.* This is obtained by comparing the relative size of the utility ranges for each attribute.

One of the greatest values of conjoint analysis is its ability to build scenarios of consumer preferences to aid in decision making. The overall utility for hypothetical products is calculated simply by adding the utility scores for the various levels of the attributes. For example, using the pharmaceutical example, the scenarios for two possible products are:

Product A			*Product B*	
Time	3 hours	−3.285	13 hours	3.070
Action	Nausea	0.375	Itch	−0.375
Claim	Beats competition	0.549	Doctor recomm.	0.873
Form	Liquid	−1.068	Tablets	1.068
TOTAL UTILITIES		−3.429		4.636

With all other things being equal, such as the cost of development and manufacturing, the product with the higher utility level would be the better bet.

Types of Variables

There are three types of variables that can be used in marketing research as input for multivariate techniques:

1. *Nominal.* People and products are often classified into categories such as male/female, users/nonusers, working/nonworking, or brand name. These are nominal variables. For tabulating purposes, numbers are often assigned to these categories, but the numbers do not have any real meaning. Nominal scales assign names but mean nothing more.
2. *Ordinal.* These scales give an order, as well as names, to the points. Examples are income categories and ranking data. On these scales there is a clear order—highest to lowest, most to least, or most preferred to least preferred. The distance between all points on the scale is not necessarily equal, but there is a clear order.
3. *Metric.* These are also called interval or ratio scales because there is a measurable interval from one scale point to the next. Volume of usage and household size are examples, as are scales that are developed to have equal intervals between adjacent points.

Each multivariate technique is suitable only for certain kinds of variables. Before you use a technique, learn which variables are appropriate for it and don't try to force another type of variable to fit that method.

Tips on Using Multivariate Techniques

Don't be like the drunk who uses the lamppost for support rather than illumination. Don't let multivariate analysis become a crutch for sloppy fieldwork or a substitute for thinking. Remember these guidelines:

• *Fit the technique to the problem, not the problem to the technique.* Don't fall in love with one method and try to force-fit it to every study. Avoid becoming technique-oriented.

• *Remember that the results are only as good as the data.* Multivariate techniques won't fix bad data. So always be careful in writing the questions and conducting the fieldwork.

• *Think before, not just after, conducting the test.* Don't dump everything you can think of into the computer in the hope that it will sort it all out and make sense of it for you. Develop hypotheses first. Then pretest your questions. You can be almost certain of finding that you need to revise some wording. In fact, it's best to think through your analysis plan at the very beginning, even before you worry about question wording.

• *Consider sequential research.* You always learn as you go along—about things you wish you'd added and other things you could have left out. One or two pilot phases will improve the quality of your final big study. Multivariate analysis is expensive, so proceed cautiously.

• *Find ways to clearly communicate results.* Most line marketing people and general managers aren't familiar with these techniques, so there's a risk of losing them in data and jargon. Look for ways to communicate the techniques and their results in easy-to-understand language.

• *Keep multivariate analysis as the means, not the end.* Running a cluster analysis isn't much help if it doesn't contribute to the overall objective of the study. Start with the problem, not the technique.

Multivariate analytical techniques can be extremely valuable tools. Sometimes these techniques are useful in supplementing straightforward analysis and judgment by bringing complex variables together in a single analysis. However, these techniques are often best used at the beginning of an analysis, before any tables are run, to help you to focus on the key elements in your data and to help you to tell a coherent story with your findings.

If you are inexperienced with these techniques, it is best to seek out expert help. Otherwise, instead of betting a whole study on a single technique, experiment with some of these as parts of studies done for other purposes, and then go ahead with a larger study after the value and applicability of the techniques have been proved.

32

Life-Style and Psychographic Research

Opinion is ultimately determined by the feelings, and not by the intellect.

—Herbert Spencer, *Essays on Education*

We know instinctively that people aren't all the same. We can sense that some kinds of people are just more likely to drive a certain make of car or smoke a particular brand of cigarettes than others are.

Using demographic characteristics (age, income, family size, and so on) is one way of segmenting a population to explain product usage. Sometimes it works, but often it doesn't—at least not as well as you'd like it to. Not all old people behave similarly, and neither do all rich people or all single people. In these cases, you often sense that there's an "internal" dimension to people that would refine the "external" (or demographic) dimensions and segment a population into useful groups—if you could just get your hands on the right internal characteristics.

The internal dimension is addressed by *psychographics* or *life-style* research. As the name implies, it attempts to use psychology in the same way researchers have long used demography to identify market segments. Specifically, psychographics seeks to explain why people behave and believe as they do by applying principles from the behavioral and social sciences.

While the terms *life-style* and *psychographics* are often used interchangeably, psychographics technically refers to general personality traits and values, whereas life-style measurements tend more toward specific activities, interests, and habits. Obviously, the two areas overlap considerably, and most projects incorporate both types of measures. So the distinction between the two has become blurred in everyday usage.

On a more commonsense level, psychographics attempts to sort people into piles so that the piles differ from each other but each pile is homogeneous. At least, that's the goal.

Uses of Psychographics

This type of analysis is usually done to understand—and then, by inference, to predict—the characteristics that most strongly affect (1) brand usage (why do some people drive Fords while others drive Chevrolets?) and (2) heaviness of usage (what are the attitudes that account for some people being heavy consumers of wine but light consumers or nonusers of beer and hard liquor?). A psychographic study must explain one or both of these variables, or it risks producing interesting, nice-to-know facts that have no practical application.

This approach is useful for helping to draw a profile of the typical user—or multiple profiles of the typical user among several segments—which most often has application to advertising problems, such as developing strategy and campaigns, writing copy, and positioning or repositioning products. In essence, psychographics helps advertising and marketing people picture the customer they're writing for or selling to. And it helps separate fads and media-created trends from reality.

Life-style analysis is most likely to provide new insight into (1) *discretionary purchases,* such as leisure-time or luxury products, with which the consumer has an interest in expressing his or her individuality or personal taste, and (2) *major purchases,* such as cars, clothes, or furniture, which the buyer may see as carrying prestige or status.

Psychographic variables often have a surprising influence on the purchase of industrial products. On the other hand, the life-style dimension is less likely to add much to the understanding of mass market products, where habit or convenience may be the primary purchase factors. Morton Salt, for example, is purchased across all life-style groups.

Collecting Psychographic Data

The first step in any psychographic or life-style study should be to develop clear, carefully worded hypotheses. This is usually done through qualitative research. The alternative is to try to collect information on every possible psychographic dimension, then hope that some clear-cut pattern will emerge from the analysis. This is always wasteful and usually unsuccessful.

After a set of hypotheses is developed, these must be translated into a series of agree/disagree statements. These statements, usually covering several subject areas, are then given to respondents for their reactions:

• *Product attitudes* related to the importance of such things as price, fashion, utility, or convenience

  "I usually buy the least expensive brand of dishwashing soap."
  "I often try the latest hairstyles when they change."
  "I consider the dog a member of my family."

• *Activities and traits* such as hobbies, work, or personal habits

  "I do a lot of work on my car."
  "Television is a primary source of entertainment for me."
  "I do not get enough sleep."

• *Interests* such as family, community, or recreation

  "I enjoy trying new recipes."
  "I like going to concerts."
  "My children are the most important thing in my life."

• *Opinions* about social issues, politics, economics, or the future

  "It's the fault of business that our lakes and streams are dying."
  "I expect my economic situation to be better in five years than it is
     now."
  "Inflation is our most important national problem."

Don't forget to include the demographic information in your analysis. This could add a valuable dimension to the psychographic measures you have gathered.

Finally, be sure to collect detailed data on brand and volume usage, because this is what you'll be trying to explain with the psychographic information.

Once this information is collected in the field, a cluster or segmentation analysis is conducted to identify life-style or psychographic groups. Then a name is usually given to each of the groups to describe its members (Retreater, Achiever, or Spaghetti Lover, for example). Finally, it's often useful to read over some actual questionnaires or to do some group interviews among life-style groups to give some flesh-and-blood reality to the research results.

Examples

Two of the organizations most active in life-style and psychographic research are Yankelovich Clancy Shulman and SRI International (formerly Stanford Research Institute). Both of them have conducted major, ongoing studies to develop life-style segments across the whole U.S. population. Although studies done on specific product categories would usually produce different groups, their segments provide a good illustration of real-world life-style research.

Yankelovich Monitor

This service tracks trends in the population among various values segments, originally identified as *old-values segments* and *new-values segments*. The old-values segments comprise two groups:

1. *Traditionalist*—middle-aged people who have accepted the traditional values of hard work and material success
2. *Retreaters*—older, poorer people who have given up on achieving success

New-values segments consist of three types of people:

1. *New Conformists*—younger people who have largely substituted self-fulfillment for traditional, work-oriented values
2. *Forerunners*—young, upscale people who place a high value on intellectual and creative achievement
3. *Autonomous*—upscale consumers who have achieved success and turned their attention to self-improvement and personal fulfillment

The Yankelovich Monitor then provides client companies with information about how these values affect consumption and trends for a large number of products and services.

SRI Values and Life-Styles (VALS)

SRI has identified nine life-style segments within three broad values categories:

1. *Need-driven*—low-income people whose consumption is driven by need, not preference. Within this category are two subgroups:
   —Survivors
   —Sustainers
2. *Outer-directed*—(the largest segment) people who consume largely for the sake of appearance and to impress others. Subsegments are:
   —Belongers
   —Emulators
   —Achievers
3. *Inner-directed*—people who purchase to please themselves rather than others. Four subsegments are:
   —I-am-me
   —Experimental
   —Societally conscious
   —Integrated

Tips on Psychographic Research

Life-style and psychographic research has limitations. The results are rarely as clear-cut and dramatic as you'd like. So it's wisest to use the approach, at least at first, as part of another study. It's risky to rely solely on the outcome of psychographic segments when you're tackling a major project.

While most researchers would agree intuitively that psychographic dimensions affect most products to some degree, the application of life-style research presents two problems:

1. *The difficulty of measuring attitudes, interests, and opinions accurately.* Whenever you're doing life-style research, you're trying to measure very subtle emotions with very approximate tools. So develop your statements as carefully and precisely as you can, but nevertheless recognize that it's going to be difficult to classify everyone into nice, neat boxes.
2. *The difficulty of finding differences between segments that justify action.* Most successful products and services are so broadly used that volume isn't restricted to one segment. Even a segment with a high index of usage may, because of its small size, account for only a small share of product or category volume.

So while psychographics isn't a cure-all, it can be a useful tool on some studies in some product categories. Here are ten tips to help you get your results out of the nice-to-know and into the real-world action category:

1. *Pay attention to sampling.* Otherwise your data may come from a subsample, which can distort the results.
2. *Avoid "don't know" choices or midpoints on scales.* Some respondents will use these instead of thinking hard to answer a question, and such responses are of little value.
3. *Use real-world language.* Make your statements sound as if they were written by real people, not by a psychologist or researcher.
4. *Include a balance of attitudes, interests, opinions, and activities.* Don't bet everything on just one or two of these areas.
5. *Include demographics.* Don't overlook their potential contribution.
6. *Try to keep statements product-specific.* That way you're most likely to get understandable segments. Try to avoid obscure relationships that give no advertising, marketing, or product direction.
7. *Use a balance of positive and negative statements.* You can't necessarily infer agreement with a positive statement from disagreement with a negative one, or vice versa.
8. *Don't include too many statements on the same topic.* This redundancy wears out respondents and often just confuses the analysis.
9. *Be careful about trying to measure illegal or socially unacceptable activities.* People may be reluctant to tell a stranger that they use marijuana or hate their kids.
10. *Use one-dimensional statements.* How does someone who likes to jog but hates swimming respond to "I love to jog and swim"?

Finally, be realistic in your expectations of life-style research. Think about yourself. How would you classify or segment your own personality or behavior? Would you be in the same psychographic segment in all aspects of your life—at work, at home, and in your leisure time? Probably not. Yet, if you have trouble classifying yourself—the one person you know better than anyone on earth—what chance do you have of neatly segmenting a thousand strangers who answered fifty questions for you?

We're all very complex people. Psychographics can often be a useful research tool, but it can't make us simpler and easier to understand than we really are.

Part VI
Working With Research Companies

33

Ten Tips on Being a Savvy Research Client

Contrary to what you might think, the best research client is a smart client. In fact, the smarter the better. The more clients know about my business, the easier they are for me to work with. The best client of all, in terms of a smooth working relationship, is often one who has actually worked on the research supplier side.

I've worked in the marketing research business for twenty-five years. My experience includes several jobs on the client side. I've also done about everything you can do on the supplier side, from interviewing to managing my own research company. (In addition, I even worked a year as a management consultant for one of the "Big 8" accounting firms, but I don't count that because I didn't do anything the whole time I was there.)

If a client who *hadn't* worked on the supplier side asked me what he or she should do to get the most from research—and research suppliers—here are some tips I'd give. (By the way, I'd bet most of these points also apply—in slightly modified form—to the advertising agency business.)

1. *Get your research supplier involved early.* The earlier the better. That's the way you'll get the most for your money. If the research company is involved up front, it can help develop the research program. Otherwise it will be reduced simply to executing your ideas. That's okay, of course. It may even be all that you want. But you'll have lost a

Reprinted and adapted with permission from *Advertising Age*, November 24, 1980, page 42. Published by Crain Communications Inc.

good chance to get some new, fresh thinking on your problem that
could have come if the research company had been involved at the start.

2. *Give your research company all the background on the project.* Surprises and secrets between clients and research companies are invariably
destructive. Openness starts at the very beginning of a project. For example:

- If cost and timing constraints exist, discuss them up front. Don't
  be afraid to talk about price at the outset.
- If there are decision rules for taking action, tell your research supplier.
- If research issues are surrounded by company politics or interde-
  partmental power struggles, give some minimal warning to your
  research company. Don't let people wander unaware into a mine-
  field.

Of course, most background material involves such straightforward
things as the history of the product and the objectives of the study. Tell
your supplier everything you can think of. Even small details help and
may support what needs to be done.

3. *Challenge your research company to give you ideas—and to save you
money.* After you fill in the background, ask your supplier to give you
some alternatives for the research that could be done to answer your
questions. If you're sincerely open to suggestions and ideas, the odds
are that you'll get some new perspectives.

Finally, after the research design is set—but *before* things get
started—ask your supplier what you could do to save money. Is there a
way to cut some fat out of the project? You'll probably be told there is, *if*
you're willing to trade off information. Of course, you may not want to
give anything up, but wouldn't it be nice to have the choice? Well, then,
ask. You'll be surprised how often the research company can tell you
how to save a buck. And you may feel that some of the "nice-to-know"
information is expendable when you see a price tag on it.

4. *Avoid last-minute changes.* This is a major cause of both aggrava-
tion and extra cost. Obviously, there are genuine last-minute emergen-
cies, but otherwise changes have to be cut off at some point. Self-disci-
pline in this respect will save you money, keep the goodwill of your
research company, and decrease the likelihood of foul-ups.

5. *Once things get under way, leave the research company alone to do its
job.* There's a fine line between client communication and hand-holding.

But if you recognize that there is a line (and that it is costly and inefficient if you cross it too often), you should be okay.

6. *Give the research people feedback.* We all like to get paid, and clients should know that compliments on a job well done are a very inexpensive way to make sure that they get a good job from their research company the next time too. Kudos from clients are rare enough that they have great impact. Their scarcity makes them valuable. At the same time, if you don't like the job you're getting from your research people, tell them about that too. Chances are they already sense that things aren't going well with you. Talking about it may help identify and fix the problem.

After a research company conducts a study on a product, it develops a sense of ownership in the study. Clients can use that to advantage. Tell the research people what happens. They'll love you for it, and they'll work harder for you next time. It's another way you can "pay" your research supplier in a currency that costs you nothing.

7. *Don't accept jargon.* Research, like most businesses, has its own special language. And that can be simple gobbledygook if you don't know the code. Don't hesitate to ask, "What does that mean in real English?" Straightforward language helps all of us to keep our thoughts straight, so your questions will probably have the side benefit of forcing researchers to examine their thinking.

8. *Remember, research is a team sport.* The legal profession is built around the adversary relationship, and some clients seem to regard research companies as adversaries. They think they'll get better work if they lean on their suppliers. They're wrong. The best clients treat their research companies as parts of their team. That doesn't mean you don't still expect the supplier to do its job, but the team attitude really makes a difference. It'll pay dividends to you. Nobody wants to feel like a lackey.

9. *Don't put your eggs in too many baskets.* Clients that work with dozens of different research companies usually lose the chance to get the full attention and commitment of any one of those companies. Find a few research companies that you can work with and trust. Then stick with them. You will be more important to them, and they'll be able to learn your business and know your products. That way you'll get better work from them—and with less learning time needed on each project, you should get it done cheaper and faster too.

10. *Work toward "partnering"—clients and research companies working as colleagues, not adversaries.* That's the trend today: ongoing relation-

ships, not project-by-project bidding wars. That's good for the research industry, and it's good for the individual research users, too. It usually results in the best-quality, most fully thought out research. And costs typically end up lower, too, since the research company has to spend less money on sales and new business development.

Good clients are demanding, but their demands are reasonable and focus on issues that really make a difference. Otherwise it becomes nitpicking, and that doesn't help anyone.

Clients usually get what they expect—and deserve. The things I've described in this chapter should help you develop the kind of relationship with your research suppliers that will get the best work for you.

34

Who's Who in Marketing Research

How many marketing research companies are there in the United States? According to a study conducted by the Center for Marketing Studies at the University of Georgia, there are roughly 4,000.

Most of the companies have names like John Doe & Associates and consist of John Doe (and often *no* associates) operating out of his home or a small office. John is most often a researcher who used to work for a large manufacturer or research company and decided to try to make it in his own business. In a couple of years, John Doe & Associates will probably disappear, as John goes back to work for another manufacturer or research company.

As in any market, the 20/80 rule applies. Twenty percent of the research companies account for 80 percent of the business. Over the past decade, Jack Honomichl, the industry spokesman, has been measuring the size of the market and which are the leading research companies in the United States. Honomichl estimates that $2.5 billion is done through U.S. commercial marketing research companies.

Regardless of the size and number of research companies, most fall into one of four categories: syndicated services, standardized techniques companies, custom research companies, and data collection services. Some of the larger companies offer more than one type of service but are generally known for one of these four categories.

Syndicated Services

Syndicated services provide information from common pools of data to different clients. Scanner data, purchase mail panels, and audience share measurements are the major types of services provided by syndicated services. For example, the same scanner sales data on volume movement and brand shares in the cake mix category are available to Pillsbury, General Mills (Betty Crocker), and Procter & Gamble (Duncan Hines). The Gallup and Harris polls are also syndicated services; they're available for purchase by any newspaper.

The companies that provide syndicated services tend to be among the largest in the research business. The major providers of syndicated research are:

- *A. C. Nielsen*—ScanTrack tracks volume and market share for food and drug products; it is also well known for its TV audience measures.
- *IMS International*—provides audit data for the pharmaceutical/medical industry.
- *Information Resources Inc.*—InfoScan provides product movement data via UPC scanners for food, drug, and mass merchandisers.
- *The Arbitron Co.*—measures TV and radio audiences.
- *The Group NPD*—offers consumer purchase panels, also ESP simulated sales tests.
- *Starch INRA Hooper*—provides audience measurements, advertising readership, and custom studies.
- *Louis Harris & Associates*—conducts the Harris Poll, also custom studies.
- *Simmons Market Research Bureau*—a division of the MRB Group Ltd., Simmons measures print audiences.

Standardized Techniques Companies

Research companies of this type conduct standardized studies for different clients—but always in the same way. Many advertising testing techniques and simulated sales tests are examples of the work they do. Results of one study are comparable to norms, or a data bank, from other comparable studies, but each project's results are proprietary to the individual client.

Advertising Tests

There are many companies specializing in advertising research. The major ones are:

- *ASI*—offers on-air pretesting of commercials
- *McCollum/Spielman*—uses theater technique
- *Research Systems Corporation*—theater setting, conducts before/after brand preference measures

Simulated Sales Tests

These techniques are described more fully in Chapter 16. The five major products and producers in this area are:

1. *BASES*—BASES Burke Institute
2. *ESP (Estimated Sales Potential)*—NPD Research Inc.
3. *Entro and Assessor*—M/A/R/C
4. *Laboratory Test Market, Litmus I and II*—Yankelovich Clancy Shulman
5. *Critique®*—Custom Research Inc.

Custom Research Companies

Most research companies (including our own company, Custom Research Inc.) provide this type of service: one-of-a-kind projects. Custom-designed projects probably account for the largest *number* of all studies done, although not for the biggest share of all research *dollars* spent.

The following list represents some of the largest companies in the custom research business (although some also offer standardized techniques):

Abt Associates Inc.	Intersearch Corp.
Audits & Surveys	J. D. Powers & Associates
Burke Marketing Research	Lieberman Research West
Chilton Research Services	The M/A/R/C Group
Conway/Millikin & Associates	Maritz Marketing Research
Creative Response Research	Inc.
Services	Market Facts, Inc.
Custom Research Inc.	Mediamark Research, Inc.
Data Development	Millward Brown, Inc.
Corporation	MOR-PACE, Inc.
Decision Research Corporation	National Analysts
Elrick & Lavidge, Inc.	The National Research Group
I.C.R. Survey Research Group	NFO Research, Inc.

Research International Group, Inc.
Response Analysis
Strategic Research & Consulting
Total Research Corporation

The Vanderveer Group Inc.
Walker Group
Walsh America Ltd.
Westat Inc.
The Wirthlin Group

Data Collection Services

Data collection services specialize in interviewing only. These companies do the actual interviewing across the United States for full-service companies. Several are large networks of interviewing services with many locations throughout the country. The major ones are:

- *Quick Test Opinion Centers*—a division of Elrick and Lavidge, it operates a national network of fifty data collection facilities.
- *Quality Controlled Services*—a division of Maritz Marketing Research Inc., it has data collection facilities at sixteen mall locations and forty-one group discussion facilities.
- *Heakin Research Inc.*—this independent company has thirty-one mall facilities throughout the United States.

In addition, there are literally a thousand interviewing services located in large, medium, and small towns to do interviewing.

Major Types of Standardized and Syndicated Data

Another way to categorize the research business is by the major types of standardized and syndicated data collected and the companies that offer each type of service.

Volume and Market Share Measures

There are two major sources of category volume and brand share tracking data:

A. C. Nielsen—gathers data through UPC scanners in a large sample of grocery, drug, and mass merchandising stores. Nielsen also provides purchase information on a national household basis and uses local household panels for test marketing.

Information Resources, Inc. (IRI)—InfoScan tracks packaged goods sales using UPC scanners in grocery, drug, and mass merchandising stores. IRI also provides scanner purchase data derived from a large national household panel.

Mail Panels

Large samples of homes agree to return custom mail questionnaires that are mailed to them periodically by these research companies:

Home Testing Institute
National Family Opinion
Market Facts, Inc.

A final note: The research field is volatile. Companies are constantly introducing new services and discontinuing others. So it's impossible to keep the list of research companies and the services they provide *completely* up-to-date. A good, relatively up-to-date list is published each year by Jack Honomichl in the AMA *Marketing News*.

35

How to Work With a Research Company

Like a marriage, the relationship between a research company and its clients is complex. And just as each marriage has its own arrangements that allow the couple to get along together, every client/research provider situation is a little different from any other.

That makes rules for the relationship difficult to establish. What works in one situation won't necessarily work in the next. Nevertheless, guidelines are helpful in that they show how other people handle similar situations. For that reason, the Council of American Survey Research Organizations (CASRO) established a Code of Business Practices to serve as a guideline for what is common practice in the research business.

The Code is included here as a reference to typical methods of handling some of the most common details of the client/provider relationship.

Council of American Survey Research Organizations
Code of Business Practices
January, 1990

This section is intended to clarify the meanings of terms used in describing certain business practices. When these terms are used in this Code, their meanings are as stated below.

THE AGREEMENT

Agreement—Legally-binding contractual relationship between the parties, describing the terms and conditions of the services to be provided by the research company in consideration for monies paid by the client. Agreements can be by letter, proposal, estimate or job authorization form, and/or separate contract. Agreement can be oral, but the most binding and effective agreements are written.

PARTIES TO AN AGREEMENT

Research company—A member of CASRO, and thus, a company that has satisfied Article IV of the CASRO Bylaws as a full-service research company.

Contractor—A research company that has made an agreement for its services between itself and a client.

Client (or sponsor)—An organization that has contracted for the services of a research company.

Prospective client—A company, organization or appropriate unit of same that a research company has reason to think will enter into an acceptable contract for research or related services.

Competing companies—Two or more research companies, or two or more prospective clients, whose products or services are such that when a customer buys from one of them, the need to buy from others is correspondingly reduced.

INSTRUMENTS TO AN AGREEMENT

Custom study—A study that typically is designed and carried out to satisfy the objectives of one client. Unless otherwise noted, all practices described in this Code apply only to custom studies. Custom studies may have commercial and/or non-commercial clients.

Proposal—A written document describing a research plan, which normally includes a statement of problem, study objectives, research method, sample design, study specifications, etc., as well as estimates of cost and time for completion. A proposal usually requires that the research company include its own recommendations about how the work should be carried out. Such recommendations for procedures may be appropriate for one or more of these reasons: (1) all specifications are not provided; (2) there are ambiguities about the specifications that require resolution; and (3) the proposal request asks for recommendations for design and procedure.

Cost estimate—A research company response to a type of proposal request: that is, when a prospective client provides a set of specifications, which are complete and which a research company can use to work out its bid price for a contract.

PRODUCTS OF AN AGREEMENT

Questionnaires—These are forms that are used for data collection, nearly always in a procedure that includes one respondent at a time. Questionnaires may be interviewer-administered (face-to-face or by telephone), or may be self-administered by respondents.

Report—The agreed-upon product(s) of a contract. Reports may be oral or written, formally or informally presented. Reports may be sets of tables, or a data tape, as well as a narrative or text.

Sometimes a report may be a set of completed questionnaires. In this instance, questionnaires are an end product of a contract, instead of a means to another type of product, such as tables or text.

This glossary is not exhaustive. There are other terms with specialized meanings in the Code that are not in this glossary. The glossary includes only those terms that especially seem to need clarification.

PRACTICES RELATED TO CONTRACT NEGOTIATIONS

As will be discussed in the following sections, it is a good practice to confirm or set forth the terms and conditions of the project in writing. In the Exhibit Section at the end of this Code is a Standard Contract Form for Survey Research Services prepared by the CASRO legal counsel and approved by the CASRO Board of Directors for use as a guideline. This contract can be tailored to fit the situation or client as needed. This contract also offers language that can be used in separate agreements with clients. It also covers limitation of liability including special or consequential damages.

A. CONFLICT OF INTEREST

It is a principle of the professional research firm to avoid conflicts of interest and to treat all information acquired from a client as confidential. It is <u>not</u> a conflict of interest to work for or attempt to work for competing clients when:

1. Both grant explicit permission.

2. The nature of the service is syndicated or shared cost.

3. The work or project involves a standard methodology offered to anyone.

4. The nature of the work that the contractor would do for Company B is completely different from what the contractor is or has been doing for its client, Company A. "Completely different" in this case means that nothing that the contractor has learned about Company A from its relationship with Company A could benefit Company B or the services rendered to Company B.

B. CONDITIONS GOVERNING <u>SUBMISSION</u> OF PROPOSALS

1. Proposals prepared in response to a client request even though entirely at the expense of a research company.

Practice—These should be submitted to the requesting client only. If that client does not authorize the work, then the proposal may be submitted to other prospective clients unless so doing would reveal confidential information.

2. Proposals for which a prospective client pays either part or all of the cost incurred by the research company in preparing the proposal.

Practice—If a prospective client does not want to go ahead with the work, a research company may submit the proposal to another prospective client only if it has received permission to do so from the original client.

C. PRACTICES RELATED TO THE <u>CONTENT</u> OF PROPOSALS AND COST ESTIMATES

The intent of this section is to ensure that both parties to the contract have the same expectations about procedures and, to some extent, how these procedures would be implemented.

A comment about applicability of procedures. Some items in this section are appropriate for some types of work and not others. For example, a proposal for a developmental study that would obtain information only via group interviews would include only some of the practices described below. The practices are mainly geared to quantitative studies in which data are from a number of separately-administered questionnaires. Many of these practices, however, may be used for qualitative studies as well, depending on the circumstances.

1. Method of communicating proposals and cost estimates.

Practice—It is good business practice to submit either proposals or cost estimates in writing. If communicated verbally, they should be confirmed in writing, especially if the project is authorized.

2. Conditions of offering services.

<u>Practice</u>—Proposals and cost estimates should specify how long a period of time after submission each of the following will be honored by the research company if the prospective client accepts the proposal or cost estimate and authorizes the work:

a. Statements about the amounts to be billed to the client.
b. The schedule for accomplishing the work.

3. Related to sharing of responsibilities with client.

<u>Practice</u>—Proposals and cost estimates should include a description of tasks that are expected of the client as part of the research procedure (for example, lists of customer names and the manner in which the lists will be provided).

4. Related to report.

<u>Practice</u>—The end product of the contract will be specified in terms of what it is and—if a written report or table—the number of copies to be supplied.

5. Related to specifications.

<u>Practice</u>—The following list of specifications for a project are suggested but may not apply to all projects:

a. Tasks to be performed

   1. by contractor
   2. by client

b. Universe definition

c. Respondent eligibility criteria

d. Estimated incidence of eligible respondents

e. Sample type and design

    f. Sample size

    g. Description of questionnaire

    h. Type of interviewing

    i. Interviewer training

    j. Respondent selection procedures

    k. Callback procedures

    l. Validation procedures

    m. Processing

        1. editing/coding
        2. data entry
        3. cleaning
        4. weighting, projecting
        5. tabulations—amount, type
        6. analysis
        7. reports
        8. presentation format

    n. Schedule

    o. Billing procedures

    p. Products—distribution/handling (and safety information)

    q. Storage—see Section II.B.2.

The following is a suggested list of specifics that could/should be included for each of the above listed topics. In some instances an illustrative wording is provided.

Tasks to be performed

    a. by contractor:
        List of functions for which contractor is respon-

sible. By omission it will specify what is not part of the project or contractor's responsibilities. For example, if the results are not to be weighted, this function would be omitted. Similarly, if no formal presentation is to be prepared, this section would be omitted.

b. by client:

List of functions for which client is responsible. If client is responsible for questionnaire design or selection of sample of dealers, employees, customers, etc., it should be specified in this section.

Universe definition:

This should be spelled out in as exact terms as possible. For example, "all persons aged 18 or over residing in households in the Houston standard metropolitan statistical area."

Respondent eligibility criteria:

This may be combined with the universe definition. For example, the phrase "who drank two or more cups of coffee in the 24 hours preceding the interview" might be inserted in the definition. On the other hand, it may be a separate statement such as "only those persons who have attended a professional sporting event within the past 12 months are eligible to be respondents to this survey."

Estimated incidence:

A statement of the incidence estimate upon which the design and cost estimate are based. This can be stated as a percent of all individuals, a percent of households containing one or more eligible respondents, a percent of business establishments meeting the eligibility criteria, etc. After the study begins, if the actual observed incidence varies from assumptions in the proposal in a direction that would increase/decrease contractor costs so substantially as to make renegotiation of the contract appropriate, the contractor should notify the client as soon as possible of such fact. As a general matter, a contractor should not seek to renegotiate a contract unless the possibility of such renegotiation, under stated circumstances, is disclosed in the proposal or cost estimate.

Sample type and design:
This should include such items as:
Probability vs. other type
List vs. area
Household vs. individual
Corporate entities vs. establishments
Quotas, if any
Listed telephone households vs. random digit dialing
Geographic definitions or number of clusters vs. sampling points

Sample size:
This may be stated either in terms of numbers of contacts attempted, numbers of completed screening interviews or number of completed interviews. If there are any quotas or specific population groups, they should be stated in this section. For group interview projects, it may be stated in terms of numbers of groups or number of individuals included.

Description of questionnaire:
The questionnaire can be described in a number of ways such as number of questions, number of questions by type such as open-ended vs. closed-ended, average duration in minutes or some combination of these elements.

Type of interviewing:
A statement as to whether the study is to be personal vs. telephone vs. self-administered interviewing. Also, the place of interviewing such as households, business offices, malls, etc. for per-

sonal interviews. For telephone interviews it should include statements on local vs. central and paper vs. CRT-type interviews. For focus groups, it should include type of questioning and responsibility for moderators.

Interviewer training:

This section should cover special interviewer training for the project, if any. Personal briefings by local supervisors, project staff, client, etc. Written or verbal subject matter instructions, special technique training, etc. should be included here.

Respondent selection procedures:

This section should specify the actual procedure to be used. For example, in a household one could use random respondent in household selected, then screened; screen all household members and select from those that meet eligibility criteria; random respondent from among those at home at time of interviewer's call; anyone who answers interviewer's call; those that fit specified quota, etc. In a mall it might be any women dressed in slacks or those who enter a particular store or all those within a specified age range.

Callback procedures:

This section should include the number of callbacks to be made and the schedule of making them if a specific schedule is planned.

Validation procedures:

Validation is "used in interview research to describe procedures employed to verify that interviews have been properly conducted" (from *A Dictionary for Marketing Research* by S. Dutka and I. Roshwald, 1974). Any such procedures such as personal vs. telephone vs. mail and local vs. central should be included here.

Processing:
  a. Editing/coding:

> Editing is the process by which inconsistent or impossible responses are either eliminated or made consistent based upon the total response pattern. Coding involves translating verbal responses into meaningful, summary response categories. The procedures by which these functions are to be carried out should be specified here, including hand editing vs. computer editing, how response categories (codes) will be set up, who will be responsible, etc.

  b. Data entry:

> This should include a statement regarding the mode of data entry such as keypunching, optical scanning, etc. and the amount of verification such as the percent key verification. Data entry may be to tabulating cards, direct to tapes, floppy disks, or some other mode

  c. Cleaning:

> This is frequently a follow-up to be used in lieu of editing. It is used to eliminate impossible or inconsistent response patterns usually after the data are in a machine-readable format. Reference might be made as to whether cleaning will be done by referring back to the original source documents or by rules programmed into the computer or both.

Product handling:

> This section should include a brief reference to any product which is to be used in the study and any special handling procedures that are required by either the contractor or client.

OWNERSHIP OF AND RIGHTS TO RESEARCH PRODUCTS, INSTRUMENTS AND SOURCE MATERIALS

A. OWNERSHIP RIGHTS RELATED TO PROPOSALS

Absent a contrary agreement between the prospective contractor and prospective client:

1. **Proposals prepared at the expense of a prospective contractor.**

   Practice—a. Such proposals are the property of the company that prepared them and may not be used by a prospective client in any way to its benefit, without the permission of the prospective contractor.

   b. Any part of the proposal, including questions or a questionnaire that is constructed by the prospective contractor, is the property of the research company that prepared it.

2. **Proposals prepared wholly or in substantial part at the expense of a prospective client.**

   Practice—Such proposals are the property of the company that has requested and paid for them and are considered to be "reports" as the term "report" is used in this Code.

B. CLIENT-SUPPLIED DATA

Scope. In view of the confidential relationship that frequently exists between a client and a contractor, the contractor may obtain, during the course of preparing a proposal or conducting a research project, private and confidential information concerning the client, its organization, personnel, business activities, policies, public relations or advertising practices, or plans or products. Customer lists, subscription lists and dealer lists are included within the meaning of this section. This information may be obtained in writing or orally.

1. Dissemination

Practice—The research company should not reveal such information to anyone outside of its own organization for any purposes whatsoever without the express, written consent of the client.

The research company should limit the internal distribution of such confidential client information to those employees who require the information in order to fulfill their duties and should inform employees of the practices to be followed with respect to client-supplied information. Many times the research company is asked to sign a separate confidentiality agreement concerning dissemination or use of client information. This is now a fairly common practice.

2. Storage

Practice—In carrying out this policy, the research company should exercise reasonable care in the handling of any client-supplied information and maintain the information in an appropriate storage place until its return to the client or its destruction, whichever is desired by the client.

3. Employees

Practice—It is considered good business practice for a research company to obtain non-disclosure statements from employees.

C. QUESTIONNAIRES

1. Ownership

Practice—Completed questionnaires on custom research projects are the property of the contractor unless otherwise specified in the client/contractor agreement.

Under any circumstances, respondent identification is subject to the conditions specified in the CASRO Code of Standards for Survey Research. If completed questionnaires are provided to a subcontractor (for data conversion or analysis, for example), the contractor retains responsibility for proper storage and disposition of questionnaires.

2. Storage

Practice—a. Absent an agreement to the contrary, the contractor is responsible for establishing a specific period of time during which questionnaires (original data forms) will be stored and for communicating this policy to the client.

b. Normal storage procedures for completed questionnaires should provide reasonable protection from external hazards, such as fire and water damage, from inadvertent misplacement or loss, and from deliberate misappropriation.

c. Completed questionnaires (paper as well as computerized questionnaires) may be stored with names, addresses, and identifying information unless the specific needs of a project require a different procedure. Survey data containing such identifying information should be kept in a locked container or locked room when not being used in routine survey activities. Reasonable caution should be exercised in limiting access to such survey data to only those who are working on the specific project and who have been instructed in any special confidentiality procedures for that project.

d. Procedures for special projects where the data have been determined to be particularly sensitive may include storage of completed questionnaires in locked containers or rooms (or if on tape then computer access-controlled) during survey activities, the removal of identifying information from the questionnaires, and coding of completed questionnaires with a number that can be linked to a special file containing identifying information.

3. Disposal

<u>Practice</u>—a. The client should be notified in writing of any plan to destroy completed questionnaires at least 30 days prior to planned destruction.

b. That notification should specify the date that the material will be destroyed if the client does not respond with other instructions by that date. A specific time-frame for automatic disposal can be negotiated with the client as part of the project agreement, but an alert prior to destruction may still be advisable.

c. The client may request continued storage beyond the specified date. If compliance with the request involves a charge to the client, the contractor should so notify the client upon receiving the request.

d. If by mutual agreement the questionnaires (paper or tapes) are to be delivered to the client, the contractor must first remove all individual respondent identification as specified in the CASRO Code of Standards.

Responsibility for shipping costs should be agreed upon, if possible, in advance of shipping.

e. Destruction of completed questionnaires should be by the normal process of the research organization for disposing of waste paper or computer tapes/disks. Procedures such as shredding and/or burning certified by a company officer are to be considered special procedures.

4. Rights to questionnaires for syndicated or multi-client studies

Questionnaires for these types of studies ordinarily are the property of the contractor.

Practice—If there is nothing about rights to questionnaires in the agreements between a contractor and its clients, then the contractor should observe the same practices regarding storage as for custom study questionnaires (see B.2.).

At the end of the stated storage period, however, the contractor may destroy or retain the questionnaires without asking permission of anyone else.

D. TABULATING CARDS AND/OR COMPUTER TAPES/ DISKS

Scope. The provisions of this section apply to all materials (e.g., codebooks) that are necessary to utilize these cards/ tapes. Specifically excluded, however, are any privately-owned programs and/or systems by which the data are processed. Included also are disks generated by personal computers.

1. Ownership

Practice—Tabulating cards and/or computer tapes/disks specifically produced for a research project are the property of the contractor unless otherwise specified in the client/contractor agreement. The contractor is responsible for storing such materials for a stated period of time after completion of the research project and for communicating this policy to the client.

2. Storage

Practice—a. These materials should be stored in such a way that any additional analyses requested by the client can be made.

b. Unless otherwise specified, the client ordinarily would be liable for charges in connection with producing duplicate cards/tapes for his use while having the research organization continue to store such material.

3. Disposal

Practice—a. The client should be notified of any plan to destroy cards/tapes/disks at least 30 days prior to destruction.

b. That notification should specify the date on which cards/tapes/disks will be destroyed if the client does not respond with other instructions by that date.

c. The client may request continued storage beyond the specified date. If compliance with the request involves a charge to the client, the contractor should so notify the client upon receiving the request.

d. If by mutual agreement the cards/tapes/disks are to be delivered to the client, the contractor must first remove all individual respondent identification. Responsibility for shipping costs should be agreed upon, if possible, in advance of shipping.

4. Rights to tab cards and/or computer tapes/disks for syndicated or multi-client studies

Tab cards and data tapes/disks for these types of studies ordinarily are the property of the contractor.

Practice—If there is nothing about rights to tab cards or data tapes/disks in the agreements between a contractor and its clients, then the contractor should observe the same practices regarding storage as for tab cards and tapes/disks generated for custom studies.

At the end of the stated storage period, the contractor may destroy or retain the tab cards or data tapes without asking permission of anyone else.

E. REPORTS

Practice—Reports are the property of the client.

The research company should include, as a part of the agreement between them, reference to the relevant sections of the CASRO Code of Standards for Survey Research on public release of information. The use of reports and/or analyses produced in connection with syndicated or multi-client research projects shall be governed by the conditions within the specific contract for the service.

Section III

PRACTICES RELATED TO THE BIDDING PROCESS

NOTE: CASRO recognizes that the following section does not pertain directly to the actions of CASRO members. Clearly CASRO members cannot dictate the actions of others. However, it is strongly felt that encouraging these practices will contribute to the professionalism of marketing and public opinion research and hence its effectiveness as a management tool. Thus, this Section III is included.

This section applies only to proposals whose cost of preparation is borne partly or entirely by the research company. Proposals whose cost is borne entirely by a prospective client are considered to be contracts and not proposals.

A. **When soliciting proposals for a research project or survey, the prospective client should inform prospective contractors, whenever possible, of (1) the specific tasks the successful contractor will be expected to undertake and (2) the criteria to be used in selecting a contractor.**

Practice—1. Research firms that are asked to submit cost estimates should be given a complete set of specifications (written if possible) covering the following items where applicable or known:

a. Tasks to be performed by the client and by the contractor.

b. Description of questionnaire (or questionnaires) by (1) number of questions by type of questions, i.e., open-ended, single response closed-end, multiple response closed-end, etc., (2) duration of interview in minutes plus number of open-ended questions.

c. Estimated incidence(s) (%) and description of incidence groups.

d. Sample design and universe.

e. Household selection/respondent selection.

f. Percent of keypunching that will be verified.

g. Type of edit/clean utilized, i.e., clean to questionnaire vs. machine clean.

h. Number of banners and banner points for tabulation.

i. Number of cross-tabs.

j. Total copies of reports and/or tabs.

k. Special hand-tabs required.

Practice—If more than one research company is asked to submit a proposal, the prospective client should indicate how the successful proposal will be determined. Factors that might be used to determine the contractor selected could include:

a. Understanding of how the results of the research will be used.

b. Recognition of the types of information that will be useful.

c. Ability to provide the necessary information—personnel, facilities, equipment, etc.

d. Relevant experience of the research firm.

e. Background/experience of the individuals to be assigned to the work.

f. Recognition of the limitations of the research.

g. Specificity, with respect to procedures to be used, can and should be outlined in detail prior to the beginning of the work.

h. Cost of services.

Section IV

PRACTICES RELATED TO FINANCIAL MANAGEMENT

A. CONTRACTOR BILLINGS TO CLIENT

1. Conditions included in proposal or cost estimate.

Practice—Payment procedures and terms should be established as part of a proposal or cost estimate.

2. Billing practices.

Practice—Invoices should include payment terms.

B. CONTRACTOR PAYMENTS TO SUBCONTRACTORS AND OTHER SUPPLIERS

Practice—Contractors should endeavor to pay undisputed bills from subcontractors (e.g., field services, data processing companies) in accordance with agreed upon terms. It is understood that the subcontractor is responsible for tendering written invoices in the appropriate amount of detail.

C. CLIENT INDEMNIFICATION OF CONTRACTOR

Practice—It may be appropriate in some circumstances to include an indemnification clause in the agreement between research company and client. Such a clause might be included, for example, in studies that include demonstration or use by respondents of products supplied by the client. Since the efficacy of an indemnification clause may be affected by varying state laws, the precise wording of the clause ordinarily should be reviewed by company counsel to ensure that it satisfies the objectives of the contracting parties. The following indemnification clause is offered for illustrative purposes only:

"The client shall indemnify and hold harmless the research organization and its agents and employees against all claims against any of them for personal injury or wrongful death or property damage caused by distribution and/or use of any product supplied by the client or its agents for the purpose of this research project and from all costs and expenses in suits which may be brought against the research organization, its officers, agents and employees on account of such personal injury or wrongful death or property damage."

D. TAXES

1. Taxes on payments

Practice—Unless otherwise stated in the agreement between the client and the research company, the research company is responsible for payment of taxes on the income received or net profits from monies paid by the client.

2. Taxes on services

Practice—In the event there are federal or state laws imposing taxes on services, the payment of these taxes needs to be clarified. Because there are newer laws, practice is still evolving.

Suggested wording for a research company to consider might be as follows:

"Client agrees to (i) pay all other taxes of any kind whatsoever imposed by any government or governmental authority with respect to the reports or services rendered or expenses incurred in connection with this agreement, whether or not these taxes are included in the invoice for the services to which they relate, and (ii) reimburse contractor for any future payments of such taxes, interest and penalties made by contractor to a governmental authority."

Section V

PRACTICES RELATED TO FACILITIES

A. USE OF RESEARCH FACILITIES FOR NON-RESEARCH PURPOSES

Research companies that utilize their survey research facilities (e.g., central location telephone facilities and mailing operations) for non-research purposes should use a distinctly different name from the research company name.

This differentiation is recommended by the CASRO Board of Directors in order to separate legitimate survey research activities from non-research activities as defined in the CASRO Code of Standards for Survey Research and its Guidelines for Telemarketing. These practices should be followed for telemarketing and any other operations that do not normally fall under the definition of survey research.

B. SECURITY

It is a good business practice to provide a safe and secure place for employees and visitors. Because of the confidential nature of the work done by research companies and the amount of information or products used for clients' studies, extra precautions should be made for security at all research facilities and locations. Restricted or controlled access to areas where products or client-identifiable information can be seen or overheard is always recommended.

C. INSURANCE

In addition to the normal business liability and employer-related insurance coverage recommended for good business, securing adequate protection against loss of client-related property or information as the result of fire, theft or other such situations is a prudent practice. Research firms may also want to consider business interruption coverage as well.

If the client and research company share in a facility lease or one or the other has a facility-related joint usage agreement, it is not unusual for each party to be named on the other's insurance policies as a "named insured." This provides each with protection.

Section VI

APPENDIX

STANDARD CONTRACT FORM FOR SURVEY
RESEARCH SERVICES*

    THIS AGREEMENT is made this _____day of _____, 19____ by and between _____, a corporation organized and existing under the laws of _____ ("Contractor"), and _____, a corporation organized and existing under the laws of _____ ("Client").

WITNESSETH:

    WHEREAS, the Contractor is engaged in the business of conducting survey research; and

    WHEREAS, the Client wishes to engage the services of the Contractor to conduct survey research; and

*The laws of the various states sometimes contain unique or special requirements as to the content and construction of commercial contracts. Consequently, it is important to obtain the advice of local counsel in adapting this model agreement to individual company circumstances.

WHEREAS, the Contractor is willing to provide such survey research services, and the Client is willing to purchase such services, upon the terms and conditions hereinafter provided.

NOW THEREFORE, the parties hereto mutually covenant and agree as follow:

Article I

Services

The Contractor hereby agrees to furnish all personnel, facilities, equipment, material, supplies and services and otherwise do all things necessary for, or incident to, the performance and providing of the following items of work:

(a) To conduct a research study in the manner and in accordance with the specifications set forth in Appendix A hereto;

(b) To prepare for the Client a report(s) summarizing the information obtained from such study, as specified in Appendix A and to supply the stated number copies of such report(s) to the Client.

Article II

Payments

(a) The Client agrees to pay to the Contractor for its services hereunder a total of $_____(± %). Such amount shall be paid to the Contractor according to the schedule provided in Appendix A. It is understood that all payments are due and payable within _____days of the date of invoice.

(b) In the event that the scope of the work to be performed by the Contractor under this Agreement shall be mutually changed by the parties hereto, the above fee shall be appropriately increased or decreased to reflect such change.

(c) In addition to the agreed upon fee, Client shall compensate Contractor for the following out-of-pocket expenses which shall be documented by the Contractor: _____

_____.

Article III

Limitation of Authority

The Contractor is and shall remain an independent contractor. Nothing in this Agreement shall constitute the Contractor as a joint venturer, agent or legal representative of the Client for any purpose whatsoever. This Agreement does not authorize the Contractor to execute any agreements, make any charges or incur or assume any obligations, liabilities or responsibilities or perform any other act in the name of or on behalf of the Client or to perform any act authorized herein other than in accordance with the terms and conditions specified herein.

Article IV

Confidentiality

(a) The Contractor shall treat all information received from the Client in the course of undertaking its responsibilities under this Agreement as confidential and shall not use such information for any purpose other than to fulfill its obligations under this Agreement. The Contractor shall exercise all reasonable diligence in an effort to cause such information to be retained in complete confidence and to prevent the use and disclosure thereof by its officers, employees, agents and subcontractors contrary to the terms of this Agreement. The Contractor's obligation of confidentiality, however, shall not apply to information which, at the time of receipt by the Contractor, is in the public domain; information which is published after receipt thereof by the Contractor or otherwise becomes part of the public domain through no fault of the Contractor; information which the Contractor possessed at the time of receipt thereof from the Client, and was not acquired directly or indirectly from the Client; or information which the Contractor received from a third party who did not require the Contractor to hold it in confidence.

(b) The Contractor shall not be required to disclose the identity of respondents to the Client, except in connection with the validation of interviews by the Client. The Client hereby agrees to maintain the confidentiality of the identity of any respondents disclosed to it.

Article V

Assignment and Delegation

This Agreement is personal in character and shall not be assignable by either of the parties without the prior written consent of the other, except that the Contractor may delegate or subcontract to agents or independent contractors certain of its obligations under this Agreement in performing the study, provided that any such delegation or subcontracting shall not relieve the Contractor from any of its responsibilities to the Client under this Agreement.

Article VI

Governing Law

This Agreement shall be interpreted and construed in accordance with the laws and procedures of the State of ____, as such laws and procedures shall from time to time be in effect.

Article VII

Notices

Any notices required or permitted to be given under this Agreement shall be deemed sufficiently given if mailed by registered or certified mail, postage prepaid, addressed to the parties to be notified at the following addresses:

TO CONTRACTOR: _____

_____

_____

_____

TO CLIENT: _____

_____

_____

_____

or at such other addresses as may be furnished in writing to the notifying party.

Article VIII

Force Majeure

Except as otherwise provided in this Agreement, each party shall be excused for failures and delays in performance caused by war, civil war, riots or insurrections; laws, proclamations, ordinances or regulations of any federal, state or local government; or strikes, floods, fires, explosions or other disturbances beyond the control and without the fault of such party. Any party claiming any such excuse for delay or non-performance shall give proper notice thereof to the other party.

Article IX

Limitation of Liability

In the event that Contractor does not or is unable to render any of the services provided for by this Contract for any reason whatsoever, the sole liability of the Contractor shall be to refund to the Client that portion of the fee for the non-rendered service as may have been paid by the Client to the Contractor. In no event shall the Contractor be responsible to the Client for any special or consequential damages by virtue of any non-performance hereunder.

Article X

Indemnification

The Client agrees to indemnify and hold harmless the Contractor and its officers, agents, employees and subcontractors against all claims against them for personal injury or wrongful death or property damage caused by distribution or the use of any products supplied by the Client or his agents for the purpose of the study contemplated by this Agreement and from all costs and expenses (including reasonable attorney's fees) and suits which may be brought against the Contractor, its officers, agents, employees and subcontractors on account of such personal injury or wrongful death or property damage.

Article XI

Ownership and Storage

(a) The Client shall have ownership rights in the report(s) prepared by the Contractor.

(b) (1) If this research project is being conducted for the exclusive use by the Client, the Client shall have ownership rights to all results of this research whether or not these results have been specifically included in the report(s) to the Client.

(2) If this research project is being conducted by the Contractor as part of a syndicated research program designed for sale to more than one client, the Client's ownership rights are limited to the report(s) provided.

(c) The Client agrees that, prior to any public release of the study findings by it, the release will be presented to the

Contractor for review and clearance as to accuracy and proper interpretation. If the study findings publicly disclosed by the Client are incorrect, distorted or incomplete in the Contractor's opinion, the Contractor shall have the right to make its own release of any or all study findings necessary to make clarification.

(d) Except as provided in paragraph (c) above, the Contractor shall make no public release or revelation of its study findings without the express prior written approval of the Client.

(e) Completed questionnaires in any form specifically produced for the study are and shall remain the property of the Contractor. All such questionnaires shall be stored by the Contractor for a period of _____ months after delivery of the report to the Client and may be destroyed by the Contractor after such period. If requested by the Client prior to the end of the specified period, the Contractor will continue to store such questionnaires beyond the specified time period and may charge the Client any additional expenses incurred by the Contractor in such storage. If the parties mutually agree, the questionnaires may be delivered to the Client provided that all respondent identification shall be removed and the _____ shall be responsible for all packaging and shipping costs.

(f) Tabulating cards, computer tapes, disks and any other data record form are and shall remain the property of the Contractor. All such data records shall be stored by the Contractor for a period of _____ months after delivery of the report to the Client and may be destroyed by the Contractor after such period. If requested by the Client prior to the end of the specified period, the Contractor will continue to store such data records beyond the specified time period and may charge the Client any additional expenses incurred by the Contractor in such storage. These data records shall be stored in such a manner that additional analyses requested by the Client can be performed. The _____ shall be responsible for all charges and expenses in connection with the Contractor's producing duplicate tapes for Client use.

Article XII

Termination

This Agreement shall continue in effect until completion of the project or such earlier termination as may be mutually agreed upon by the parties.

Article XIII

General Provisions

(a) This Agreement constitutes the full and complete understanding of the parties hereto with respect to the subject matter. All prior written or oral agreements concerning the subject matter hereof are hereby cancelled and terminated.

(b) The captions contained in this Agreement are inserted only as a matter of convenience and for reference and in no way define, limit, extend or describe the scope of this Agreement or the intent of any provision hereof.

(c) Each party represents to the other that it is authorized to enter into this Agreement and perform its obligations hereunder.

(d) No change, waiver or satisfaction of any of the provisions of this Agreement shall be valid unless in writing and signed by the parties.

(e) The invalidity or unenforceability of any particular provision of this Agreement shall not affect the other provisions hereof, and this Agreement shall be construed in all respects as if such invalid or unenforceable provision were omitted.

(f) This Agreement shall be binding upon the parties, their successors, assigns and transferees.

IN WITNESS WHEREOF, the parties hereto have caused this Agreement to be executed by their respective corporate

officers, thereunto duly authorized as of the day, month and
year first above written.

ATTEST: CONTRACTOR:

By: _____   By: _____

ATTEST: CLIENT:

By: _____   By: _____

36

Ethics in Research

Knowledge without integrity is dangerous and dreadful.

—Samuel Johnson

All marketing research is based on an assumption of public trust and cooperation. We assume that people will agree to be interviewed and that they will give honest responses to the questions we ask.

But what's the source of people's trust and willingness to cooperate? It's *their* assumption that researchers will not abuse them, that it's in their interest to cooperate and allow themselves to be interviewed.

That's why ethical business practices are so important in the research business: We have to constantly protect the foundation of trust on which our whole profession is built. Congress is continually being pressured to pass laws to protect individual privacy. Only through the research industry's self-regulation can we protect our raw material—the respondent.

General Guidelines

It would be impossible to draw up a list of ethical practices that covered every possible situation. But a few general guidelines may help you to make the right decision in many situations.

1. *Act with integrity. Integrity* is a good word, because it connotes more than just a minimal adherence to legal and ethical standards. We all like to deal with people whom we feel have integrity, so that's a good standard for our own behavior too.

2. *Compare how much to how little.* It's sometimes tempting to ask, "How *little* do I have to do to avoid clear violations of ethical standards?"

A better question might be, "How *much* can I do to ensure that all my actions will be above reproach?"

3. *"Do unto others . . ."* That's a very old rule, but still the best one. Would you feel okay (as a respondent or as a client) being on the receiving end of the action you're considering? If not, chances are that your behavior isn't completely ethical.

4. *Ask, "What if they knew?"* If everyone involved knew exactly what you were doing and why, would it make a difference? Obviously, some things, like explaining the purpose of projects to respondents, have to be disguised somewhat to ensure objectivity. But that's a separate issue. It probably wouldn't make a difference to most respondents' willingness to cooperate. But could your actions stand the scrutiny of others for fairness? If not, think again.

5. *Prepare for the long run.* None of us are in business for just today or tomorrow. We intend to be around next month, next year, and for many years to come. Yet most questionable business practices have very short-run benefits that almost never justify the long-run risk of losing goodwill and trust.

Respondents and the Public

Most ethical issues in the research business relate to dealing with respondents. There are very clear, generally accepted practices for handling these issues.

Anonymity

Most survey respondents assume that their answers are anonymous and that they won't be associated with their responses individually. It's a reasonable assumption, even when they aren't told specifically that that's the case. And because the guarantee (implied or stated) of anonymity is an important component of cooperation, that anonymity must be protected. This means that names of individual respondents generally should not go beyond the questionnaires. Identifying respondents risks their being contacted for sales purposes or other reasons that would violate the respondents' anonymity.

One caution: Anonymity may be difficult to protect on some government-sponsored studies because of provisions of the Freedom of Information Act. On these projects, then, it may be necessary to tell respondents that their responses may *not* be entirely anonymous.

Privacy

This is perhaps more a matter of courtesy and politeness than of ethics. Nevertheless, it's important to remember that we risk invading respondents' privacy if we don't first ask permission to conduct an interview and give a sincere "thanks, anyway" if they refuse to cooperate.

Respondents in a group interview should usually be told that the session is being observed by closed-circuit TV or through a one-way mirror. That's good practice, even though most people would probably assume that comments made to seven other group participants and a moderator aren't completely private. The situation can usually be explained by the moderator in this way: "There are some people who are interested in hearing what you have to say, but we decided it would be better for them not to crowd into this room with us, so they're behind this mirror." This seems to satisfy respondents; in fact, they seem to quickly forget that anybody is watching.

Disguised Sales Efforts

One of the most common abuses of research is the telephone caller who introduces himself as a survey taker but later turns out to be a salesman for aluminum storm doors, magazines, or whatever. You have an obligation as a professional researcher to object to this practice and to try to stop it whenever you learn about it.

But beyond this you should make sure that you never contribute to research abuse by misrepresenting *any* type of sales effort—even if it only involves developing sales leads through a survey.

"Sales waves" of some research techniques, such as simulated sales tests, can fall into a gray area and require special attention. This includes things such as calling people back after a product test and asking if they'd like to buy some of the product they just tried in the test. The distinction here is that the purpose is really to do research (get a behavioral measure of buying intent) and not to make a profit (in fact, the prototype samples sold in such tests usually cost many times the price respondents are charged). The danger, however, is in giving respondents the impression that they have been deceived into a sales situation. So some introduction should be used to clarify the situation, such as "As you know, the product you tested is new and not available in stores. As part of the research study, however, we're making it available to people who want to buy it. Would you care to purchase any?"

Industrial Espionage

This is much less common than novelists and TV scriptwriters would have us believe. But it does exist. Using research as a guise for obtaining confidential information is clearly unethical. For example, contacting XYZ Company and asking about its sales (or number of employees, or product line mix) as part of a fictitious survey that is actually a fact-gathering effort for a competitor is clearly unethical.

Clients and Research Companies

Research companies often need to have access to their client's confidential information to conduct a project. Indeed, the very fact that a research project is being done on a new product is itself often confidential. So special care must be taken to protect the confidentiality of this information.

Conflict of Interest

These days, as corporations become more diversified, it's nearly impossible for research companies to avoid working for clients that compete in some line of business. So it usually isn't practical for research companies to eliminate every possible conflict of interest by the companies they work for.

The key is this: *Can research providers be fair to, and give their best efforts to, both companies they work for?* As a rule, it's impossible for a research company to work for two clients on a directly competitive issue. The company can't give its best effort to one without compromising its relationship with the other. Since it's impossible for any client to monitor this situation directly, it becomes the research company's responsibility to decline work that would create such a conflict.

Sponsorship

The name of the client sponsoring a study should not be divulged to respondents without the client's consent. This is the other side of respondent anonymity: Respondents can be sure the sponsor doesn't know who they are; likewise, sponsors know respondents won't be aware of the sponsor's identity.

Some industrial-survey respondents, because of concerns about industrial espionage, won't take part in a survey without knowing the identity of the sponsor. In these cases, the study sponsor should be asked if the respondent's cooperation is worth revealing the client's identity.

Professionalism

Often the sponsor of a study hopes the results will come out a certain way: The new product is better than the current one; the product beats competition; and so on. For the researcher, there is a real risk of misinterpreting these hopes as pressure to affect the outcome of the study. But a researcher always has a professional obligation to provide unbiased design, honest fieldwork, and objective analysis. After all, what's the point of trying to believe that the new product is better if it really isn't? The marketplace doesn't lie, so the truth will eventually come out anyway.

Competing Research Companies

Research is an idea business. Researchers have little to sell but their thoughts, usually in the form of designs for research studies. And these designs are rarely protectable in any formal, legal way (such as by copyright).

As a result, pirating other researchers' ideas is primarily an ethical issue. Where the study design is a unique, original one, it's unethical to steal a research company's idea or for a customer to give a proposal on a unique project design to another research company.

Appendix

Several industry groups in the marketing research field have developed codes of ethics or business practice guides. These include:

American Marketing Association (AMA)
American Association for Public Opinion Research (AAPOR)
Market Research Association (MRA)
Council of American Survey Research Organizations (CASRO)

The CASRO Code of Standards is included here for reference because it covers the ethical responsibilities of all the parties connected with research: respondents, clients, the public, and interviewers.

Council of American Survey Research Organizations
Code of Standards for Survey Research

Introduction

This Code of Standards for Survey Research sets forth
the agreed upon rules of ethical conduct for survey research
organizations. Acceptance of this Code is mandatory for all
CASRO members.

The Code has been organized into sections describing
the responsibilities of a survey research organization to respondents, clients and outside contractors and in reporting
study results.

This Code is not intended to be, nor should it be, an im-
mutable document. Circumstances may arise that are not covered by this Code or that may call for modification of some
aspect of this Code. The Standards Committee and the Board
of Directors of CASRO will evaluate these circumstances as
they arise and, if appropriate, revise the Code. The Code,
therefore, is a living document that seeks to be responsive to
the changing world of survey research.

I. Responsibilities to Respondents

A. Confidentiality

1. Survey research organizations are responsible for protecting from disclosure to third parties—including clients and
members of the public—the identity of individual respondents as well as respondent-identifiable information, unless
the respondent expressly permits such disclosure.

2. This principle of confidentiality is qualified by the following exceptions:

a. The identity of individual respondents and respondent-identifiable information may be disclosed to the client to
permit the client: (1) to validate interviews and/or (2) to deter-

mine an additional fact of analytical importance to the study. In these cases, respondents must be given a sound reason for the re-inquiry. In all cases, a refusal by respondent to continue must be respected.

Before disclosing respondent-identifiable information to a client for purposes of interview validation or re-inquiry, the survey research organization must take whatever steps are needed to ensure that the client will conduct the validation or recontact in a fully professional manner. This includes the avoidance of multiple validation contacts or other conduct that would harass or could embarrass respondents. It also includes any use of the information for other than bona fide survey research purposes or to respond to customer/respondent complaints. Assurance that the client will respect such limitations and maintain respondent confidentiality should be confirmed in writing before any confidential information is disclosed.

b. The identity of individual respondents and respondent-identifiable information may be disclosed to other survey research organizations whenever such organizations are conducting different phases of a multi-stage study (e.g., a trend study). The initial research company should confirm in writing that respondent confidentiality will be maintained in accordance with the Code.

c. In the case of research in which representatives of the client or others are present, such client representatives and others should be asked not to disclose to anyone not present the identity of individual participants or other participant-identifying information except as needed to respond, with the participant's prior specific approval, to any complaint by one or more of the participants concerning a product or service supplied by the client.

3. The principle of respondent confidentiality includes the following specific applications or safeguards:

a. Survey research organization staff or personnel should not use or discuss respondent-identifiable data or information for other than legitimate internal research purposes.

b. The survey research organization has the responsibility for ensuring that subcontractors (interviewers, interviewing services, and validation, coding, and tabulation organizations) and consultants are aware of and agree to maintain and respect respondent confidentiality whenever the identity of respondents or respondent-identifiable information is disclosed to such entities.

c. Before permitting clients or others to have access to completed questionnaires in circumstances other than those described above, respondent names and other respondent-identifying information should be deleted.

d. Invisible identifiers on mail questionnaires that connect respondent answers to particular respondents should not be used. Visible identification numbers may be used but should be accompanied by an explanation that such identifiers are for control purposes only and that respondent confidentiality will not be compromised.

e. Any survey research organization that receives from a client or other entity information that it knows or reasonably believes to be confidential respondent-identifiable information should decline to use such information unless the information was disclosed in accordance with the principles and procedures described in this Code.

f. The use of survey results in a legal proceeding does not relieve the survey research organization of its ethical obligation to maintain in confidence all respondent-identifiable information or lessen the importance of respondent anonymity. Consequently, survey research firms confronted with a subpoena or other legal process requesting the disclosure of respondent-identifiable information should take all reasonable steps to oppose such requests, including informing the court or other decision-maker involved of the factors justifying confidentiality and respondent anonymity and interposing all appropriate defenses to the request for disclosure.

B. Privacy and the Avoidance of Harassment

1. Survey research organizations have a responsibility to strike a proper balance between the need for research in contemporary American life and the need to respect the privacy of individuals who become the respondents in the research. To achieve this balance:

a. Respondents will be protected from unnecessary and unwanted intrusions and/or any form of personal harassment.

b. The voluntary character of the interviewer/respondent contact should be stated explicitly where the respondent might have reason to believe that cooperation is not voluntary.

2. This principle of privacy includes the following specific applications:

a. The research organization shall make every reasonable effort to ensure that the respondent understands the purpose of the interviewer/respondent contact.

(1) The interviewer/research company representative must provide prompt and honest identification of his/her research firm affiliation.

(2) Respondent questions should be answered in a forthright and non-deceptive manner.

b. Deceptive practices and misrepresentation, such as using research as a guise for sales or solicitation purposes, are expressly prohibited.

c. Survey research organizations must respect the right of individuals to refuse to be interviewed or to terminate an interview in progress. Techniques that infringe on these rights should not be employed, but survey research organizations may make reasonable efforts to obtain an interview including: (1) explaining the purpose of the research project; (2) providing a gift or monetary incentive adequate to elicit cooperation; and (3) re-contacting an individual at a different time if the individual is unwilling or unable to participate during the initial contact.

d. Research organizations are responsible for arranging interviewing times that are convenient for respondents.

e. Lengthy interviews are a burden. Research organizations are responsible for weighing the research need against the length of the interview and respondents must not be enticed into an interview situation by a misrepresentation of the length of the interview.

f. Research organizations are responsible for developing techniques to minimize the discomfort or apprehension of respondents and interviewers when dealing with sensitive subject matter.

g. Electronic equipment (taping, recording, photographing) and one-way viewing rooms may be used only with the full knowledge of respondents.

II. Responsibilities to Clients

A. Relationships between a survey research organization and clients for whom the surveys are conducted should be of such a nature that they foster confidence and mutual respect. They must be characterized by honesty and confidentiality.

B. The following specific approaches describe in more detail the responsibilities of research organizations in this relationship:

1. A survey research organization must assist its clients in the design of effective and efficient studies that are to be carried out by the research company. If the survey research organization questions whether a study design will provide the information necessary to serve the client's purposes, it must make its reservations known.

2. A research organization must conduct the study in the manner agreed upon. However, if it becomes apparent in the

course of the study that changes in the plans should be made, the research organization must make its views known to the client promptly.

3. A research organization has an obligation to allow its clients to verify that work performed meets all contracted specifications and to examine all operations of the research organization that are relevant to the proper execution of the project in the manner set forth. While allowing clients to examine questionnaires or other records, the survey research organization must continue to protect the confidentiality and privacy of survey respondents.

4. When more than one client contributes to the cost of a project specially commissioned with the research organization, each client concerned shall be informed that there are other participants (but not necessarily of their identity).

5. Research organizations will hold confidential all information that they obtain about a client's general business operations, and all matters connected with research projects that they conduct for a client.

6. For research findings obtained by the agency that are the property of the client, the research organization may make no public release or revelation of findings without expressed, prior approval from the client.

C. Bribery in any form and in any amount is unacceptable and is a violation of a research organization's fundamental, ethical obligations. A research organization and/or its principals, officers and employees should never give gifts to clients in the form of cash. To the extent permitted by applicable laws and regulations, a research organization may provide nominal gifts to clients and may entertain clients, as long as the cost of such entertainment is modest in amount and incidental in nature.

III. Responsibilities in Reporting to Clients and the Public

A. When reports are being prepared for client confidential or public release purposes, it is the obligation of the research organization to ensure that the findings it releases are an accurate portrayal of the survey data, and careful checks on the accuracy of all figures are mandatory.

B. A research organization's report to a client or the public should contain, or the research organization should be ready to supply on short notice, the following information about the survey:

1. The name of the organization for which the study was conducted and the name of the organization conducting it.

2. The purpose of the study, including the specific objectives.

3. The dates on or between which the fieldwork was done.

4. A definition of the universe that the survey is intended to represent and a description of the population frame(s) actually sampled.

5. A description of the sample design, including the method of selecting sample elements, method of interview, cluster size, number of callbacks, respondent eligibility or screening criteria, and other pertinent information.

6. A description of results of sample implementation including (a) the total number of sample elements contacted, (b) the number not reached, (c) the number of refusals, (d) the number of terminations, (e) the number of non-eligibles, (f) the number of completed interviews.

7. The basis for any specific "completion rate" percentages, fully documented and described.

8. The exact wording of the questions used, including interviewer directions and visual exhibits.

9. A description of any weighing or estimating procedures used.

10. A description of any special scoring, data adjustment or indexing procedures used. (Where the research organization uses proprietary techniques, these should be described in general and the research organization should be prepared to provide technical information on demand from qualified and technically competent persons who have agreed to honor the confidentiality of such information.)

11. Estimates of the sampling error and of data shown when appropriate, but when shown they should include reference to other possible sources of error so that a misleading impression of accuracy or precision is not conveyed.

12. Statistical tables clearly labelled and identified as to questionnaire source, including the number of raw cases forming the base for each cross-tabulation.

13. Copies of interviewer instructions, validation results, code books, and other important working papers.

C. As a **minimum,** any general public release of survey findings should include the following information:

1. The sponsorship of the study.

2. A description of its purposes.

3. The sample description and size.

4. The dates of fieldwork.

5. The name of the research agency conducting the study.

6. The exact wording of the questions.

7. Any other information that a layperson would need to make a reasonable assessment of the reported findings.

D. A survey research organization will seek agreements from clients so that citations of survey findings will be presented to the research organization for review and clearance as to accuracy and proper interpretation prior to public release. A research organization will advise clients that if the survey findings publicly disclosed are incorrect, distorted, or incomplete, in the research organization's opinion, the research organization reserves the right to make its own release of any or all survey findings necessary to make clarification.

IV. Responsibility to Outside Contractors and Interviewers

Research organizations will not ask any outside contractor or interviewer to engage in any activity which is not acceptable as defined in other sections of this Code of Standards for Survey Research.

Glossary of Marketing Research Terms

Like every business, marketing research has its own terminology and jargon. Here are some of the most frequently used terms that have unique or particular meanings within the research field.

AAU   See *awareness, attitude, and usage study.*

AID (Automatic Interaction Detector)   A method of multivariate analysis often used in market segmentation studies.

analysis of variance (ANOVA)   A method of analysis for determining the level of statistical significance of differences between two sets of data.

audit   A method for measuring sales in a store by counting beginning inventory, adding new shipments, and subtracting ending inventory.

awareness   The proportion of people who have ever seen or heard of a product or brand name.

awareness, attitude, and usage (AAU) study   A type of tracking study that monitors changes in consumer awareness, attitudes, and usage levels for a brand or product category.

balanced incomplete block (BIB)   An experimental design procedure for rotating a large number of products or items in a test.

banner   The series of column headings, or cross-tab breaks, that runs horizontally across the top of a computer table.

base   The number on which the percentages in a table are calculated.

BIB   See *balanced incomplete block.*

bipolar scale   A scale with opposite end points and a "just right" midpoint. Examples: spicy/bland, moist/dry, large/small.

buying intent   A scale used to measure respondents' likelihood of purchasing a product.

callback   A second attempt to interview a respondent, either because the person could not be reached on the first try or to complete an after-use interview in a product test.

cathode-ray tube (CRT)   A TV-like terminal with a keyboard, used for getting data to or from a computer. Often used in research to display questions and enter responses into the computer for tabulating.

CATI   See *computer-assisted telephone interviewing*.

central-location study   A survey conducted at a conveniently located site to which respondents come to be interviewed. Sometimes used to mean any location where respondents are interviewed, such as shopping malls.

chi-square test (χ^2)   A test of statistical significance.

clarifying   A follow-up technique for getting complete responses to open-ended questions by asking respondents to explain vague or general terms in their answers. Also see *probing*.

closed-ended question   Any question with a limited number of pre-listed answers.

cluster analysis   A multivariate technique for identifying homogeneous groupings of products or people.

coding   The process of translating responses to questions into numerical form for data processing.

computer-assisted telephone interviewing (CATI)   A system for doing telephone research where the questionnaire is programmed into a computer and the interviewer works from the computer screen, instead of from a questionnaire printed on paper.

concept description   A brief description of a new product or service.

confidence range   The range around a survey result for which there is a high statistical probability that it contains the true population parameter.

conjoint analysis   A multivariate technique for separating consumers' judgments into their components.

convenience sample   A sampling procedure that leaves the selection of respondents totally to the interviewers, with no quotas or qualifications imposed.

criterion variables   The variables being predicted or explained in a study. Examples: volume of category or brand usage. Also called *dependent variables*.

CRT   See *cathode-ray tube*.

customer satisfaction research   Surveys conducted to measure the customers' level of satisfaction, overall and on specific dimensions, with a company's product or service.

day-after recall An advertising testing technique that measures the proportion of people recalling seeing a TV commercial within twenty-four hours of its airing.

demographics Personal or household characteristics, such as age, sex, income, or educational level.

dependent variables See *criterion variables.*

disappointment score The proportion of respondents in a product test who indicate, after trying the product, that they would not buy it.

discriminant analysis A multivariate technique for analyzing the predictive value of a set of independent variables.

discussion question See *open-ended question.*

distribution check A study measuring the number of stores carrying specified products, along with the number of facings, special displays, and prices of the products.

editing The process of checking questionnaires for completeness and accuracy.

exhibit Anything shown to respondents during an interview. Examples: a print advertisement, a card listing income categories.

factor analysis A multivariate technique for analyzing interrelationships among variables.

frequency A measure of how often repeat buyers repurchase and how many units they purchase each time.

group interview A qualitative research technique involving a discussion among eight to ten respondents, led by a moderator. Also called focus groups, group discussions, panels, and group depth interviews.

hedonic scale A scale for measuring general, overall opinion of a product.

incidence Any figure referring to the percentage of people in a category. Examples: incidence of users, incidence of people qualifying for a study.

independent variables See *predictor variables.*

intercept study An interviewing method whereby people are stopped in stores or shopping malls for an interview.

interval scale See *ratio scale.*

judgment sample A sample containing certain types of respondents, who are selected on the basis of the judgment that their attitudes or behavior will be representative of the population.

life-style research Research that attempts to explain behavior by analyzing people's attitudes, interests, activities, and opinions. Often associated with psychographic research.

mall intercept See *intercept study.*

MAPPing   Mathematical Analysis of Perception and Preference. See *perceptual MAPPing*.

marginals   A computer-generated frequency count of the number of people giving each answer to all the questions in a questionnaire. Also called an 80-column dump.

marketing concept   The business philosophy that a company's effort should be adapted to the needs and wants of its customers.

metric scale   See *ratio scale*.

monadic   A test in which a respondent evaluates only one product.

multidimensional scaling   See *perceptual MAPPing*.

multivariate analysis   Any analysis that analyzes several variables together.

nominal scale   A scale that classifies people into groups that have no inherent numerical order or value. Examples: male/female, user/nonuser.

nonprobability sample   Any type of sample that is not a probability, or random, sample.

nonsampling error   All the sources of bias or inaccuracy in a study besides sampling error. Examples: leading by the interviewer, recording errors.

objectives   The information to be developed from a study to serve the project's purpose.

open-ended question   A question that has no prelisted answers. Example: "Why do you say that?" Also called *discussion question* or *subjective question*.

ordinal scale   A scale that classifies people into groups that have an inherent order. Examples: preference data and rankings.

paired comparison   A test in which a respondent evaluates two products.

panel   "Purchase panels" are composed of people who record and report their purchases in specified product categories. "Mail panels" are made up of people who have agreed to participate in mail surveys. Group interviews are sometimes called "panels."

perceptual MAPPing   A multivariate technique designed to represent consumers' product perceptions and preferences as points on a map or graph. Also called *multidimensional scaling* or *MAPPing*.

placement interview   An interview in which a respondent is recruited and given the product to use in a product test.

population   See *universe*.

positioning   Location of a brand or product in consumers' minds relative to competitive products.

predictor variables   The variables that explain or predict the differences in dependent variables. Examples: demographics, attitudes. Also called *independent variables.*

prerecruited central-location test A survey conducted at a conveniently located site to which respondents—who have been previously contacted and qualified—come to be interviewed.

probability sample A sample in which every unit has an equal and known probability of being selected. Also sometimes called a *random sample.*

probing A follow-up technique for getting complete responses to open-ended questions by asking, "What else?" until the respondent has nothing more to add. Also see *clarifying.*

product placement study A type of test in which respondents try a product under normal usage conditions. Example: in-home test of a food product. Also called a product test.

psychographics Research that attempts to explain behavior by analyzing people's personality traits and values. Often associated with *lifestyle research.*

purpose The reason a research project is being conducted; usually focuses on the decisions for which information from the study will be used.

qualitative Exploratory research involving small samples. Example: group interviews.

quantitative Research done with large samples to provide definitive, quantified results.

quota sample A sampling procedure that includes specified numbers of respondents having characteristics known or believed to affect the subject being researched.

random digit dialing A telephone sampling procedure that generates random combinations of telephone numbers in order to include unlisted numbers in a survey sample.

random sample See *probability sample.*

ratio scale A scale with measurable intervals between scale points. Also called *interval scale* or *metric scale.*

regression analysis A multivariate technique that relates a dependent variable to one or more independent variables.

repeat-pairs technique A product testing procedure in which respondents express a preference between two products, then repeat the task with an identical pair of products.

repeat rate The proportion of first-time triers of a product who purchase the product at least a second time.

sample A proportion of the population selected for a research study.

sampling error   The range, usually expressed as ±X percent, attached to a survey result to estimate the likely population parameter.

sampling frame   A physical listing of all units in a population used to draw a sample, or a procedure for producing a result comparable to such a physical listing.

scale   A closed-ended question for measuring attitudes.

sequential testing   A testing procedure in which a respondent tries one product, evaluates it, then tries and evaluates a second product. (This is also sometimes called a sequential monadic test, which is technically a misnomer, since use of the second product is by definition not monadic.)

simulated sales test   A procedure designed to estimate a product's sales potential by simulating trial and use conditions of the marketplace.

single-source data   Information on a product's sales and distribution obtained from in-store scanners. Often tied to customer purchase and advertising response data so that all information comes from a single source.

stratified sampling   A procedure that groups the population into homogeneous segments (or strata) and then samples from each of the strata.

stub   The responses to the question being tabulated, which run vertically down the left side of a computer table.

subjective question   See *open-ended question.*

systematic sampling   A procedure that selects every *n*th unit for inclusion in the sample.

tachistoscope (T-scope)   A device for controlling the intensity and duration of light exposure. Sometimes used in package testing.

topline   Preliminary results from a project, usually showing responses of the total sample to a few key questions.

tracking   Studies repeated over time to monitor changes in a brand or product category.

trial rate   Measures the proportion of people who buy a product at least once.

T-scope   See *tachistoscope.*

unipolar   An ordinal scale with one positive end and one negative end.

universe   The set of all the units from which a sample is drawn. Also called the *population.*

validation   A procedure for recontacting respondents to confirm that interviews were conducted correctly.

Index